All Joy

Models for Our Daily Lives

Compiled by:
Dr. G. Louise Byrd

ROYSTON
Publishing

BK Royston Publishing
Jeffersonville, IN
http://www.bkroystonpublishing.com
bkroystonpublishing@gmail.com

Copyright – 2024

All Rights Reserved. No part of this book may be reproduced, stored in a retrieval system, or transmitted by any means without the written permission of the author.

Cover Design: Elite Cover Designs
Back Cover Photo: Robert L Byrd, Jr

ISBN-13: 978-1-963136-09-8

Library of Congress Control Number: 2024903739

Common English Bible (CEB) - Copyright © 2011 by Common English Bible

English Standard Version (ESV) - The Holy Bible, English Standard Version. ESV® Text Edition: 2016. Copyright © 2001 by Crossway Bibles, a publishing ministry of Good News Publishers.

King James Version (KJV) – Public Domain

The Message (MSG) - Copyright © 1993, 2002, 2018 by Eugene H. Peterson

New Century Version (NCV) - The Holy Bible, New Century Version®. Copyright © 2005 by Thomas Nelson, Inc.

New International Version (NIV) - Holy Bible, New International Version®, NIV® Copyright ©1973, 1978, 1984, 2011 by Biblica, Inc.® Used by permission. All rights reserved worldwide.

New King James (NKJV) - Scripture taken from the New King James Version®. Copyright © 1982 by Thomas Nelson. Used by permission. All rights reserved.

New Living Translation (NLT) - Holy Bible, New Living Translation, copyright © 1996, 2004, 2015 by Tyndale House Foundation. Used by permission of Tyndale House Publishers, Inc., Carol Stream, Illinois 60188. All rights reserved.

Living Bible (TLB) - The Living Bible copyright © 1971 by Tyndale House Foundation. Used by permission of Tyndale House Publishers Inc., Carol Stream, Illinois 60188. All rights reserved.

Printed in the United States of America

Dedicated To:

This book is dedicated to Gladys and Odell Spease, my parents; Lester, Barbara Jean, Charlie Frank, Diane, my siblings; Robert Byrd, Sr., husband; Robert Jr., son; Rob III, Daniel Byrd, grandsons; nieces and nephews; Jerry Thomas, Beverly Wells, best friends and writers who opened their hearts to help witness to the world.

Special Thanks

To all writers, who were willing to share their testimony as a tribute to God whom they love and serve.

To Linda Pope, who is home with the Lord. Her testimony will live forever in our hearts.

To Karen Mize, Dr. Sharon Moore, Dr. Jewelene Richards, and Beverly Blount Hill for their support and prayers. I appreciate your spiritual guidance and continual encouragement.

To Dr. Julia Royston and the team at BK Royston Publishing Company for their professionalism, editing and patience. Dr. Royston worked overtime to make All Joy: Models of Our Daily Lives, a reality.

> **Consider it pure joy, my brothers and sisters, whenever you face trials of many kinds, because you know that the testing of your faith produces perseverance." James 1: 2–4 (NIV)**

TABLE OF CONTENTS

Dedication iii

Special Thanks iv

Introduction xi

Defining Joy xv

The Journey xx

Let's Prayerfully Begin xxii

Chapter 1: JOY OF SUFFERING 1

Joy of Suffering Introduction 7

An Overcomer **Eloise Greer** 9

Strengthening My Faith **Alice and James Binford** 11

Count It All Joy **Pastor Willie M. Byrd** 13

Mama's Love **Gwen Johnson** 16

Free at Last **Sandra Whiteside, MSSW, CSW** 18

Out of the Puddle **Patrick Sullivan** 20

In the Midst of the Storm **Elizabeth Caples** 22

Count It All Joy: A Testimony of Faith **Joyce Mayes** 24

Potter's Hands **Kim Jackson** 27

Resting in Jesus **Mildred A Binford Smith** 29

Discovering Joy Through Devastation **Carolyn Collins** 31

Questions to God **Desiree Anthony** 33

Finding Joy in the Midst of Trial **Michael E. Johnson** 35

Good Can Come Through Suffering **Linda Martin** 37

Testimony of Joy **Janice C Collins** 40

Walking with God **Debbie Maldonado** 42

The Joy of the Lord **Dr. Moniqueka E. Gold** 47

One Day at a Time **Judy Waller** 51

My Search **Mildred Byrd** 52

From Darkness to the Marvelous Light **Jean Griffin** 58

Memories **Beverly Wells** 60

All Joy: My Testimony of Faith **Candace Strong** 62

Joy Comes in the Mourning **Damon L. Armstead** 65

Only God **Odell Reliford** 67

From Birth to Rebirth **Tanisha Ortiz** 69

Barren **Shaun Nelson** 71

His Protection **Elizabeth Rose** 73

Are You Mad at Me? **Paulette Jewell** 75

New Kidney **James Harrell** 78

A Reflection **Loretta Gillenwater** 80

Just My Story **Mildred James** 82

God Has the Final Say **Dr. Anthony Sanders** 83

Second Chance **Abe Drake** 86

Success Through Perseverance **Robert Byrd, III** 88

And Yet... **Sue Terdan** 89

My Career Testimony: The Real Estate Promise **Diane Ulmer** 91

A Five-Year Walk of Faith **Beverly Barbour** 94

A Cry of Joy **Alphonsa Fowler** 97

The Enemy **Richard McKnight** 99

Under Control **Anthony Lamb** 101

Best Friend **Lena Lewis-Harrell** 103

Always Looking **Cynthia Lusco** 105

Small Beginnings **Rebehak Dow** 108

Count It All Joy **Candace Johnson** 110

Defying the Odds! **Evangelist Karen Hatcher** 112

How to Be Joyful During Trials **Dawnene Byrd** 113

It Can't Be Real **Linda Pope** 115

I Had Fallen, But God Lifted Me Up! **Jerry Jim James Thomas** 117

My Savior, My Healer, My Deliverer **Ann Elliot** 120

Joy of Suffering Reflections 123

From the Heart 124

Prayer 125

God's Process (Poem) **Robert L. Byrd, Jr.** 126

Chapter 2: JOY OF BELIEVING 127

Introduction 129

Joy of Believing Testimonies 133

All Joy **Sandy Miller Jones** 135

Journey to Joy **Leisa Martin** 137

Joy Comes In The Morning **Diana L. Mott** 140

Second Angel **Joseph Wiley** 142

Down in My Heart **Barbara Lyons** 144

My Amazing Experience **Tacia Lyman** 146

Counting It All Joy During Trials and Tribulations **Dr. Jewelene Richards** 149

Working Weights **Daniel Byrd** 151

A Way Out of No Way **David Byrd** 153

I Made It Through **Dennis Prince** 155

Returning to the Word and the Awakening of Faith **LeDoan C. Smith** 157

Cancer, Children, and Christ **Durell Hall** 161

He Makes the Final Decision **Frank Thomas** 164

Trust Him **Susie Grady** 165

Invisible **Niyetta Williams-Hill, Ed.D.** 167

My 3 P's That Lead to Joy (Prayer, Patience, & Peace) **Karen Mize** 170

God's Joy **Rev. Keith Williams** 171

The Ripple Effect **Charmaine Ward** 173

This Joy **Sandra Malone** 175

Unspeakable Joy **Toni Byrd** 177

Blessed, Anyway! **Veronica McGill** 179

Who's in Charge? **Wanda Mitchell-Smith** 181

Your Joy Is Returning **Nancy E Hall, MSW, LCSW** 182

Self-Discovery **Felicia Smyzer** 184

Joy of Believing Reflections 186

From the Heart 187

Prayer 188

A Reason to Rejoice **Rev. Bob Byrd** 190

Chapter 3: THE JOY OF GIVING 193

Introduction: The Joy of Giving 195

The Joy of Giving Testimonials 199

God's Blessing **Linda Kennedy** 201

Blessed with Joy **Dr. Gail Clark Dickson** 204

Caregiving with Joyful Heart **Dr. Pam Randolph** 208

How Could You, Lord? **Dr. Louise Byrd** 210

Giving Love **Yolanda Farris** 213

Let's See **Dr. G L Byrd** 215

The Gift Goes On **Rev. Robert Lee Byrd, Sr.** 217

Only You **Dr. Louise Byrd** 219

Joy of Giving Reflections 221

From the Heart 222

Prayer 223

Chapter 4: JOY OF HUMILITY 225

Introduction: Joy of Humility 227

Humility Testimonies 231

Change of Life to Bring Forth a Better Life **Dr. Victoria Felicia Hanchell** 233

Count It All Joy **Rev. David Dow** 236

Joy of Humility **Pat Richardson** 237

Loving Energy **Mary Lou Bryant-Reid** 239

Joy of Humility Reflections 242

From the Heart 243

Prayer 244

"Which One Would You Choose?" 245

Chapter 5: STEPS TO A JOYFUL LIFE 247

Renew The Mind – 249

Renewing the Body 251

Inward Disciplines 254

Outward Disciplines 260

Corporate Disciplines 264

I Have a Choice to Make! 268

Invitation: A New Life in Christ **Rev. Robert L. Byrd, Sr.** 270

Inspiration 272

Biography 274

Bibliography 277

INTRODUCTION

All Joy: Models for Our Daily Lives is based on the scriptures that read as follows:

> *"Consider it pure joy, my brothers and sisters, whenever you face trials of many kinds, because you know that the testing of your faith produces perseverance."* James 1: 2–4 (NIV)

The world has sold us the hype that having material things will fill our lives with Joy and happiness. The media has convinced us that artificial implants to change facial and body structures will make us glamorous and provide a fountain of youth that attracts a desirable mate/companion. Advertisements suggest the more money you make, the more successful you will become. The world implies you will live a more joyful and fulfilled life. While in pursuit of these treasures, the world is in a chaotic state. Violence escalates, the family structure has declined, and our communities are compromised.

According to *National Geographic* (June 11, 2020), 1,100 people are killed annually by police. As a result of the U. S. Capitol riots on January 6, 2020, Americans are concerned about civil unrest and increased violence. Some students bring guns to school to resolve conflict. Since Columbine, there have been 386 school shootings. Guns used in these shootings came from home (April 5, 2018, *Wall Street Journal*).

The family structure has changed. Many single parents are trying to raise their sons/daughters alone with limited financial and human resources. In 2022, there were about 15.78 million children living with a single mother in the United States, and about 3.44 million children living with a single father (U.S Census Bureau, 2021).

According to the Pew Research Center (2018), neighbors don't interact with or know each other. This generation of children is missing the uniqueness of what belonging to a community is all about. When I was growing up, you knew all the neighbors, and the elders were given the authority to supervise your behavior. There were consequences if you disobeyed. In my community, if there was a need, someone would help fulfill it. Respect, courtesy, kindness, fairness, patience, obedience and reverence to God were valued.

As of September 23, 2023, America experienced 1,141,782 deaths due to COVID-19. Many deaths occurred because wearing a mask and getting the vaccine made people feel inconvenienced or unhappy. According to the Centers for Disease Control and Prevention (CDC), life expectancy has dropped considerably for Americans due to an epidemic that is highly treatable with vaccines and precautions.

Growing up in a home with mother and father to instill important values was the norm during my youth. Going to church and school demonstrating obedience and respect were expectations, and there were no exceptions or excuses accepted. Since communities were close knit, everyone knew your mother and father. If you got off track, your parents would know before you got home. Believe me, there were consequences.

When I was a classroom teacher, I asked students, "What did you learn in Sunday school this week?" Only one child out of 30 had attended Sunday school. Since the majority of the students didn't attend church or were not required to go to church, they missed learning the truths that helped them develop into responsible adults who feared and showed reverence to God. Sunday school for me provided examples of how God wanted me to live.

Unfortunately, the enemy (Satan) is roaming the world seeking whom he shall devour. How can we consider it pure Joy when the world is in such a disarray and chaotic state?

The world has embedded a lot of untruths in the way we live. These untruths have led to the chaos we see today because the world cannot offer us truth, only God will. How do we overcome the "trials and tribulations" of the world? James states: "Consider it pure joy whenever you face trials of many kinds, because you know that the testing of your faith produces perseverance." James 1:2–3 (NIV)

The concept is mind-boggling. How in the world can I find "pure Joy"? In the world, we see limited examples of Joy. The solutions to our problems will not be of the world, but found in knowing, trusting, and believing in God.

The world uses the words "Joy" and "happiness" interchangeably, as if they mean the same thing. Some people think they have Joy in their lives, but may only be experiencing happiness. A few elements of happiness are as follows: an external focus, conditional demands, self-centeredness, dependency on others, temporary emotions and worldly choices. As a result, a person is never satisfied because their happiness becomes a fleeting moment. If their desires/demands are not met, they become very unhappy. When we don't become richer, meet a mate, or lose those desired pounds, happiness eludes us. I have heard people say, "If I am not happy, you won't be happy, either." They will try to make your life miserable if you allow them. What a stressful way to live! Life isn't all about you. My parents used to remind me that the world doesn't revolve around me.

This is a biblical example of how temporary happiness is: In Exodus 32:1-35 (NIV), Moses left the Israelites along as he went to receive the Ten Commandment from the Lord. They became restless because they wanted a god they could see to worship. They knew that God had forbidden them to worship any golden idols but this act would make them happy. So, they pressured Aaron, the priest into supporting them. After offering sacrifices to their golden image, they ate, drank, and sang. However, their happiness was short lived. Once Moses returned and destroyed the image, the people endured consequences for making bad decisions. Instead of enjoying all the Promised Land had to offer, they died in the wilderness for not obeying God.

When I first married, I was so happy. Soon I realized happiness fades when you don't agree on issues for a long time and don't have enough money to pay living expenses. Happiness fades when you can no longer do what you want because you are a couple now. I had to learn the meaning of "we" versus "me" in a marriage. I was truly self-centered and had to make a different choice to remain married. My concept of marriage was you worked hard to get what you wanted and had fun on the weekend.

Do those examples sound familiar to you? We have substituted other images to replace God and put ourselves before Him. There are dire consequences for our bad decisions. That is why God provided another plan, Jesus Christ. Pure Joy comes from knowing, trusting, and believing who Jesus Christ is with all our hearts, minds, souls, and strength.

Even though I grew up in the church, I had to learn what Joy really looked like. Learning about Joy was a process that required spending time with Jesus. I made a conscience, deliberate decision to live a Christian life with Jesus Christ as the center of my life. The closer I got to God, the more I experienced His Joy.

Kay Warren, in her book *Choose Joy: Because Happiness Isn't Good Enough* (2013), points out that "Not only is God a God of joy, but God's Word to us is a Word of joy." She found 545 references to Joy, merriment, happiness, laughing and rejoicing in the New International Version (NIV) of the Bible, while 158 verses talk about sorrow (*Choose Joy: Because Happiness Isn't Good Enough*, p. 104). We can infer that God wants us to experience more Joy than sorrow in our daily life. This book invites you to learn more about Joy and experience how your life will be blessed forevermore. *All Joy: Models for Our Daily Lives* provides 70 Christians' examples of what Joy "looks like." You will discover how Christians overcome the trials and tribulations of the world and how you may begin to live a joyful life.

Background Scripture for Testimonials

The main text for the book is James 1:2–4 (NIV). James, a servant of God and the Lord Jesus Christ, wrote these scriptures. His mission in life was to spread the Word of God throughout the 12 tribes, who were scattered across the nations. The 12 tribes of Israel were scattered because of their **unrighteousness, disobedience, and rebellion** against God (Leviticus 26:33). In other words, they continued to sin against the Lord — and He abhors sin. The Lord also used the scattering of the tribes to bless other nations. In doing so, the Word was preached, not only to the Jews, but to the gentiles as well.

As leader of the Jerusalem Council, James discussed the Laws of Moses and the Gentiles, in Acts 15:17–21. He preached to the people of Jerusalem in the company of Paul and Barnabas and encouraged them not to make it difficult for the Gentiles, who were turning to God.

The scriptures reiterate the trials and tribulations of James and Paul. James was called "Son of Thunder." He worked fervently and passionately to share the Word of God. James' writings illustrate how he found contentment in all things because God is a provider who can do all things.

Due to the hands of unbelievers, Paul was beaten, imprisoned many times, and threatened, and he labored, toiled, and went without sleep, and more (2 Corinthians 11:16-33). Through his trials and tribulation, he remained humble. Even though he boasted, it was not of the world, but for Christ. He states:

"If I must boast, I will boast of the things that show my weakness. The God and Father of the Lord Jesus, who is to be praised forever, knows that I am not lying." 2 Corinthians 11:30–31 (NIV)

I bring these facts to your attention because James and Paul were disciples who worked together to spread the Good News including the message of Joy. The work of these apostles is intertwined, and their names appear often. In Paul's writing to the Philippians, he defines four areas that embrace Joy. They are as follows: Joy in Suffering (Philippians 1:1–30),

Joy in Giving (Philippians 4:2–23), Joy in Humility (Philippians 2:1–30), and the Joy of Believing (Philippians 3:1–4). Therefore, *All Joy: Models for our Daily Lives* has four chapters using these titles.

The main message of the Book of James challenges believers to walk by faith and to put into practice what they have learned. In other words, they must become doers of the Word of God and not just hearers only.

The concept of pure Joy makes you pause. At one time, I walked in your shoes. When I submitted to God and allowed Him to lead my steps daily, I began to experience His joy. I'm glad I learned there is more to life than the pursuit of things. When I experienced His Joy, I gave away the majority of what I had. Less became more. The consequences of seeking more isn't worth it. Keeping up with the Joneses is a burdensome thing. My dad would say, "When you get tired of being sick and tired, you will do something about it." When I let go of worldly things and thinking, weights were lifted from my shoulders.

There are living examples of Joy in this world. As you read this book, I pray that God will bless you. My desire is that you share what you learn with family, friends, relatives, and associates. They, too, deserve to spend eternity with God and begin to live life more abundantly.

As you examine testimonies in each section, take your time and absorb the commonalities. Begin to associate with people who have chosen Christ as their Savior and glean wisdom from their experiences. Remember, the world cannot give you Joy: only God will. Seek Him first!

DEFINING JOY

God is the source of all Joy. He sent His son, Jesus, into the world as a sacrifice for our sins. He hung, bled, and died on the cross, so that we may be reconciled back to God, the Father. Previously, an unblemished lamb was used, and the priest followed specific instructions as he prepared the altar to atone for our sins. God developed a new plan for the world and sent Jesus as the ultimate sacrificial lamb, who takes away the sins of the world.

As I developed the definition for Joy, I considered the following truths from scriptures:

First, God is forever present in our lives. His presence fills us with Joy. In Psalms 16:11 (NIV), scripture says, "You make known to me the path of life; you will fill me with joy in your presence, with eternal pleasures at your right hand." As life offers its challenges, God assures us: "Never will I leave you; never will I forsake you" Hebrews 13:5 (NIV).

Second, trusting and believing in God provides us with power. Scripture states: "May the God of hope fill you with all joy and peace as you trust in him, so that you may overflow with hope by the power of the Holy Spirit" Romans 15:13 (NIV). Notice you will overflow with hope by the power of the Holy Spirit. The hope of God provides us with the confidence to boldly address the trials and tribulations of life. Proudly, I proclaim the scripture, "I can do all things through Christ which strengthens me" Philippians 4:13 (KJV).

Third, God sends the Holy Spirit, who lives within us. *"This is the word of the LORD to Zerubbabel: 'Not by might nor by power, but by my Spirit,' says the LORD Almighty"* Zachariah 4:6 (NIV). The Holy Spirit leads, guides, counsels, instructs, convicts, and intercedes on our behalf. Scripture reminds us, "But the fruit of the Spirit is love, joy, peace, longsuffering, gentleness, goodness, faith" Galatians 5:22–23 (KJV).

With the guidance of the Holy Spirit, we look internally for answers to the world. We deny self and follow Christ's examples. When we use the fruit of the Spirit, we demonstrate love for people and God-like behavior to draw the world toward the Lord Jesus Christ. Jesus' Sermon on the Mount reminds us: "In the same way, let your light shine before others, that they may see your good deeds and glorify your Father in heaven" Matthew 5:16 (NIV).

Do you remember as a child singing, "I have that JOY down in my heart to stay" from the song "I've Got the Joy, Joy, Joy, Joy (Down in My Heart)" (by George William Cooke)? I loved singing that song. As a child, I never understood the meaning behind what I was singing. As I spent more time with Christ, I realized the song is so true. He has given

> As God's children, we have the Holy Spirit living inside us, and with Him come all the fruits of the Spirit, including joy.

joy to us and it will stay forever and ever. I thought this JOY was warm and fuzzy, never encountering problems, but this JOY is about the confidence in knowing that God is with you. He will never leave you nor forsake me. Since He is a God of every nation, I am assured He is in control of every detail of our lives. As believers, we are called to trust in the Lord with all your heart and lean not on your understanding. What another wonderful and comforting assurance that gives us confidence to walk boldly before the Lord in everything we do without being anxious or afraid. God loves us so much. He provided over 8000 assurances for us to stand firmly on and believe.

Additionally, Paul reminds us: "And we know that in all things God works for the good of those who love him, who have been called according to his purpose." Romans 8:28 (NIV) Therefore, let us "Rejoice in the Lord always. I will say it again: Rejoice." Philippians 4:4 (NIV) Abiding in the Lord allows us to sustain trials and tribulations, because true Joy comes from Him, and no one will take away your Joy. (John 16:22)

As we navigate through the book, the definition of Joy below will guide us as we read each testimony.

> Joy is a gift from God, who assures us that He has total control of our lives. We are confident that all things will work for the good and make the decision to praise and worship Him at all times.

THE JOURNEY

What does Joy "look like" and "sound like" in the life of those who know, believe, and love the Lord? It's easy to say, "Count it all Joy," but how do I do this? Are there "real people" that actually "Count it all Joy?" This book answers these questions and more. The reason this idea/concept challenges most people is because they have associated happiness with Joy. This book focuses on Joy not happiness, because happiness is temporary, conditional and comes from the outside. Joy is a gift from God: unconditional, last forevers, and an internal choice. No one can take away your Joy unless you allow them.

At the end of each chapter, there are questions entitled **Reflections** that provide an opportunity for the reader to make application to their lives; they are joined by **From the Heart**, which promotes a deeper understanding of the messages, and a **Prayer** thanking God for His Wisdom and Mercy.

The four chapters of testimonials are entitled *Joy of Suffering*, *Joy of Believing*, *Joy of Giving,* and *Joy of Humility,* represented by Christians/believers from all walks of life and various states, such as Kentucky, North Carolina, Texas, Alabama, Georgia, Ohio, Tennessee, Illinois, and New York.

As I present this collection of testimonies, I'm reminded of King Jehoshaphat of Judah in 2 Chronicles 20, who was told that a vast army was coming to destroy him and the people. The king and the people prayed together to God. On their way to battle, the king reminded them by saying: "Listen to me, Judah and people of Jerusalem! Have faith in the LORD your God and you will be upheld; have faith in his prophets and you will be successful." 2 Chronicles 20:20 (NIV)

In the end, Judah saw that the battle was not theirs but God's. In life, keep in mind that whatever you encounter, God has all power in his hands. Therefore, the battles of life are not yours, but God's. The trials and tribulations of life are unavoidable, but with God, we will overcome them.

My personal battle with loss of hearing greatly challenged me. I have purchased hearing devices every two years with increased technology to help me communicate better. Every time I take a hearing test, my hearing loss increases. I reminded the Lord that I'm expecting a miracle, sign, or wonder to overcome this trial. Since I am His creation, He can mold and shape me into whatever is best. The audiologist says I'm a candidate for a cochlear implant. I am going to wait for God's prognosis. He has the final say. I know His grace is sufficient. I have what I need to make it through each day.

As an educator, I enjoy learning and group activities. I have petitioned the Lord often about my situation, and He has heard my cry. Two years ago, I was told to advocate, don't give up and speak boldly about my hearing loss. As a result, He gave me a platform to testify, facilitate Zoom meetings, and advocate whenever needed for people with hearing loss. Not being able to hear does not mean I am not able to think.

Armed with God's directions, I proceed confidently into the world knowing the Holy Spirit will reveal to me what is important. Therefore, I can speak boldly. Most people are caring, open, patient, responsive, nurturing, and sensitive to the needs of those with hearing loss.

Some days are very challenging, but I remind myself that the battle is not mine. Without God, I would have given up. Hearing people really don't hear. They don't always listen to the needs of others or forget. Hearing loss affects one out five people, who often isolate themselves from the world. They end up being very lonely. When persons with hearing loss are overlooked, they sometimes give up and remain at home to avoid the humiliation or insensitivity of the world. Therefore, I am going to continue to advocate to make a difference.

If it wasn't for the Lord, I don't what I would have done. With him, I gain strength on those tough days. I am thankful for the tools that are available to me. Hearing loss advocacy groups provide signals, alarms, and communication devices to enhance my living environment. Only God has the power to win this battle, not the world. I am going to take each day and be thankful for what the Lord provides.

All Joy: Models in our Daily Lives is written as an invitation to persons who do not know the Lord and an inspiration to believers, who witness for Him. God wants all to be saved and none lost or left behind. He loves you so much! Open your minds, hearts and souls to the wonders, signs, and miracles of the Lord Jesus Christ. He has a message of Joy for you!

LET'S PRAYERFULLY BEGIN!

O, Lord our God, I thank you for your spirit of understanding and leading me to write this book to share with the world. I know that there are many people who still do not know who you are, but you are waiting patiently to receive them, because you want them to have eternal life with you.

There are a lot of people struggling who need to know that you have provided them with the tools of life to be successful. You, O Lord, are not a spirit of fear but of power, love, and a sound mind. The battles we try to fight by our might are impossible to win. The fight is spiritual, a warfare encountered in the spiritual realm, therefore, we need a savior who can do supernatural things. We need a Savior who has assigned angels in the spiritual realm to help guard, guide, and protect us. Thank you, Father!

I thank you, Lord, for the persons who are reading this book. May they grow strong in your power and know that only God provides joy that is everlasting. Above all, Lord, we praise and honor you for what is about to happen in our lives. We know that victory is yours, that you love us with an everlasting love and want us to live life more abundantly. May the Joy that is in you, Lord, prevail in our lives forever and ever. Amen.

Chapter 1

THE JOY OF SUFFERING

> "Suffering is intrinsic to human existence. There is no joy without its attendant pain."
>
> Peter Ackroyd

> "Struggles not only make us into stronger, better, and wiser people, they also let us learn more about ourselves and our purpose in life."
> Auliq Ice

There is no way to get through life without pain, suffering and struggling. No one is immune to it. With ourselves and God, we struggle with our health, jobs, families, finances, politics, relationships, racism, and abuse. Why does this happen? How do we become overcomers?

The Apostle Paul lived his entire life suffering 2 Corinthians 11:23–33 (KJV). He calls this pain and suffering momentary/light when you compare eternity with the Lord. Paul was imprisoned for teaching the Word of Jesus Christ. In verses 26–27, an excerpt of his suffering reads as follows: "… in journeys often, in perils of waters, in perils of robbers, in perils of my own countrymen, in perils of the Gentiles, in perils in the city, in perils in the wilderness, in perils in the sea, in perils among false brethren; in weariness and toil, in sleeplessness often, in hunger and thirst, in fasting often, in cold and nakedness." 2 Corinthians 11:26–27 (NKJV)

Getting through the tough times of life requires focus. If you take your eyes off Jesus, you lose sight of who is in control. I had my son at 32 years. During my second doctor's visit, I was told that I had a fibroid tumor larger than the baby and needed to go to the hospital immediately. I was traumatized. My family was shocked and thought I needed a second opinion. After gathering more information, the family realized that time was of the essence. I immediately checked into the hospital.

Weeks earlier, I knew something was wrong inside my body. I could feel it within my spirit. Eating and sleeping were difficult, but I would go to work hoping that things would get better. I was losing weight, but my stomach continued to grow.

Having a baby was not in my plans. I thought I could wait until I was 35 years old to have my first child. God knew differently. When I heard the news I could lose the baby, I cried out to God, prayed and stayed on my knees petitioning before Him. Christian friends and family came to pray and intercede on my behalf before God for health and strength.

When I came out of surgery, the doctor was not sure if the baby would survive. When the doctor said the tumor was the size of a grapefruit and successfully removed, I felt hopeful that everything would be just fine. Even though the tumor pressed against the baby, I still felt peace. As I stayed home six weeks recovering and praying, God was faithful. I rested with the assurance that He is in total control.

The rest of the story is that the baby is now 48 years old with two sons. As I think back on the encounter, I find this experience was a steppingstone in developing my trust and belief in Christ. He heard my prayers, and I know I can trust Him in all things.

In the Bible, Job is another example. He suffered and lost family, children, house, possessions, health, and friends. Job's response was, "the Lord giveth, and the Lord taketh away; blessed be the name of the Lord." Job 1:21 (KJV) He lived with the unshakeable confidence that the Lord was the source of everything. Regardless of Job's situation, he was going to praise the name of the Lord.

In *Book of Joy: Lasting Happiness in a Changing World* by the Dalai Lama, Desmond Tutu, and Douglas Carlton Abrams, they describe how Nelson Mandela was imprisoned in a travesty of justice from 1964 to 1990. Upon his release, Mandela soon became the deputy president, then president of the African National Conference (ANC) because he wanted to destroy the enemy of his people. During his imprisonment, the Lord had revealed to him that he would serve 27 years. Through the discomfort, pain, and suffering, he emerged kind, caring, and ready to trust his enemy (*Book of Joy: Lasting Happiness in a Changing World*, p.153).

The greatest and most memorable example of suffering was Jesus on the cross. Christ felt abandoned and forsaken, so he cried out, *"My God, my God, why have you forsaken me?"* Matthew 27:46 (NIV) If He had not gone to the cross, we would not know of salvation and eternity with Him.

How do we live in the midst of suffering if it cannot be avoided? Baptist minister Edward Mote stated it best in his hymn "My Hope Is Built on Nothing Less,": "My hope is built on nothing less than Jesus' blood and righteousness." There is Hope in suffering.

In the book *Torn* (2011), Jud Wilhite points out that it is not about the "why" questions, but the "who." He states the following: "Why is not the most fundamental question when it comes to suffering. The most fundamental question is who. Who will we trust in the calamities of life?" (*Torn*, p.7)

Elisabeth Elliot and her husband, Jim, were missionary workers in Ecuador. The Waodani Indians killed her husband and four other missionaries. Even though her friends and family said to leave immediately, she yearned to live with the Waodani Indians while raising her daughter Val. She wrote the Bible in the Waodani language and trained men to carry on the ministry as a previous promise to her husband before his death. Without a doubt, whom we trust can only give us the strength and power to persevere in this situation. She said, "Pain is never for nothing. In our suffering, we learn something. Most important lesson is that God loves us."

I empathize with Elisabeth Elliot. When my husband passed, the pain was unbelievable, shocking and excruciating. I couldn't stop crying. Dying to me would be easier than going through the agony of missing a loved one. Separating from someone you loved for 38 years is hard to do. I couldn't think straight, eat, or sleep. Transacting all the paperwork was insurmountable. Without my sister-in-law Mildred's help, I would not have been able to do it. I asked a lot of "why" questions.

> The suffering is what makes you appreciate the joy.
>
> Dalai Lama XIV

In order to survive, I had to stay in the Word of God. I found peace and comfort reading daily. I am so glad God's Word was available to me. When I didn't think I could move one foot in front of the other, He was there. When He said to cast all my cares upon Him, I was glad to do so. I needed Him to carry them because my burdens were too heavy.

I finally understood what the Lord's Prayer meant. I began to take one day at a time. The Lord was my shepherd, provider, protector, teacher, and comforter. Fifteen years later, I am stronger, wiser and willing to serve Him. The more time I spent with Him, I began to see His plan for me unfold. God sent people to comfort me, and now I am comforting others through grief counseling. He led me to writing this book, so the world will learn more about His joy. He has turned my mourning into dancing again.

My sorrow has been lifted. Only God can do this! In and of myself, I can do nothing.

Suffering is something that no one wants to happen, but it brings you to your knees and shows you that life is not about you, but Jesus Christ. In the book, *Choose Joy (2012),* Kay Warren reminds us that God uses dark times in our lives to reveal his majesty. He ultimately shows us he is the Creator, Sustainer, Deliverer, and Redeemer (*Choose Joy*, p.103).

In the Book of Joy, the Dalai Lama states, "the suffering is what makes you appreciate the joy. In spite of difficulties and suffering, you can remain firm and maintain your composure" (*Book of Joy*, the Dalai Lama, p. 146). He also points out that when you see your suffering having meaning, it becomes ennobling versus embittering (*Book of Joy*, the Dalai Lama p.153).

In this section of the book, testimonies of sufferings demonstrate how Christians counted it all Joy, because Jesus Christ revealed wonderful and mighty things in their lives. As a result, they became stronger witnesses and drew closer to Him. They walked not by their might, but of the Lord. The testimonies reflect that in this twisted, chaotic, distorted, confused, and evil world, God has the last Word. His mercy and grace give them a chance to "get it right" before judgment occurs. One day, our tears will be wiped away, no more pain or suffering, only eternity with Him.

Joy is a gift from God, who assures us that He has total control of our lives. We are confident that all things will work for the good and make the decision to praise and worship Him at all times.

JOY OF SUFFERING TESTIMONIES

"Joy is not in things; it is in us." Richard Wagner

AN OVERCOMER

By Eloise Greer

> "My brethren, count it all joy when ye fall into divers temptations;
> Knowing this, that the trying of your faith worketh patience.
> But let patience have her perfect work, that ye may be perfect and entire, wanting nothing." James 1:2–4 (KJV)

Joy is that positive attitude that rises above circumstances and focuses on the character of God and His love for us. The Joy required of the righteous is given by the Spirit of God.

When the trials of our lives come, we must be able to determine if these trials come from the world and Satan or from God. If they are from God, we will know that these experiences are a test of our faith and as such should be accepted as Joy. My trial came on a quiet Sunday afternoon in August 1983. At the time, we had just relocated to the area. My family included my husband and 7-year-old daughter. My daughter and I were preparing to return to evening service at church, while my husband was preparing to drive to his job, which was about two hours from our home. After prayers and goodbyes, we went our separate ways. Just as I backed out of the driveway, I sensed a "pop" in my head and immediately my head began to ache, and I was unable to turn my head left or right. At the time, I was not worried because I had only been hospitalized for the birth of my daughter. We worshipped for two hours and upon leaving the church to head home, my vision became blurry. Although this was concerning, I still did not panic, but when I blinked my eyes to clear my vision, everything went dark.

At this point, I began to panic and pulled the car over. My daughter called our emergency contact and once she arrived, I was transported to the hospital's E.R. At the end of a five-hour examination, which included brain scans and a spinal tap, I was admitted to the ICU because I had blood in my spinal fluid. I was placed under sensory isolation, which includes complete darkness, no outside stimuli (e.g., television, radio, phones, or magazines). My visits were limited to my husband who was instructed not to give me bad news! I was hospitalized for 30 days following this episode.

My diagnosis, while in the hospital, was a brain hemorrhage, causes unknown. The only lasting effect was a change in my vision, requiring new corrective lenses for my glasses.

There were many days and nights to reflect on my condition and I could have taken this as a trial from Satan rather than God. I believed that it was a sign from God, and I chose to show my love for Him out loud among my peers and family.

One of my many works of joy was teaching Sunday School classes, setting up the church nursery and organizing the Dorcas Ministry, a community clothing closet.

I take time each day to give thanks for my trials and tribulations and the grace and mercy God has shown me, in allowing me to overcome them. I know that these things have made me a stronger Christian and follower of Christ.

STRENGTHENING MY FAITH

Alice and James Binford

I counted it all Joy when I fell into trials and tribulations. I accepted Christ at an early age in Athens, Alabama. Here, I was in Christ Jesus, but my faith wasn't as strong as I thought it should be. Even though I was attending Sunday School every Sunday, singing in the male chorus, and a deacon serving on the board, I thought that I was putting my trust in God.

So, one day I asked the Lord to strengthen my faith, not realizing how or when He was going to do what I had asked. One day, I went to work, and my supervisor met me at the door and said, "As of right now, we are closed and not in business anymore." At that moment, I didn't know what to do or say, but I knew that I had to tell my wife and children about not having a job any longer.

My first response was to cry and say, "What am I going to do now?" The Lord spoke and said unto me that He was going to take care of us, and provide for us without the job just as He had done when I had a job. The Lord let me know that He was our provider and sustainer and not we ourselves. At this time, our daughter had just graduated from high school, getting ready to go to college at Western Kentucky University, and our son was preparing to go to college in the next two years. The Lord, proving himself to us, gave our son a full scholarship in football at the same university. Won't God do it?

During this time, my faith was strengthened by reading Psalms 37. The Psalm taught me patience, because God's time is not the same as ours, therefore, we must endure our trials and tribulations. I read it over and over again until I realized what God as telling me. I learned that the trials I had experienced were a test of my faith and without a doubt He would supply all of our needs according to His riches in Glory.

The trials and tribulations are not to destroy you, but only to make you strong in Him. I have matured in a stronger walk with the Lord and believe that no matter what may come my way, the Lord is working it out for my good. Know that if God brings you to a situation, trial, or tribulation, He will see you through it. What the devil meant for evil, the Lord turns into good.

What I would like the world to know is just because you are going through trials and tribulations, it isn't necessarily because you have sinned or are not living in the right relationship with God. It possibly can be that the Lord is using you to bring Glory to Him, just as He did with Job, who had no knowledge of what God was doing when he lost everything.

During this process of strengthening my faith, I held on and continued to walk with Him, worship Him in spirit and truth, and not forget to tithe with what I have. I remained faithful unto Him. He restored me back with a job, truck driving, just as I had in the beginning. The new job was at a better place with better supervisors.

COUNT IT ALL JOY!

Pastor Willie M. Byrd

"My brethren, count it all joy when you fall into various trials, knowing that the testing of your faith produces patience. But let patience have its perfect work, that you may be perfect and complete, lacking nothing." James 1:2–4 (NKJV)

James' messages to me about counting it all Joy, have been very inspiring and enlightening when facing great trials or troubles during my many years trying to do the Master's will. It has caused me to be steadfast and unmovable despite the storms I've had to face as an ordained pastor these 36 years.

At times while carrying out the divine purpose of God's calling on my life, I've faced some challenging moments of disappointments and adversities that could have caused me to give up. But nevertheless, the inspired words from James have caused me to persevere and be encouraged, knowing that my trials and tests were only there to make me wiser and stronger.

Being a devoted husband, father, and full-time pastor of a large congregation at times can be very challenging and overwhelming. The many responsibilities that you often having to face can easily cause you to burn out; however, allow me to say this in a respectful way. It is a great price in following Jesus.

The most active moment of my life happened after the calling to be a full-time pastor of a church. I was holding a full-time job and was now providing leadership as a pastor. This alone is too much for any human being to do, but nevertheless, I was obedient and determined to serve in this capacity. The Lord spoke to me when I was 38, and He said, "I have the power to bring you out of the workplace." Now, of course, this was very challenging for me, because my family was depending on my income for provision. However, I was obedient to do this although it was not all popular or pleasurable for my family. To step out of my comfort zone into the unfamiliar was something different.

Now, I was giving up a very well-paying job with bonuses and benefits to trusting God for daily blessings. Now remember, my three children were young and in grade school. Often, I had to encourage myself in the Lord, when so many others were concerned about my welfare. What I do know today is God honors faith. Also, He is a rewarder of those who seek him and step out to do His will (Hebrews 11:6). Above all, He is faithful.

Many times, my family and others who were close to me were very concerned about my well-being because they too had witnessed the crisis of painful heartaches and disappointments I had endured. So, praise the Lord. He kept me safely through my many storms; that is why I can count it all Joy. His grace sustained me through every storm, and I've been kept by His grace and anointed and covered by His blood.

My personal response, now after looking back over my life these many years, has caused me to better appreciate life and the love He has for me. God's grace has been sufficient, "more than enough," to keep me through it all so that I can still have Joy. At times I must admit that I felt like those three Hebrew boys who were put in the fiery furnace; but now I know I was never alone, because the fourth one was there with me in the midst keeping me all along. So, counting it all Joy has taught me so many valuable lessons in how to survive the pitfalls of trials in my life. Also, to have faith is to believe that all things are working together for my good (Romans 8:28). To have faith is to trust God even when I can't trace Him, and to believe that if He brings you to it, He (God) will bring you through it. Today, I can truly testify that the Lord has been faithful. He has taught me to stay in the faith no matter what I am going through. Also, to count it all Joy even when it doesn't seem to make sense how "weeping may endure for a night, but Joy comes in the morning." Psalms 30:5 (NKJV)

Finally, it is my Christian confession to let you know that the Joy of the Lord is my strength Nehemiah 8:10 (KJV). It has truly been a blessing sharing my personal testimony about how invigorating it has been laboring as a full-time pastor these 36 years. Although I've had my share of trials, heartaches, and disappointments, God has kept me covered with His grace, and today, I count it all Joy. Everything that the devil has done to distract and harm me, God has used it for His glory to elevate me. Also, I can tell you that He has favored me. So, whoever happens to read my story, always remember you can always count it all Joy when you fall into great trials and tests of troubles. Keep the faith and give God praise. Let patience have her way, because it produces fruits in your life. So "being confident of this very thing, that He who has begun a good work in you will complete it until the day of Jesus Christ." Philippians 1:6 (NKJV) So beloved, I pray this message will cause you to be encouraged and motivated to be all God has called you to be.

MAMA'S LOVE

Gwen Johnson

I got up that morning in February 2015, knowing I had to tell Mama a secret I had been carrying around for over 50 years. It was important that I tell her that day because I knew she did not have much time left. I packed a bag, jumped in my car, left Maryland, and headed for Salisbury, North Carolina, where she was in hospice. I only stopped once to refill the gas tank because I could sense time was running out. I called Mama's room and did not get an answer but left a message that I was on my way. When I arrived, the nurse said, "Your Mother died a few minutes ago." I cried knowing that I did not make it in time.

The lady I called Mama did not give birth to me. I was the child of my daddy and his first wife, when they were both teenagers. At the age of 14, I was spending time with my birth mother, two half-brothers, a half sister and her second husband, when it happened. My stepfather drank a lot, I often watched as he beat my mother and when she wasn't around, he would beat me. My stepfather returned home one night, wanting to know where Mother was. Even though I was sleeping in a room with my siblings, he came in and got on top of me and raised my gown up. I started screaming, it woke up the other kids and in a drunken stupor, he rolled off the bed onto the floor. Then, he staggered out. I ran out of the house and hid in the woods.

That night, I prayed for God's help. I recited the 23rd Psalm. I didn't know what I needed, but I decided to kill myself if I couldn't get away from him touching me again. I couldn't call Mama without permission, so I wrote her a letter begging her and my daddy to please come and save me. I never told them why. I didn't hear anything for a couple of weeks and decided I couldn't stay in that house any longer, so I was planning to run away. I had no idea where I was going. Suddenly, one morning, my birth mother told me I needed to pack my clothes and get ready to take the train back to California — alone. At 14, I knew God's grace had delivered me from evil.

I learned by accident, years later, that my daddy and Mama had a terrible fight back then. He wanted to fight it out in court, and she said, "No!" that I needed to come back immediately. She somehow knew getting me back could not wait. When Daddy left to visit his father (my grandfather) in Colorado, Mama had bought the train ticket and sent it to me without telling him. God had used her as the instrument for His work.

Mama's love was my guide throughout my life, and I learned to define the love of children and family not by blood, but by God's lessons of caring for all of us. I gave birth to two girls, but I also have a spiritual son who found himself alone and I brought him into our family.

When Mama's cancer became terminal in 2014, without hesitation, I committed to her being as comfortable and at peace as possible as she ended her journey on earth. She let me know she was ready. Together, we made her final arrangements. I was blessed to be able to spend most of her last days at her bedside.

When I entered her room for the last time, she was still warm; I cried as I laid my head on the bed beside her. I told her that one of the reasons I had always loved her so much was because she had saved me from evil all those years ago. I told her I was sorry, because I never revealed my thoughts. It saddened me that I had not told her when she was alive.

A few days after her death, I was sitting alone in the house, where she and I had shared so many conversations. Suddenly, I felt at peace. I felt Joy! My Joy was in the revelation that she had known all along what I never said, and God's love combined with hers had saved me.

FREE AT LAST

Sandra Whiteside, MSSW, CSW

My tribulation occurred many years ago in the early seventies. I worked at night and was waiting in my car for a friend to get off work as well. It was a hot summer night, and my car window was down. Suddenly, out of nowhere, a strange man appeared at my car door with a knife in his hand. Before I knew what happened, the knife was thrust at my throat! I tried to scream, but terror claimed the sound. I grabbed at the knife, and he yanked it back, cutting my hand. Again, the knife was at my throat. He grabbed me by the hair and dragged me out of my car, cursing at me the whole time. So now I found myself in a vacant lot, terrified with a knife-wielding stranger. He used that knife to cut my dress off of me. I was sexually assaulted that night in the vacant lot with freshly mowed grass.

I wasn't ready to die! I had been brought up in the church but had fallen away. All I could think about was my children at home. What would they do without their mother? The Lord gave me His prayer to say, and I prayed the Lord's prayer over and over. When he was done, the stranger cursed at me and kicked me, leaving me there with my hand bleeding, crying with no clothes on. I was able to gather myself and staggered back toward my car. By that time, my friend came out of the house, got me clothes to wear and saw me home.

I called the police once I arrived home. They were so very rude, asking if I had been wearing "one of them there mini-skirts" and "whether I was sure it wasn't one of my boyfriends." I never heard from the officers for follow-up after that night. It felt as though I was raped for a second time by the police officer.

For years, I hated the man who did this to me. I would wonder if I had passed him on the street or seen him in the grocery store. Whenever I smelled freshly cut grass, I would have a flashback and throw up. I couldn't help it. Hatred consumed me for years as I felt that I had a RIGHT to hate him. God told me over and over to forgive the man, but I flatly refused, thinking, "But God, you don't understand the violation and the humiliation," (as if He had not suffered violation and humiliation for me on Calvary's cross). For years I felt unworthy, that I was damaged goods, a dirty rag.

Some decades later, I heard a sermon in which the preacher declared, "God has freed you from Egypt, and you're dragging Pharaoh around with you!" She then asked anyone in the congregation to come to the altar and thank Him for his deliverance and pray for Pharoah! At that moment, I decided to forgive the man who had violated me and to ask the Lord to forgive me for hating him all these years. FREE AT LAST! My life blossomed after that experience. I decided to return to school and obtain my master's degree in social work, giving my life to helping others, particularly women who had been abused and neglected. I was 53 years old at the time, but that did not lessen my resolve to do my part to make the world a better place for those who are bruised and battered. I learned that day that God is a healer, and forgiveness is not for the person who wronged me, but forgiveness is for ME!

For those of you who feel that you have been wronged, think about Jesus, how He suffered, bled, and died. *He paid a debt that He didn't owe because we owed a debt that we couldn't pay.*

Don't waste your time hating; work through your pain and grief. God has something special for you. Just believe the things that God says about you, not what the world says. He declares that you are fearfully and wonderfully made. Walk in that and be blessed!

OUT OF THE PUDDLE

Patrick Sullivan

I was baptized at 5 years old and had to go faithfully to church every Sunday. Mrs. McDaniels, my Sunday School teacher, taught us how to pray and shared stories in the Bible. In the youth choir at church, we did plays for Christmas. My dad, sister, and I helped clean the church and kept the grass cut — even at the graveyard.

My biggest problem was knowing right from wrong. At first, I thought everybody was just nasty and mean. I knew that I was to always treat everybody the way you wanted to be treated. I have been in some situations where I was doing more of what I knew was wrong. Seemed like God would let me know it was just wrong. Growing up, there were some situations I thought that I would never get out of, but God straightened me up by putting people in my life who helped me.

When I was run out of my hometown, I came to Louisville. Even though I would try to do right, I would still get hurt. I remember one time when I met my future wife, I thought it was going to be a struggle at home. When I got here, it was different; there were brothers here that wanted to embrace me, talk to me, and try to help me stay on the right path. I thank God for that, and I gradually caught on to how to do things from being around Godly people. I liked how they were living their lives. The person who helped and pushed me the most was my wife. She introduced me to God.

I have been transformed. My previous life looked like a person jumping into a mud puddle while everyone is looking. I was a dirty mess. Now I am out of that mud puddle and cleaned up. Everyone is saying, "wow!" It feels good that people now see me in a different way. When they see me, they see how God transformed me by cleaning my body and my mind. I see things differently and want to please God in what I say and do. I would say to you don't give up, because there is always somebody out there that will show kindness and will push you toward doing the right things so you may live the right life.

You have to show a kid right from wrong, because life is a learning experience. I finally caught on. Thank you, God. I stepped up in my life. At first, being a dad was scary and embarrassing, but I got the hang of it. I didn't want to be as rough on my son as my father had treated me. Thank God, I had a good son! I provided for him and my wife. He is still a little distant with me in his behavior, but we have a good relationship.

He knows who Christ is because we went to church as a family. Church members helped my son choose a college and find a scholarship. This year, he graduated. I am thankful God transformed me as a testimony to the entire family.

IN THE MIDST OF THE STORM

Elizabeth Caples

Is Joy within our reach as we watch, look, and listen to daily reflections of sorrow, grief, and sadness? Challenging situations are ever present in our lives, and we wonder which way would be the best way to turn.

As I continue to read and study the scriptures, I find clarity, and it becomes clearer daily that we all can be joyful in the midst of any predicament or dilemma.

Times of trouble, struggle, or unhappiness must be met with acceptance, perseverance, and continuous staying power. Strength of mind allows one to endure pain or adversity with courage and tenacity.

As I look back over my life and think things over, I am a witness that trouble and misery have been in existence. Joy in the midst of it all was very difficult to see; however, I began to realize that my loved ones remain in my heart and spirit.

As I catch a glimpse of the past, I think about my dear mother. We made use of all the time that we had together. We spent time talking in person several times a day, traveling together, and having all holiday meals and Sunday dinners together. I was at her house almost every day. My mother was my best friend! I also have Joy in knowing that we were together in her last weeks, days, and hours on this earth. She called me her "angel" from her hospital bed. Those words remain with me now from 20 years ago. Her love, care, and teaching has carried me thus far and it has been a true blessing from God.

When I meditate on the past, my mind allows me to think of my one and only daughter who passed away 10 years ago. Her passing was truly something that could not come close to allowing any Joy to inch in. Small cell lung cancer was something that I never anticipated, because this information was never shared with me by her. I knew that she was getting sicker, but I never knew a specific reason. Joy in the midst of a storm will probably not come at the time of great pain; however, trust in God can ease that pain, and Joy will come knowing that her spirit remains with us.

She loved her five children dearly and they also loved her very deeply. Joy truly came when her third son became the national winner of Season Nine on the televised Master Chef television program. This Joy was unspeakable!

We all knew that his mom was definitely smiling down on him as he cooked his way to stardom.

I once heard a person say that trials, tribulations, and disappointments take away the joys of life. I say that when you grow closer to God, you will be filled with Joy in the midst of a storm.

As a retired teacher, I have watched many students struggle with many adversities. Great Joy came when I was able to say a kind word, lend advice, pronounce a word, help a student learn something about music, or uncover a hidden talent.

In summing up Joy in the midst of a storm, I realize that our lives are full of love, pain, Joy, and sorrow. It is up to us to face trials when they arise and seek the Joy that our Lord and Savior freely gives. We must strive to count everything as Joy in Christ Jesus.

COUNT IT ALL JOY: A TESTIMONY OF FAITH

Joyce Mayes

I was blessed to be born into and raised by parents in a home where Christian principles and faith in God were taught and demonstrated in the lives of my parents. My dad was the breadwinner in a family with eight children, while my mom stayed at home and took care of the daily needs of our family and the household. My dad, besides working an eight-hour job, also pastored a church. I've seen my parents go through life struggles such as financial crisis, sickness, and sadness due to the death of close relatives and friends, all while maintaining a strong faith in God.

I was a "pew" baby, and was taught at an early age about God's love for me and all of mankind. I learned about the life of Christ, and the sacrifice He made through His death on Calvary. I accepted Christ as my personal Savior at 12 years of age, was filled with His Spirit, and thus began my walk with Christ.

In over 60 years of walking with Christ, I've learned and experienced many things that have solidified my relationship with Him. I was married for almost 41 years before the passing of my husband, and we were the parents of nine children. I needed God's guidance as I navigated through marriage, raising children, financial issues after income loss from job changes, sickness, and death. I've learned that in times of trouble, God is always with me, and it's been during turbulent times that my relationship with God has been truly developed. I've learned to respect God's sovereignty. I've come to realize that whatever the trial of life or how hard things appear to be, life events do not negate who God is! Nothing can separate me from the amazing love of God! I have experienced what is found in Psalms 46:1 (KJV), "God is our refuge and strength, a very present help in trouble."

One of the most significant events that I've experienced in life was the illness and death of my precious son, Michael. He was a junior in college, majoring in biology, with aspirations of becoming a doctor when he became ill. He appeared to have flu-like symptoms and went to a clinic where he was given medication. (The office of our neighborhood doctor was closed at the time and was to reopen later during the week.)

Michael attended class the following day, as he was preparing for mid-term exams. When he returned home from class, while in conversation with Michael, I noticed that he seemed extremely tired, and it was something unexplainable about his countenance that caused me to be so concerned that I insisted we go to the emergency room of one of our local hospitals. In recalling this experience, I began to see how God is in control and how He has orchestrated my life.

Michael was diagnosed as being in complete renal failure and his condition was critical. I was in the emergency room not knowing whether my son was going to live or die. I do believe had I not gotten him to the hospital with an urgency, Michael would not have lived to see another day. I would also like to mention the fact that because my husband and I had recently changed jobs with less pay, we had no medical insurance on Michael. One of the nurses on duty in ER recommended a specialist in nephrology to me and agreed, with my permission, to call him to see if he would be willing to treat my son. Shortly after the call, Dr. Sidney Marcum arrived at the hospital, examined Michael and agreed to take charge of Michael's care. Michael was admitted to the hospital and once Michael was stabilized, Dr. Marcum discussed Michael's condition with me. He further stated that he was aware that Michael was uninsured, and that Michael had a condition that even he could not afford. Dr. Marcum sent his office social worker to talk to me and Michael qualified for resources that paid for all of his medical expenses, which included hospitalizations, dialysis, doctor's visits, and a kidney transplant. I might also add that because I had changed jobs, prior to Michael's illness, the hours of my new job allowed me to go through the training I needed to give Michael dialysis at home as he waited for a kidney transplant.

Michael received a kidney from his brother, and the quality of his life improved. He was able to graduate from college and marry his high school sweetheart. Although he never became a doctor, he became employed as a certified expert in the field of technology. Michael's life was productive, and he was a gift to his family, friends and co-workers.

God added additional years to his life for my family to love Michael and for Michael to show us love in return. Unfortunately, Michael contracted the COVID-19 virus and expired on January 10, 2022.

Presently, I am still going through the grieving process. There are times when I sometimes cry (unexpectedly) because of a memory that I attach to some incident or event that reminds me of Michael. I've learned during those times not to suppress the tears or the feeling of sadness because I miss my son. I am also aware of the fact that there are more instances when I smile remembering something funny that he'd said or did in the past. I do know that the Holy Spirit has brought me comfort through God's Word and through hymns that exalt Him.

I can rejoice in the Lord because of God's goodness to me! I am grateful for past and present blessings. I have Joy when I think that God gave me the precious gift of Michael! He allowed me to be his mom, and to be a part of Michael's journey on earth. Since Michael's death, I find Joy and appreciation for so many more things that I once took for granted. I love my family and friends profoundly, and I am more appreciative of their love and the kindness they show me. I wake up seeking for purpose and asking God to help me to be a reflection of Him. The Joy of the Lord is my strength!

THE POTTER'S HANDS

Kim Jackson

I came to Christ around the age of 6 under the leadership of the Rev. C. D. Simmons at the Friendship Missionary Baptist church, located at 1200 Zane Street, Louisville, Kentucky. My family was significantly involved in the church and contributed to my spiritual education and belief in Christ. I am thankful for the expressions of faith I witnessed in my great grandmother, Eula Bell High-Beach; grandmother, Julia Cockrell Beasley-Washington; my mother and father, Birdell Beasley-Jackson and Lee M. Jackson, as well as various aunts and uncle who were all active in the church. My mother constantly poured into my life by teaching me to utilize my prayer closet and to serve God in my youth.

I believe that I have always carried a faith and belief that I am filled with the blessings and favor of God. My first experience at really experiencing that covering was as I left home as a teen to join the United States Air Force. I didn't realize it then, however God was molding and shaping me into the person that I am today. I remember having a peace that was beyond understanding as I felt nervous and a little bit scared about being so far away from home with people, I didn't know for the first time. I remember having the spirit of encouragement with the members of my squadron that were also far from home. Joking, laughing, and encouraging them and how they noticed that I was always happy and in good spirits no matter the challenges we faced. That peace, comfort and encouragement followed and covered me then during those 9 years as it does now in my later life.

First Peter 5:7 says to cast all your fears/cares upon the Lord because He cares for you. I did this as I moved home after those 9 years as my mother was being diagnosed with pancreatic cancer. God through His infinite wisdom, grace, and mercy sent me home to be with my mother during her final months of life. This decision was a gift beyond measure that allowed me to grow closer to God and to gain a greater understanding that He is my source and my strength. I have seen this throughout my life as I raised my daughter as a single mom; lost my father to lung cancer; lost my older sister, Pamela to a rare form of cancer; lost my older brother, Antonio, to suicide; and most recently lost my cousin Walt to COVID-19. Through all these trials, losses, and events, God has been right there with me, making a way, carrying me through, and letting me know without a doubt that I can lean on Him, depend on Him, and be comforted by Him. During my darkest moments, God would whisper to me, reminding me that I am His child and that He cares for me.

The good news is that I carry with me every day of my life, that God has my back, that He is there for me, and what He will do for me, He will do for others. You only need to trust Him!

Thanks be to God and for all that He has allowed to be poured into my life!

RESTING IN JESUS

Mildred A. Binford Smith

I gave my life to Christ at the age of 12. As I realized later, when I walked out of the church building, I took back the gave part. I did not completely understand what happened. Thank GOD I continually went to church, sang in the choir, attended Bible studies and Sunday school. When I did this, I began to understand.

Most important, my father was a deacon in the church, so we were required to attend services. When I became an adult, between the ages of 18 through 31, I got married, had four children and continued to go with my children to the church. One thing I realized, I never left the church when trying times would come from raising children and other trials of life. Don't misunderstand, I still don't have it all together, but I still know where the House of the Lord is.

However, the real desire to follow Jesus came around the age of 32. One day I said to the Lord, "I have done everything there is to do, what do I do now?"
I heard him say, "Follow me."
I replied, "I can do that!"
I have been running for the Lord for the last 40 years.

My testimony is Resting in Jesus through the passing of my daughter last year from COVID. Going through this trial was nothing like any other. God kept me in His REST. All of my emotions were wrapped up in the Savior's arm. I was at peace during this trial, which went on for six months. Everyone was praying and fasting for her recovery, but the Lord made the choice to take her home.

Something good happened during the home going services of my daughter. There was something different about the services. The pastor gave an altar call and the soloist sang the song *Tomorrow* by the Winans and five of my grandchildren gave their lives to Christ that day. I cried and gave glory to God.

I have learned what it means to be in His rest and to count it ALL JOY. I discovered in His rest there is Joy, in His Joy there is peace, and in His peace, there is comfort. I found Joy, even in grief.

People say you must show grief, cry, and feel bad. Well, I never felt those emotions during this trial. Since I didn't feel these emotions, I thought there was something wrong with me. Don't think for a minute I don't miss her. I do, but I know where she is.

Now, I understand clearly what "Count It All Joy" really means. I want others to understand to remain in Joy all the time. I learned a lot about grief. With much prayer and praise, Joy is one of the fruits of the spirit, and the Joy of the Lord is my strength. I believe grief is not filled with negative emotions, but Joy covers all emotions. I now understand what "Count It All Joy" means.

DISCOVERING JOY THROUGH DEVASTATION

Carolyn Collins

On Sunday October 26, 2011, my husband of 42 years unexpectedly died without any warning. We were married at the ages of 17 and 18 years, respectively. My world was focused on my husband and children. I had a serious surgery which caused me to have a sense of personal mortality. It led me to a lifetime of medication; consequently, I felt I was going to be my the first one to die. My husband had never been sick or in the hospital; therefore, without any hint of expectation, my world shattered into tiny pieces, and I lost any reason to continue on in this existence.

I was brought up in the church and I was baptized at the age of 6 years. Sundays were special days filled with various church services from morning to night. I loved church, especially Sunday School, because I had a thirst for learning about God's Word. I knew I could pray about all things and God Loved Me Unconditionally. Throughout those 42 years of marriage, I knew without a shadow of doubt that God Answers Prayers. Many times, people would ask me how we stayed together for so long from teenagers through adult years, and I gave all the glory to God. It was not us. Faith and Prayer overcame the obstacles of life.

Now, on this special 10/26/11 day, where is God? Why has He forsaken me? My emotions ran from shock, confusion, anger, abandonment, depression to complete devastation. I knew God had all power and He could have saved my husband. So, why didn't He save him? I became determined that I could not live in this world any longer. One night after I had a major breakdown. I shouted at God asking, "Why did you take him from me?" I threw things around my bedroom until I fell, exhausted onto the floor. In the midst of the quietness, I heard a very clear voice say the following, "He was never yours in the first place. He was always my child. I allowed you to have him for a little while then I decided it was time for me to bring him home." Thus began my journey toward healing, discovering Joy through devastation.

My relationship with God changed throughout the emotional rollercoaster of grief with God becoming my best friend and developing a closer more consistent relationship with deeper insight into God's Word. Making sense out of the nonsense helped me to develop the Grief Ministry to give others hope in life by sharing my story and informing them their key to survival is developing a relationship with God. I share all my thoughts with God, both good and bad. Of course, he knows everything anyway. I still deal with bouts of depression and loneliness, but I know where my help comes from. I am discovering who I am as a person without the lifetime titles. I believe God still has several purposes for my life. Therefore, I walk into and throughout the challenges of life with renewed confidence that I am God's child. "I can do all things through Christ who strengthens me." Philippians 4:13 (NKJV) I feel Joy in knowing that, regardless of my circumstances or the world's situation, God is in Control. God answers **prayers!**

QUESTION TO GOD

Desiree Anthony

WHY? That's the question I had for God November 1984 after my mother Winnie, that's what we called her, was diagnosed with lung cancer. Growing up as a youth in Versailles, Kentucky, attending First Baptist Church, I always heard pastors say, "You don't question God." I never understood why, but that November I did question God! Winnie was experiencing a cough that wouldn't go away. She went to her primary care physician, who eventually sent her to a specialist. A mass was found on her lungs. I can recall that day just like it was yesterday. I couldn't believe what I was hearing. I was in total disbelief! The news came as a complete shock. It felt like someone hit me so hard and knocked the wind out of me that it was hard to breathe. I was so angry and disappointed with God that I needed and wanted an answer now. I continued to question God and ask why He was allowing this to happen to my mother.

She went in for a biopsy and was diagnosed with carcinoma of the lung: lung cancer. You're talking about a punch to the gut. My emotions were all over the place. Surgery was imminent! The morning of her surgery, my stomach felt as if I were riding a rollercoaster that would not stop. I wanted to throw up, but nothing was in my stomach. I prayed all night long and that morning, but nothing would settle my nerves. The rest of the family was just as nervous as I was. Although I had been praying and asking God for her to make it safely through, I was scared. I was being optimistic and full of faith, but I had to realize that God was not obligated to answer my prayer in the way I wanted Him to. I just had to believe that He knew what was best for my mother.

While in surgery, we waited and prayed, and prayed and waited. A few hours later, the surgeon came in and told us he removed three-fourths of her cancerous lung, and that he believed he got it all. Praise God! He told us she would need chemotherapy and radiation. Although that's great news, I'm still asking God, "why?" There has to be some purpose in this pain. At that moment, I felt like our lives would never be the same again as we knew it, especially for my father. My parents had been married, at that time, 30+ years, and Winnie was the glue that held our family together. Winne being sick was a big shock to our family and friends in our small community. Everybody knew everybody and everybody cared about everybody.

Her cancer treatment went extremely well! In January 1985, Winnie went back to work. If you didn't already know she had lung cancer, you wouldn't have known it, because she didn't look like what she had been through. HALLELUJAH! At that point, I stopped asking God why, and asked the question, "What is it that you want me to learn from my mother's illness?" I finally realized and learned through this process that God is in control, and His plan is not always what our heart wants. You have to trust God like never, because in His word He promises never to leave us or forsake us. He is true to His Word, even when we may not understand and even though it's not easy. Keep trusting, keep praying, and keep on believing!

I want the world to know that you can question God, but it should come from a humble spirit. God knows our hearts and He is not intimidated by our questions.

On November 22, 1985, my mother lost her battle to cancer. I was no longer angry or disappointed with God. I had to give Him all praise, honor, and glory that He allowed me the time I had to be with her. I am so glad that God can turn valleys into victories, midnights into days, and pain into praises. Unfortunately, if we live long enough, we will all face calamities in life. We should be glad that we can rejoice in the Lord and that God allows us to embrace the simple joys that each day has to offer!

"You will show me the path of life; in Your presence is fullness of joy; at Your right hand are pleasures forevermore." Psalms 16:11 (NKJV)

FINDING JOY IN THE MIDST OF TRIAL

Rev. Michael E. Johnson

I have to be honest: when it comes to experiencing Joy, my first thought typically does not focus on being in the midst of a trial or adversity. Yet James 1:2–4 makes the bold declaration that we should consider it pure Joy when we do encounter trials of many kinds. The combining of Joy with trials seems illogical, but I've come to learn that there is always a meaningful purpose behind God's seemingly incongruous methods. In particular, I've found that trials and adversity in my life have a way of drawing me closer to God (in His presence), which in turn, as Psalms 16:11 (KJV) tells us, we will find fullness of Joy. Ten years ago, I experienced this promise of Joy from God while going through a real-life physical trial.

My family and I were on our way to Toledo to visit my wife's parents. As I was driving, I received a phone call that was audible to everyone in the car over the car speakers. The call was a message from my doctor's office informing me that the test results from an earlier procedure that I had done were back. The voice said in a sterile, unfeeling, matter of fact way that I had prostate cancer. The lighthearted mood in the car quickly turned to silence, and I could feel that all eyes were focused on me, wondering how I might react. It was strange, but my initial reaction was not one of being fearful, in disbelief, or even surprised. My initial reaction was one of calm and an almost immediate sense from God that said, "I've got this." Not "I" as in me, but "I" as in God. This initial thought was comforting and reassuring, even without knowing any further details as to what my prognosis might be. I can't even remember exactly what I said to my family in that moment, but they, too, seemed to understand that our mutual Father was already on the case.

When I returned home to Cincinnati from Toledo, I made an appointment with my doctor to find out what my next steps were. Although I had questions and some concern of the unknown, God continually reminded me that He was with me. In fact, He turned my attention to how just in the last five years, He had delivered my wife from ovarian cancer. As I recalled how faithful He was to her and how He protected her from her fears and the Joy she experienced being able to come through her trial victoriously, I knew I was in the best hands possible. As I journeyed through the process of diagnosis, treatment, and recovery, I continually saw God bring Joy (which Dr. Tony Evans defines as internal stability in spite of external struggles) into the experience. Instead of approaching visits for radiation treatment with dread, I responded with the Joy of knowing I was spared chemotherapy. Instead of being caught in a negative cycle of "what if's" regarding a series of surgical procedures I had to have done, God replaced it with a flow of good news and good reports after each doctor visit; that buoyed my spirit and, yes, brought me Joy.

Needless to say, I came out of that life trial successfully from a physical standpoint (cancer free since 2012). More importantly, the trial allowed me to experience what it means to count a trial pure Joy. Being in God's presence when there is darkness and negativity swirling about, is a most reassuring feeling. Even though I don't go seeking trials, I'm confident when one occurs. I know for myself that I can find Joy in the midst, because I lived it. All praises and glory be to God our Father!

GOOD CAN COME THROUGH SUFFERING

Linda Martin

When I was expecting my youngest child, I was thrilled that I would once again get to experience the Joy of childbirth. My husband and I had four other children ranging in age from six years to 13 years. I experienced love at the deepest level during their births and realized childbirth was truly an encounter with God. In addition, my husband and I had gained so much parenting experience that I felt Caroline would have advantages that could lead to an almost perfect childhood for her. Of course, that was an unrealistic expectation. Like other children, she experienced teething pain, caught colds and stomach bugs, and had her share of bumps and bruises.

When Caroline was in kindergarten, she began to complain of bizarre symptoms that bothered her physically and psychologically. My husband and I had never seen these symptoms with our older children and thus had no experience to guide us in helping her. Many evenings, she had a dull look in her eyes, ran a low-grade fever, and had a stomachache. Some mornings, she awoke groggy and had trouble eating breakfast and getting dressed for school.

Caroline reported other bizarre events, such as seeing triangles in the air, having "ping pong ball" headaches, or hearing something she knew was not really there. Little did I know that it would take six years to get a diagnosis and another three years for her to outgrow the syndrome from which she suffered.

Caroline had innumerable appointments with pediatricians, neurologists, counselors, and psychiatrists. She had many MRIs, EEGs, blood tests, and counseling sessions. The professionals seemed as confounded as we were, and we were given conflicting diagnostic opinions. During one office EEG, her readings went wildly erratic, and she had to start anti-seizure medication that very night. Another neurologist took her off that medication, while a third feared she was having complex partial seizures during her sleep and determined she need to be on anti-seizure medication.

Twice during those six years, she had periods of obsessive-compulsive thoughts necessitating more medication.

Caroline's problems affected our entire family. My frantic worry and the research I did to find answers took up as much time as her numerous appointments and tests. It was hard for me to be available to the rest of the family. Once when we were traveling to visit their grandparents, Caroline had one of her episodes. She felt so poorly, we thought we were going to have to return home. Her siblings expressed their disappointment and her brother commented, "You have to be sick to get any attention around here."

I worked tirelessly to find answers. At first, I had only a nursing textbook and articles from medical journals sent to me by Caroline's uncle, who was a doctor, to help in my research. The language was over my head, and it wasn't until a neurologist connected me with the Epilepsy Foundation that I had material written in layman's language to help me in my quest to understand Caroline's case.

Although I was frantic with worry, I experienced moments when an aura of peace would envelop me. My parish priest told me that those moments were gifts from God. I also felt God sent people who kept me going during those long years. Two neurologists we met through the Epilepsy Foundation and a local support group went out of their way to help us. Out of the blue, one of those neurologists called me and spoke at length about Caroline. I remember thinking, after that call, that if someone who barely knew us and cared that much, we would be okay. I had previously thought of love as the most important virtue, but I have come to realize that having hope is equally important. Nothing had changed in Caroline's life, but that phone call gave me hope and the desire to carry on.

Six years into Caroline's ordeal, she was hospitalized for a week of seizure monitoring. Those tests revealed she had benign focal epilepsy of childhood with migraine headaches. We learned she would outgrow the seizures, but the migraines could remain with her for life. Fortunately, over the next three years, she outgrew them both. She is now 37 years old, married, with three children of her own.

Having lived through these challenges, I feel God taught me three main lessons. First of all, I have learned to be patient, trusting God's timing for troubling situations to work out. Second, I learned that God can and does bring good out of suffering. When I was able to help lessen the suffering of another child from the research I had done, a weight was lifted off my shoulders and I experienced Joy. Finally, I learned the enormous value of hope. I try to reach out, whenever I can, to return the hope graciously given to us by people who cared deeply enough to help others whom they barely knew. What seemed to be the worst trial ended up being a period of growth and blessings.

TESTIMONY OF JOY

Janice C. Collins

Before I committed my life to Jesus, I only focused on material things. I loved shopping and at all cost never focused on the price of anything. Yes, I overspent and never appreciated or understood the true value of money and the results of living beyond your means. In addition to overspending, I was focused on being successful as a manager in the healthcare industry.

While sitting in church in 2015, there was a special announcement that a class "Freed-Up Financial Living," by authors Dick Towner, John Negovetich, and Shannon Plate through the www.goodsensemovement.org, would be taught, and the cost was only $20.00. This announcement motivated me because I wanted to change my attitude about money.

 I enrolled in the course, and throughout the time I was working on class assignments the Holy Spirit reminded me that in order to fully be the person that God created me to be, I **MUST** become financially free.

Now, fast forward to February 2016, while lying on my back in bed, I saw a black cloud that covered my body from head to toe. As I opened my eyes, all of sudden my body felt numb. I closed my eyes and said a prayer, as I attempted to get up — I could not move. One could imagine all kinds of crazy thoughts entered my mind. I continued to lie in bed for about an hour. At the time, my husband hadn't made it home from work. I did not want to call my family, who lives in Tennessee and wasn't comfortable with reaching out to a female friend in church. I lay quietly, until my husband arrived home.

UNFORTUNATELY, this black cloud that I felt ended up being medically diagnosed as depression. Everything I was doing in my life (job, hobbies, social life and marriage) was not focused in the direction that God had designed for me. I was going in two different directions. I could not fulfill my legacy because the seed that God had planted inside me was not being utilized. Unfortunately, I was not a blessing to others.

With the help of Rev. Yvonne D. McCoy, I sought professional counseling at the Transformation Institute — Holistic Life Healer. For the first time in my life, the holistic counseling has taught me the importance of meditating and praying. As the result of reading the book *Who Am I? Identity In Christ* by Jerry Bridges, I'm no longer ashamed to speak freely about my emotions and speak up when faced with challenges in my life.

As a result of my depression, I was forced to address the root of limiting myself in knowing who I am in Christ. The time I took in understanding who I am through the holistic counseling, I had to understand that the black cloud hovering over my body was that God was merely trying to get me to recognize — I'm now into a new level (new season) in my life and I was being elevated.

During my elevating period, in order to get where God wanted me to be, I had to go through several layers of testing to see if I understood who I am and make application in my everyday life. Through numerous days of fasting and praying, God revealed that even though He has given me administrative skills, my main purpose in life is connecting with people at the heart level.

As I continue my walk with Christ and seek to live the life that has been so graciously granted to me, my focus scripture until eternity is: "Above all else, guard your heart, for everything you do flows from it." Proverbs 4:23 (NIV)

I view my heart as a spring that flows from one person to another with God as the foundation.

I count it all Joy, because without any hesitancy, my relationship with Jesus Christ provides me with intimacy and the security of knowing that He totally has accepted me for me. He has created me with purpose. When I was at my lowest, deep into depression, He was demanding my attention to remind me that I **MUST** be totally dependent on Him and not material things.

WALKING WITH GOD

Deborah Maldonado

God is Sovereign. God's character is good, faithful, and loving. God is the Giver, Keeper, and Taker of Life. I believe these truths. I also believe that **I am** fearfully and wonderfully made in the image of God who promises to give me, His beautiful brown skin daughter, an abundant life. So, the question beacons, what is abundant life? The verse in James 1:4 (KJV) tells me that If I want to be complete (whole) and if I want to be mature (wise) and not lack anything, then, I need to let perseverance finish its work. That work only occurs not in the midst of happy circumstances, but in unhappy circumstances — aka "trials." I think that just as lifting 10-pound kettle bells for three repetitions builds my biceps, likewise my walking through trials with an attitude of pure Joy builds my faith. I know my purpose in life is to live by faith for His glory.

This attitude of pure Joy was not only a heart seed planted by God but was also cultivated and shaped by the role models in my life. Real life is wisely and purposefully deciding to use your time for fruitful relationships, work, finances, and hobbies, for His purposes. With that in mind, I'm grateful to these role models and the way they poured into me at various stages of my life.

My role models were my parents, grandparents, and family who modeled giving of 3 T's (Time, Talent, and Treasure). My professional relationships modeled global perspective, purposeful research, and grace for the ungrateful. Finally, my spiritual family modeled a hunger to love and live by the Word of God, serve in the Kingdom of God, and love mercy.

As I reflect over my 60-plus years, there have been many ups and downs of life, some very serious. I have not always had an attitude of Joy or contentment. It is something the Holy Spirit gave and has been cultivating in me over many years. As the scripture tells us, the trial is a test of our faith— proof of our allegiance to God the Father — a test of our obedience. It allows an opportunity for God to demonstrate to us (and others) His authority, power, loving care; and that He can produce a Christ-like spirit within us. As a potter shapes a clay vase, He is shaping us into His image daily. We are becoming Christ-like each day if we are obedient to His ways.

I value all 60-plus years of my life story. The foundation of my life is the Word of God because as the designer of life, I trust Him to know what is best. I understand that just like the body needs food to be energized, so does my spirit need to be fed for abundant life. Life for me involves listening to God as I read, study, meditate. That involves living out scriptures to build up my spirit, soul, and body with an attitude of Joy. The gift of Joy only comes from being in the presence of God Psalms 16:11 (KJV). While in His presence, He instructs me on decisions in life through wise thinking from His point of view. Seeing life from His point of view is the key to experiencing pure Joy in the midst of trials. His point of view often is different from my point of view, and I have to submit or be willing to live with the consequences instead of receiving the reward. Often, I don't know what to do in circumstances that are out of my control. I send up what I call "Arrow Prayers" in situations where a trial suddenly comes upon me. Sometimes the answer is to wait and be still. I don't always agree, understand, or want to do what He instructs me, but it is and continues to be a process of navigating through daily ups and downs of life. I hope that I am growing wiser!

Now that you know what I believe and what I value, let me share one or two examples that have shaped my belief to allow perseverance to finish its work in you. But before I share, I think it's important to discuss the definition of pure Joy. Pure Joy cannot be purchased from the store. True Joy (pure Joy) is a gift from the Holy Spirit that comes up from the inside out, and is expressed with shouts, cries, or singing.

One of my life experiences involved the doctor's report that they found a lump in my breast. If you are familiar with the process, as I had been from previous surgeries, I had to go for the biopsy and an ultrasound two times. Between the first and second ultrasound, I remember pleading with God to not be cut again and for the test results to be benign. He answered my prayer and the pure Joy I experienced was hearing the oncologist doctor not being able to find the lump on the second ultrasound. She responded,

"Can you explain this?" and we had a moment of sharing how I believe in prayer and how God was faithful once again.

Another one of my life experiences involved the birth of my fourth child. After having three previous healthy full-term pregnancies, I was faced with health issues which were out of my control. No vitamin, exercise, or medical procedure could alleviate the diagnosis.

I was working as a teacher and pregnant. I was starting to hemorrhage slightly. My doctor had said to stay off my feet as much as possible, but it was okay to continue working. The school and coworkers were wonderful. I received so much loving care. Staff escorted my students to their other classes, restroom, and lunch. I taught from my desk with an elevated footstool under the desk. All the human efforts to continue working and to bring in the second income for the household were exhausted. I'm sure others were praying for me, but I don't recall praying for God's viewpoint on my circumstance. He shortly made my next step clear.

Life took a turn. At school one day, I started hemorrhaging again. I was put by the doctor on complete bed rest at three months. My bedrest lasted for five more months. If that wasn't enough of a trial, during that time our house caught on fire, and we were living out of a hotel for four months. I could not stay in the hotel with my family because there were stairs, so the solution was to move in with my parents. From my perspective, I was a sick, pregnant, homeless woman separated from my family and confined to a bed.

Although there were times I was depressed, stressed, and questioning the trial, I remember to this day the Joy I felt then and feel today when I think about how God showed His gracious loving care for me through my husband, family, and friends. It was in this season of my life that God's word of counting it all Joy when faced with trials became real. The test was this: did I still believe that God was good and loved me? In the midst of it then and even now I would say, yes!

Love is a verb and is shown through unselfish action. I experienced the love of my husband caring for me and the other children with great responsibility. I experienced love from my parents caring for me at bedside with meals and rides in the car for fresh air. I experienced love from friends standing in for me at school events and making play dates for our children. I experienced love from church family and neighbors helping to clean up the fire damaged home. Not only did God show His love for me through all these relationships but He also showed me his power by giving me a healthy baby girl. She is 27 today and a beautiful testimony of the blessings of our heavenly Father. Every time I look at her, I am reminded of God's goodness and power.

This experience is one of many encounters of God's goodness in my life. He has been faithful with my health, work, and relationships. I chose to share my health journey because it reminds me — and I hope proves to you — how powerful He is in all of life. His unfailing love and continued faithfulness are the reason I believe that all things are possible. He is powerful and I can rejoice in the Lord Always. The rejoicing is not in the circumstance but in the relationship with Him as I wait to see how He will work things out for my good.

In closing, may you discover and surrender to the pure Joy that comes from waiting and walking in and through trials with the God as our guide.

> Remember these truths:
>
> God is in control of the time and intensity of trials.
>
> God has a specific purpose for my trial.
>
> God has designed a specific need in my life.
>
> God will walk with you through the trial.
>
> The trial will be for our good if we respond in faith.
>
> The trial can strengthen my faith — grow me up.
>
> The trial is an opportunity to demonstrate perseverance.
>
> The trial will develop Christ Likeness in me — transformation
>
> The trial will help you measure your spiritual maturity — make you the person He designed you to be.

The blessings are many:

May you know you are loved and unique.

May you know your uniqueness and grow, blossom, and be fruitful.

May you grow wisely so you can help the community.

And may you live with purpose and with a servant's heart.

By God's grace and power, may you overcome trials with an attitude of pure Joy!

THE JOY OF THE LORD

Dr. Moniqueka E. Gold

In 2009, my college did not have any departments; we were one big college. Our new president decided we could operate better if we divided into two separate departments, so I threw my name in the hat for faculty to vote on. It was unanimous: I became department chair of one of the departments.

My department focused mostly on graduate programs and had a team of 11 people. The faculty who made up my department were selected based on whether they taught undergraduate or graduate courses.

We were a good team. Everyone was amiable, professional, courteous, and collaborative. We ranged in age and rank from approximately 30 years old and tenure-track to full professors in their 70s. I, the department chair, was the only person of color.

Before I threw my name in the hat, to be voted on as chair, I prayed. Once selected, I prayed and all the time I was department chair, I prayed for guidance, patience, discernment, and covering from God. I was chair for nine years without any problems, until my dean retired. Once she left, I was asked to serve on the search committee for the new dean.

The search committee worked well together. We made a selection in the spring of 2017 for the dean to begin fall 2017. Approximately 60 days in, it was clear to me (and probably others) that the new dean was absolutely "CRAZY!" The dean was cordial when he met me in the hallway or saw me across campus. However, working with him was awful. He was a manager and not a leader. He would hold meetings, but actually prior to the start of the meeting, it was clear he already knew exactly what he was going to do because all he wanted us to do was rubber stamp his decisions. I was unhappy. Other faculty members voiced their discontentment privately.

Still praying…

With my previous dean, I could always be transparent. She would at least listen. I believed in giving the new dean his respect as our dean, so I thought I could continue the same tradition with him of being transparent in meetings, as I did with my previous dean. NOT so. Well, that did not work with this dean.

Believe me, I "checked myself in meetings." I worked especially hard to make sure I listened to what he said, smiled, showed him respect and everything I needed to do before I shared my opinions.

Still praying…

I think it was the fact that I thought I could share my opinions that he did not like. If I said up, he said down, so you know how it went.

Just typing this makes my blood pressure go up because he was so rude, ugly, disrespectful, and threatened by my mere presence. Sad to say, but that man was very insecure. Each time I would have meetings scheduled with him, I always prayed before I went in. I needed God to keep my blood pressure down and my demeanor professional, and I needed to represent who I was, as a Christian woman and professional. He seemed to not compromise well, so meetings became more contentious as time went on.

Still praying…

A lot happened over the fall and spring semester of 2017–2018. When the fall of 2018 came along, I was still prayerful we could start fresh and figure things out. Seemingly, the semester got off to a good start, but some paperwork was due that I had not submitted. Long story short, the dean was asking me to submit the work, and I could not figure out why I could not see what he wanted me to submit when I was in this electronic platform. Later, I found out that he had not submitted my name to the higher ups, which was required, in order for the higher ups to give me access to the section of the platform he needed me to complete. He never admitted that he forgot to submit my name to the higher ups.

Still praying…

I scheduled a meeting with him one day to talk about this platform. We tried two different dates before we finally agreed on a date/time. When his administrative assistant sent me the meeting invite, it was labeled performance review. That was puzzling to me because **I** had scheduled the meeting, and it definitely was not a performance review. All performance reviews were conducted annually in the spring. The first performance review I had with him was for merit pay that took place in the spring of 2018. A satisfactory score was from 3 to 6; my score was a three. The three qualified me for merit pay.

Still praying…

When I walked into the dean's office, surprisingly, the Director of Human Resources was sitting there. The dean began the meeting and spoke very few words only to say, "Effective immediately you will no longer be the chair of your department." He went on to say, three times, "I am sure this makes you mad, but this is the decision that came down from Academic Affairs." He put this entire issue on Academic Affairs, when it was he who did not want me to be chair. Academic Affairs was in a different building and never encountered me. When it was time to place blame or take responsibility, he always found a surrogate to take his place.

Even while in the meeting, still praying…

At that moment, I knew it was pointless to attempt to defend myself, ask any questions or even try to gain any clarification. Therefore, I simply said, "No, being removed does not make me mad, and if you feel removing me is in the best interest of the department, I will comply." I just felt fighting back would have been pointless, it would have made me seem combative, and I had nothing to prove. He knew I did not have access to the platform and wasn't able to load the required material because he did not put me on the list to have access. He knew it!

When I tell you God will give you peace that surpasses all understanding, that was exactly what he did. Peace is what I had when I left his office. I was over it.

Still praying… moving forward—

Today, he is still the dean and although I am no longer a chair, I am still a full professor; he did not attack my rank. Slowly, since the time he removed me from being chair, he has done other unmerited things, mean things, unnecessary things, tried to demean my character among other faculty in my college and across campus, but in my prayers, God assured me that if I remain steadfast and unmovable, those around me will see my character and the dean's as well. As faculty stood on the sideline and watched him do wrong to many people, I believe they are done with him, too. Morale in the college is definitely under the basement. At this point, many of us are in continual prayer that God sees fit for his skills to be used elsewhere.

I am waiting on God. I know he is in control, and I know thy will be done so I am just praying and waiting. I know, when I least expect it, everything will fall into place. It will happen so beautifully and when it does, I will understand why God made me wait!

Even though you might feel your situation is wrong, you were treated in a disrespectful way, etc., just know that you must trust God for there is something he wants you to learn in the process. Going through this dark place has taught me about myself and my strengths and has drawn me closer to God. For I know he is my sustainer! This journey is a part of my testimony.

Just keep praying…

ONE DAY AT A TIME

Judy Waller

My husband and I had been married 34½ years when he was diagnosed with cancer. We fought the battle for nine months, but he died. I was not prepared for the total feeling of hopelessness. We were a team. Everything that could go wrong did, and the problems were mine to solve. I became so overwhelmed I wanted to give up.

The devil had me convinced that life was not worth living. What little self-confidence I had took a beating. One night, while trying to fall asleep, I asked God to help me. He told me to take one day at a time. He was the ultimate consistent problem solver, and I should have depended on him from the beginning. My church family and pastor were tremendous support. Every sermon and song seemed to address what I was experiencing. God did not forsake me. He rescued me from my period of depression. He sent new friends and acquaintances to replace the ones that drifted away. I have been financially secure. I have had reasonable health and strength. I just can't tell it all.

I still miss my loving, beautiful husband. Each day is still a challenge, but I am stronger. My prayer is that anyone who witnessed my 19-year journey will be encouraged if they experience loss. God's grace and mercy brought me through.

My Search

Mildred Byrd

Before I came to know Jesus as my Lord and Savior, I knew about Him through the missionary ministry that came to our school each month to share teachings of Bible stories and memorization of Bible verses. Those were days of joyful times for my siblings, classmates, and me. We did not have to be in the classroom listening to the teacher talk, or take a test. It was delightful to listen to stories and engage in learning new music and singing new songs. That experience was a joyful event because my mother played the piano, and my daddy loved to hear her play hymns. He had a habit of asking her to play for him. Today, I carry those scenes in my heart and I, too, love music and the hymns.

In early days of growing up, we were sent to church, and at the age of 13, I heard the teaching of how God loves us and what He did for us, so I believed and accepted Jesus as my Savior. At that time, I trusted in people, what they said and did, and I learned to be obedient to my parents and others of authority. I grew up thinking I was living a Christian life or a life pleasing to God.

In our home, we had joyful times of playing board games, learning to love others as we saw our parents love each other, and love us (their children) and other children in the neighborhood. My mother fed and nourished others as if they were hers. She loved and disciplined us when we were disobedient, and my daddy would come home from work and love on us by patting and rubbing our heads. He would ask, "Have you been giving your mother a hard time?" What an example of the love of God implanted in my mind at an early age. At that time, I had no understanding of the true goodness of our God.

From the care of my parents, God allowed me to meet the real world full of distortion, lies, etc. I was introduced to people who influenced my way of living. It was the beginning of doing things and making decisions my way. My problems, hope, belief, trust, etc. were the results of listening to the wrong voices of people who were caught up in the world's way of seeing and doing things.

My problems became our troubles within our home. I became "Miss Fix It." I dropped out of college to marry. Neither one of us was ready for this event. God gave us precious gifts of children to love, and to nourish (as it reads in His Word, "Train up a child in the way he should go, and when he is old, he will not depart from it." Proverbs 22:6 (NKJV) He enabled us to do so, in spite of our faults.

There came a time when we did not want to be together in marriage. God allowed that to happen and at the same time He had plans for our future. Having failed to have a stable home, He allowed us to move from the place of our trials and learn whom to trust, how to live together, how to live to glorify Him, what voice to listen to, who to follow, what to do, and how to live a life pleasing to Him.

Before moving to another city and coming to know God, our prior lifestyle was one of hypocrisy. People looked at us thinking we were the ideal couple. However, God knows the heart of all of us, and He knew we needed more than each other.

At one time, my children and home were the most important things in my life, and I spent my time being defensive and suspicious of people. When our son was born with a birth defect, I really took control of trying to protect our children and centered more attention on what I thought should be my priorities.

When I stopped listening to people, who were telling me what they thought and ran to a person who knew God and His Word, I made the right choice for the benefit of family and others. I learned that God created me and everything belongs to Him. He knows my name. One of my favorite Bible verses and hymn is Psalms 139: 23–24 (KJV) that says, "Search me, O God, and know my heart: try me, and know my thoughts: And see if there be any wicked way in me, and lead me in the way everlasting."

We moved to another city and state, and I met a person who became my friend; then I came to know what was important in my life. While attending a lady's "Caring and Sharing" luncheon, I heard a message concerning God's goodness and eternal life. I was motivated to seek and live a lifestyle that was pleasing to God.

Moving and being flexible became a way of living for our family. We were trying to satisfy our inner needs of love and Joy in the wrong places and with the wrong people. But God, in His love and care introduced me to my friend and her husband who lived a lifestyle different from what we had been taught, embraced, and lived.

Moving was the beginning of something new and the continuation of my missionary schooling. The Bible reads in 2 Corinthians 5: 17 that if anyone is in Christ, he is a new creature. The old is gone; the new has come (paraphrased). I learned to reach outside of my immediate family with love for whomever. I do not concern myself with what people think, but rather what God says. This revelation has been and is a Joy to grow spiritually and at the same time to give to others outside of my family and home

Over the years and presently, my Joy is serving with missionary outreach, learning and supporting those who train young people into go to the mission field. During this time of commotion, diversity, violence, etc., the Lord is still using me to be available to care and share where there is a need. It is a joyful time to encourage others, all for His glory.

We continued to grow spiritually, and after several years, we moved again to what was or is called the Bible Belt. On April 25, 1982, we had found a church home, and we rededicated our lives to God our Creator and Jesus our Savior, Lord, and Redeemer. .

God allowed us to move several more times, and each time He equipped us with all we needed to continue to grow in our relationship with Him. He taught us to trust Him to fight our battles, provide for our needs, and be the source of our Joy.

An awakening of peace and Joy occurred when my husband and I met a Christian family in Pennsylvania, where I heard Bible teachings and saw applications of the Word of God being illustrated. For me, it was what the missionaries had taught when I was in grade school. This family became our joyful teachers and an example of being a believer of Christ and a follower of His will and way.

The mother of this family became m" fri'nd for 40 plus years. She encouraged me to join a Bible study, and introduced me to a minister of the Word, who opened my eyes to see and understand how to come to know God the Creator and all He has freely given us. She invited me to fellowship with a group of women who studied God's Word, spent time bowling, having lunch together, visiting the nursing homes, helping with children's Bible class after school, etc. That time of learning demonstrated the ways of God.

God brought me from thinking that I could fix whatever problem confronted me or my family to understanding the knowledge of knowing He is our source of help. My attitude of boasting, seeking wisdom, following the world's way of solving situations, focusing on myself were no longer healthy, peaceful, joyful or beneficial. A transformation started for me.

After several years, we moved to another city and state, where God kept His promise to never forsake us. God brought a young woman into my life for His purpose. One day while my husband was at work, I ventured out to explore the city. When it became time to drive home, my sense of direction failed me, I approached a young lady for help and God provided all that I needed.

She was one of His missionaries. He was teaching me to rely and call upon Him first for all my cares. I asked the young lady, a total stranger, for physical directions to where I lived, and after some time of interacting and verbalizing, by God's grace, she gave me the physical directions and God's spiritual directions also, as she invited me to a women's Bible study group. What a joyful time! It was the joyful continuation of interacting with people from all walks of life and nations.

My husband and I rededicated our lives on April 25, 1982, to the Father. With the help of other believers, God taught us to live as followers of Christ: share the gospel, serve the needy, bless and encourage others, worship and praise Him and trust and obey Him with words of adoration, Joy and peace. Now, God is teaching me how to be more like Jesus and pleasing to Him. He has provided someone by which I can be accountable. My spiritual missionary will ask me, "Have you prayed about it?" Is there anything that you think you can control or provide the answer for without seeking the help of God. At this time of my life, He has taught me to seek His will; walk and talk with Him, using His tool (THE WORD); listen to His voice as I read His word; and He has given me a spirit of discernment to listen to His messengers. In today's world, we are facing so many evil ungodly acts of violence, misuse and abuse of children, parents, and neighbors. There are assaults of all matters, selfishness, and a long list of uncaring acts, but as I live according to His word, my days are joyful ones regardless of the circumstances. I have learned to be content where I find myself and I begin my day with thanksgiving and a joyful heart to glorify Him with praise and to sing of His goodness. He is awesome and nothing or no one else is entitled to that description.

We are rich in Him, so we should help others with a grateful heart because everything belongs to Him. As the missionaries shared with me in my early days, I have been taught He is in control of everything. God has allowed me to see myself and to use that which He owns wisely. He prepared me to be a joyful caregiver of my children, other children, my husband, and others. He has given me a heart of love, compassion, and patience for those in need.

He has given me His gift of eternal life. He has adopted me as His child. He has given me a passion for many things that are pleasing to Him; however, the one thing, Mission Ministry, has a special place in my heart. I am His servant to others, I will go where He sends me, and do what I believe He would have me do. We can only live one day at a time, and I pray each day is pleasing to my Lord.

Psalms 19:14 (NIV) states, "May these words of my mouth and this meditation of my heart be pleasing in your sight, Lord, my Rock and my Redeemer."

My prayer is to be bold in sharing the gospel as the missionaries were bold in visiting my school and sharing the word of God with other school children and myself. I am forever grateful for their service. I identify with the writing of Paul as he wrote in Philippians 1:3–6 (NIV), "I thank my God every time I remember you, in all my prayers for all of you, I always pray with Joy because of your partnership in the gospel from the first day until now, being confident of this, that he who began a good work in you will carry it on to completion until the day of Christ Jesus."

Today, He is still working with and in me. This testimony is what He did, is doing, and will do in your life as well.

He is the Potter. I am the clay.

He taught me to trust and obey, to love Him first and then my neighbor (those who cross my path), He healed and mended my marriage, He chose and anointed my children to identify with Jesus His Beloved Son, to serve and please Him, to be more like Jesus. I am still moving and being flexible because of His goodness and mercy. He allowed me to learn through my troubles and heartaches how He is the healer and fixer of the broken hearted; He is in control of everything. He has given us a guidebook to read, learn, and meditate upon the words to know Him in His fullness and for our Joy.

"…for the joy of the Lord is your strength." Nehemiah 8:10 (KJV) And "the Lord is my strength and song: And He has become my salvation." Psalms 118:14 (NKJV) I still love music and enjoy listening to singers who praise the Lord with songs. I am thankful that He knows me and my heart, for I, too, sing and play the piano for my enjoyment and for His glory. I make a joyful noise. He has given me a voice to make a joyful noise. "The Lord has done great things for us, and we are filled with joy." Psalms 126:3 (NIV)

He is still filling me with Joy as a missionary friend. My missionary's children are coming to visit this week; I pray they will be blessed with safe travel, that our visitation gathering will be a great time of sharing and rejoicing and God will be glorified.

"To God be the glory, great things He has done!" proclaims the 19th century hymn by Fanny Crosby and W. Howard Doane. Therefore, we will lift our voices in spiritual praise to the Lord for He is worthy!

FROM DARKNESS TO THE MARVELOUS LIGHT

Jean Griffin

I count it all joy because God turned my darkest day into sunshine. I almost lost my house and came within a day of being homeless because I was trying to help someone else. Have you been in a situation where you loved a family member so much that you would do anything to help them?

A family member asked my husband and me to help keep his home from foreclosure. If not, he would lose everything. With his promises to pay us back if we obtained a loan, we felt confident that everything would work out. So, we borrowed the money in our name.

Upon my husband's graduation, he took over the family member's business but unknowingly, the business name and equipment were sold to someone else therefore limiting my husband's ability to bid on jobs that would pay back the loan. Now my family was placed in a bad financial situation in addition to the fact that we never received help that was promised by my family member to pay back the loan.

During the entire time, I asked God to guide me through paying of bills with limited income. As a result, I prioritized what bills to cover. Our income was reduced, and we were not able to pay bills for a while; therefore, our own house payment was jeopardized. We got three months behind, and the dark clouds began to gather around us. Isn't that ironic: we helped someone else save their mortgage and now we needed to save our own mortgage.

Upon receiving foreclosure notices ourselves, we tried getting a new loan approval but faced challenges. I was just about to give up and a Christian friend called to encourage me to pray in all rooms in the house. So, I cried out, "Lord, help me keep our home. I come to you as humble as I know how. Heavenly Father, please help me. I know you have the power. Please help us save our home so our children won't be homeless. Save my home." Every day for a week I humbly prayed this same prayer. My father always told me that God will not put anything on you that you can't bear. Sometimes, I would cry and ask God, "how much more do you think I can bear?"

Then, my darkest day arrived. A letter arrived in the mail indicating the house was being foreclosed. However, there was another letter that I reluctantly read. As I slowly unveiled the letter, that very day God turned my midnight into day. The second letter said that we were approved to refinance our home. How humbling for me and my family. I did not want to be homeless or see my children in an unstable situation.

Today, I still thank God for saving our home. I knew that God would work it out for His good because going through this trial/tribulation built my self-confidence. By trusting Him, I have become stronger. As a result, I am more active, supportive, and open to sharing Christ on the job or in church. I learned that if you lean on God, He answers prayers. If you pray and ask God to help, He will show you a way out of no way. Even if we were not able to save our home, God would have something better in store for us because our trust was in Him.

The rest of the story is that the company's name was changed to incorporate my husband's name. Business was restored. Thank you, God! Just be patient and wait on the Lord! The sun will shine in the morning.

MEMORIES

Beverly Wells

Today is my mama's birthday. The last time we celebrated in person was July 1, 2006. At that time, she was battling stage four lung cancer. She never smoked, was not a drinker, ate healthy, and in general led a very wholesome lifestyle. She was a tiny thing, only four feet ten or eleven, but a power house. She was the rock that held us together, battling school officials in Chapel Hill, Tennessee, and driving me to Marshall County High during my senior year of high school. One would describe her as feisty.

We were baffled by the prognosis given by doctors at Southern Regional Hospital in Nashville and an oncologist at Vanderbilt Hospital who agreed with the previous doctors.

I remember vividly my mother's reaction after the second opinion. She sat in her living room quietly staring into space. She did not ask for anything, but I knew her strategy would be to think of next steps for her care and how she would relate her wishes to her children. My sister Judy and I were by her side constantly. Deep down, I wanted her to try anything to save her life, but she refused to do anything experimental. She shared that being a Christian, she wanted to remain home as long as she could (hospice); she did not want to die at home; anything in disrepair she wanted fixed; and of course, her will would be updated. I don't think I could be that brave. In later weeks, she was in great spirit, talking on the phone (one of her favorite things) to her friends, accepting visitors, joking with us, and watching movies. She viewed this juncture as a time to eat everything that had been restricted from her diet. We granted her every wish.

I can remember bathing her, combing her hair, rubbing lotion on her skin and sitting with her as she watched one judge show after another. On one occasion, she asked me if I thought she would get better. My response centered on her eating to gain strength and taking her medicine. I'm sure she saw through my attempt to make her feel hopeful. There were days when she felt really good and others that confirmed how terminal her illness was. We did anything to make her comfortable. My sister Judy and I never left her bedside. While one of us slept in the recliner in her room, the other slept in bed.

My heart was so heavy. As teachers left for summer break, in June, I told my co-workers that I would be in Nashville as long as my mother needed me. I spent the month of July doing my best to help take care of her. Seeing her slowly die before my eyes is an image I will never forget. I wished for the miracle of life on earth. I knew I would miss our Sunday morning talks or impromptu discussions throughout the week. I tried to remember her resolve when asked if she wanted to enter trial treatment. Her response was that she wanted to spend her last days aware of her surroundings. Being a Christian meant that she would go to a better place. She left us painfully on August 2, 2006. Because she was our glue, life seemed uncertain without her. My sister and I were a united front. My brothers were in a flux.

I am reminded of her strength as a wife, mother, grandmother, member of community associations, and of course a Christian. She read her newspaper with great interest and resolved to keep us informed about local and national politics. She would periodically send me clippings from the Nashville paper, the *Tennessean,* that were of interest to me. During conversations with my siblings, constant references to words of wisdoms were shared. Most have come to pass, or they reflect that following her suggestions would have been wise. I remember the love she had for all her children, grandchildren, and great-grandchildren. July first would have been her 92nd birthday.

She was first born to Luther Bell and Sally Bea Green, in Chapel Hill, Tennessee. I know she was proud of my accomplishments. In life, I strove to be the person she wanted me to be. I have faith and works in my life.

ALL JOY: MY TESTIMONY OF FAITH

Candace Strong

I have been on this Christian journey for a long time. I was baptized at an early age of 6 years old, and even then, I knew there was a God that had something special in store for my life. I had no idea of how much turmoil would come into my life but knowing that God was a "very present help in trouble" helped me understand who God is and how much I needed him in my life.

When I reflect on the scripture passage James 1:2–4, I become more confident in the message James was conveying to the Christians who were being persecuted. I honestly felt like I was being tested and could not understand why I was going through such a hard trial. I had always tried to do the right thing but being homeless and dealing with my daughter's illness at the same time was more than I thought I could bear.

I would like to share how I worked through the trial of being homeless with a family of three and soon to be four. The scripture states to "Consider it pure joy, my brothers and sisters, whenever you face trials of many kinds, because you know that the testing of your faith produces perseverance." James 1:2–4 (NIV)

I did not find any "Joy" when my daughter could no longer work, and I had the only income to support us. My income is challenging sometimes, especially paying bills for myself, but how was I going to make it stretch for a family? I did not have the answer, and it seemed that the prayers I was praying were falling on deaf ears. I lost my apartment because I could not make the rent payment after a while, but I knew I had to make sure to hold on to my car because I knew the time was coming that we might have to sleep in my vehicle. It was getting cold outside, and I had already borrowed from a couple of relatives and repaid them, so I had run out of options. We stayed a couple of nights with relatives, but they really did not want us to be there long, so we packed up quickly and I continued to pray that God would make a way. I learned how to stretch a dollar for us to eat daily and I would take my daughter and her son to the library to stay all day while I went to work and would pick them up later. We slept in the car a couple of nights, and I would get clothes out of my bag each day to change for work. I was angry at God, my daughter, and all those I felt had turned their backs on us. I thought to myself on many a day, "how did this happen? What could I have done to prevent it? I am a Minister and had preached the gospel — why has God forgotten all about me?"

I would continue to pray and speak scriptures, especially Psalms 23 and my favorite scripture Psalms 121, over our lives. One night as we sat in McDonald's parking lot, my phone rang and a man from Southeast Christian Church called me and asked if I could meet him at the church, and I said, "sure." We had decided to go to Southeast for a service and I had one of the people pray with me after the service. They took my name and number, and I didn't think any more about it because friends and family had let me down — so why would strangers help us out? The man was sent from God as he paid for us to stay in a hotel for months, and his wife's group at church gave us gift cards and money to sustain us for a while. I cried while he was talking to me and presenting all of this to us. I thanked God that night over and over for rescuing us from sleeping in the car once again. My daughter was so thankful along with my grandson who began doubting that God existed.

For months we stayed in hotels and prayed each week for God to open a door for a home of our own and money to make it through another week. God was faithful even if it was last minute before a payment was made to the hotel we were staying in, but God made a way. I went back to my church, but I was ashamed of how we were living without an address of our own. My daughter was getting close to her due date with her second child and was dealing with a tumor in her brain as well. In September of 2019, my grandson was born, I was trying to figure out how in the world we were going to take care of this baby in a hotel, and my daughter was getting weaker and sicker. I cried out to God over and over to please fix our situation. I told God he said in his word "if you have faith of a mustard seed" the mountain would be removed. I wondered — did I not have enough faith? I reached out to my dear sisters in ministry, and they provided for a night's stay in a hotel, then a wonderful sister came to the hotel and paid for an entire week. I was so filled with gratitude that Jesus was moving on our behalf and opening some doors after a year.

The Lord began speaking loud and clear that others needed to know that we are hurting and could use some help and He would use people I hadn't considered to show us His love. My daughter and I prayed together more frequently and had my grandson to pray also so he could see that God would profoundly move on our behalf. I reached out to one of my former bosses and told her what was going on. She told me to continue to look for an apartment. I began to call around to see about getting somewhere convenient and affordable for my grandson to get to school and my daughter to chemo appointments.

Suddenly, God was answering our prayers! My former boss' daughter had sent word that she would pay our deposit and first month's rent when we found an apartment. My daughter called an apartment and we declared that we would be moving and packed up our things. The apartment accepted our applications and in two weeks we could move into our new place. I fell on my knees and praised God until my voice was hoarse from crying and shouting. We have been settled in our apartment for a couple of years now and every day we are so grateful that we have a place to call home.

I learned that life isn't easy and having faith in God doesn't make you immune to challenging times. It is in those seasons of loneliness and discontentment that I find solace in the only one who can understand my moods and pain. This was a testing of my faith and I thank God that I persevered through this painful, dark valley. Since then, I have read and heard about so many people who have been homeless, and I try to help others. The stigma of being homeless is harsh, and people think they know why things happen without having a clue to why a person may be in this predicament. I now have a greater appreciation for the scripture James 1:2–4 because it has matured my thinking as I go through other trials in my life. Jesus came, bled, and died to give me and others who accept Him as their Lord and Savior an abundant life. Jesus lives and I intend on living my best life serving Him and trusting Him to the fullest. We can count on God when everyone else has counted us out!

JOY COMES IN THE [MOURNING]
Damon L. Armstead

On a day that should have been routine — morning coffee, family time with the kids and grandkids, karaoke, video games, selfies and pizza — my wife and I unexpectedly spent the morning co-writing our eldest son, William's obituary. Instead of celebrating his 28th birthday, (which was just a few short days away) we were tasked with planning a memorial service in honor of a life gone too soon: suddenly, senselessly, tragically, permanently.

"What the hell just happened? GOD, please tell me this ain't real. Please tell me we didn't just watch our son take his last breath." I mean we cried. We prayed. We trusted GOD to save him and now they're calling for the coroner and telling us it's over? This doesn't make sense! He's too young. He's a father. He's a son. He's a brother. He's a fiancé. He's a friend and now…he's gone."

And just like that, a tsunami of emotions overtook us, destroying everything in its path, rendering us helpless to fight against the violent waves of shock, awe, and anguish. We were, and still yet are, beyond devastated by the loss of his spirit, his smile, his passion, and ultimately, his presence. The wounds of William's death remain fresh in our hearts and minds and are as deep as the ocean is wide. He's not coming back, and that fact is as traumatizing and tragic as it is true.

But what is also true (in fact eternally so) is that GOD is ever-present, particularly in our times of trouble, and with HIS presence comes the unspeakable JOY of knowing that we are not alone, and that death is not the end. Make no mistake, as parents we miss him terribly and are heartbroken. Yet as followers of Christ, we must believe by faith that somehow, some way, GOD is working all things (tragedies included) together for our good.

My faith tells me that weeping may endure for a night, but Joy comes not only in the morning (at the dawning of a new day) but *in the mourning* (amidst our pain).

To the parents of children gone too soon, I feel your pain, firsthand, and I and my wife pray for your comfort and peace. If I may, allow me to make a recommendation from one hurting heart to another: Let your tears flow and within that flow find your place of worship; a place where you can be honest about your pain, transparent about your fears, truthful about your anger and vulnerable about your vulnerabilities, a place of meditation, revelation, restoration, comfort, and care, a place of peace, a place of praise, a place of power. Abide in that secret place where GOD exchanges our weaknesses for HIS strength, HIS beauty for our ashes and the garment of praise for the spirit of heaviness.

You've experienced a great loss, and your tears are valid. So let them count, not just as weeping but as JOY, watering the seed of your greatness and producing a peaceable fruit of righteousness, all to the glory of GOD. We are not a people without hope. We have a Great High Priest who can be touched by the feeling of our infirmities. In short, God cares about us. Thus, we must never let our weeping stop our worship. Because worship is the secret ingredient that turns death into life, hurt into healing and mourning into everlasting JOY.

ONLY GOD!

Odell Reliford

"Lord, help me! I have no money, no savings, hungry babies, and the rent isn't paid," I cried out loudly because I was in a troubled marriage with only $20 to live on. After paying back what I owed a friend, I was left with only $3. So, I believed that if I prayed and cried out to the Holy Spirit, the Lord would show me what to do next.

With $3, I found someone who changed the lock to my apartment. Isn't that unbelievable? That's just like God! I immediately packed his belongings. When he finally came home and tried to enter the property, the keys didn't work. After sobering up, he returned and still was unable to enter the home. So, I made sure he received his clothing and other belongings. He wasn't happy about the situation, but he got the message and didn't return for a long time.

Now, I was on my own with no money and no job. I told the people that I was renting from that if they will give me 30 days, I will have both month's rent because I had a job lined up. Thankfully, an accountant told me previously to always call him when times got tough. So, I did. Whatever the pay was I was willing to accept. I worked and saved in order to meet my obligations.

Another friend, who was a maître d' at a rich country club, was having a party and needed help. All I needed was a white uniform and white shoes. I borrowed these items from my mom and at the end of the party, I had money everywhere I could put it. I paid my rent for two months and had enough to stock up on food supplies.

"Now, I am on my way," I thought. To top things off, I lived on a bus line. All I had to do was come out of the house to catch a bus and, it stopped where I worked. As I trusted God and followed His guidance, now I am retired from an administrative job with income and opportunities to help family, friends, and others.

My experiences with God started when I was 3 years old. I had visions and dreams that came true. They scared me at first, but my mom told me to embrace them and not be afraid because it was a gift from God. For example, I dreamed that there was blood in the bed. I shared this with Mom, and we found out that Dad had pancreatic cancer. My dad had blood in his bed. Another time, a family member was in a dire situation, and I saw all parties involved in the altercation and told my parents when I was 3. Then, I saw a serious car accident that involved relatives in a vision: it appeared on tv just as I shared with my mom. Today, I still have visions but do not always share them. So, I have learned how to trust God.

As I reflect on my ability to have visions/dreams, God probably show me signs before I married, but I chose to ignore them because I didn't know the difference between love and infatuation. Even though I was blinded by love and didn't listen, I repented and got back on the right path with God. Even though I didn't have a clue how I was going to overcome this situation, God did. From the outside looking in, this situation looked hopeless.

I want the world to know that if you call on the Lord, He will hear your cry. He was always there guiding me, showing me, and speaking to me the entire time. He will do the same for you. During these trials, I asked God to just lead me, and I followed. So, I want you to just let God be in control of your life. Trust Him! When you meet me, we are going to talk about the goodness of God. I have to always testify about who He is and what He has done in my life. Nothing in life matters more than a relationship with Him.

FROM BIRTH TO REBIRTH

Tanisha Ortiz

It was June 2015 when I decided to give my life to the Lord, formally. I had grown tired of simply going to church to tag along with my parents. I needed more. I needed to surrender. Although it did not happen immediately, I could feel the Holy Spirit pulling and tugging on my heart as the years went by. It was in 2018 that He truly met me where I was. Alone in my apartment, He called out to my heart yet again, and I finally surrendered. Little did I know that was only the very beginning of the shaking he was about to bring into my life.

I want to share my testimony of how one of my greatest blessings also forced me to go through the fire. It is a story about my struggles with motherhood and how God was molding me and pushing me to a deeper intimacy with Him.

In November of 2021, I gave birth to my son by way of cesarean delivery. The birth did not go as I had planned or prayed for, leading me into a downward spiral of emotions that left me feeling out of control. I was upset with everybody including the doctors, nurses, my husband, and with God because I could not understand why this happened. I asked myself so many questions including, "What did I do wrong?", "Did my body fail me?" and "Why couldn't I give birth naturally?"

For the first six months of my son's life, I was filled with so much sadness and fear that it caused a lot of stress and strain on my marriage and friendships. I was in such a dark place that I struggled to enjoy being a new mom. I cried a lot. I felt alone and cut off from the people I thought would be around to comfort me.

The only thing I held on to was praise and worship. Even when it was difficult, I would play instrumental worship and declare that God was still good even in the midst of my circumstance. I began to declare who He said I was. I would hold my baby boy and sing or hum allowing the presence of God to wash over me. It was not easy, but I knew that the enemy would prefer to let me dwell on my sadness, and I could not let that happen.

I finally got to the place where I was constantly talking to God, journaling, and staying in a place of worship. I had to ask God to shift my perspective and grasp the understand that my journey into motherhood was not some sort of punishment. I needed to be shown how to enjoy moments of motherhood and how it mirrored my walk with Him by trusting Him and letting Him be the Father in this situation. There are so many titles you can call Him, but I needed Him to be my Father, Abba. Being a mother to my son, the way the Father wants me to be, is my desire.

Motherhood caused me to step back and reflect because it is a blessing. I believe that God had so much transformation He had to do within me. It wasn't just about giving birth to my son in the natural. God was pushing me through the birthing of a new me. I do not believe I would be where I am today without the stretching He did during my postpartum period. That is not to say that I have somehow arrived and reached my end. This is a continual process, and He is looking for my daily "Yes" to trusting Him. Now I am walking in boldness and encouragement in my faith as a mother.

He has given me this blessing of being a mother and wants me to be joyful. I went from distrusting Him to completely surrendering to Him because I could have easily chosen to give up or stayed in the dark place of depression.

I'm continuing to learn even in my moments of frustration and when I'm thinking how hard this is that I can still be joyful about my struggle. For the past few months, I've been a stay-at-home mom and the Joy in this experience is greater than I could have imagined. I am able to pray over my son, be with him every day, see him grow, teach him, and share the Word with him. I have freedom to set the tone for my household, and that brings me Joy in this season. I'm adjusting to what motherhood looks like for me.

I want the world to know that even in the toughest of times, God remains the same. He is the PERFECT Father. He loves us and we are His most prized possession. Stay close to Him, dive into the Word, and remind yourself of what He says about you. When the season feels unbearable, remember this: *"Yes indeed, it won't be long now."* Amos 9:13 (MSG)

Barren

Shaun Nelson

Desolate. Despairing. Unfruitful. Infertile. Barren. These words depict how I felt on May 18, 2005. You see, just a few short days prior to that, my then-husband and I were ecstatic! A couple of weeks before, we had just found out that I was pregnant. We were making so many plans joyfully beginning our family. And then I had some cramping and very sharp pains within my right lower abdomen that lasted for what felt like hours but probably had only been minutes. We made a trip to the doctor the next day just to "make sure." The nurse exclaimed, "Oh look! There's the heart beating!" The doctor then said, "I'm sorry but the heart is beating, but the egg did not implant in the uterus — it's in your tube and cannot survive there. I'll have to remove it."

In not even 15 seconds we went from ecstatic hearing the heart beating to heartbroken after being told I had an ectopic pregnancy, which would have to be surgically terminated. I was truly despondent. We were older trying to start our family and had been facing infertility and had finally conceived. I was beyond disappointed. I was in a broken place. You see, because I was a child of faith: I believed in God and believed in His promises. Why was this happening to me/us? I was deeply hurting and was so mad at Him because I felt "why did you allow me to become pregnant only to take the baby away in such a quick time!"

A very dear Canaan church sister called me a few days after my surgery to check on me, and I confessed to her how very angry at God that I was. She simply said to me, "It is OK to be mad at Him. He already knows and can handle your anger." That was so freeing to me to be able to admit what I was feeling, so that I could begin the healing process. What I know beyond a shadow of doubt is that my God is Faithful! What I know is that He is a Healer! What I know is that He keeps His promises! I have learned truly how to trust God when I cannot trace Him. I have learned what my elders used to say that His timing is not our timing.

In my case I was able to conceive and carry a healthy 9-pound, 20.5-inch baby girl who is thriving physically, emotionally, mentally — but most of all — spiritually. The Joy of being Olivia's mother was able to happen because it was not yet her time to bless us as parents. We had more growing to do as a couple. I am now confident that I may have possibly missed out on the blessing of her if that pregnancy had survived. Sometimes our prayers are answered the way we ask but sometimes they are not. In this spiritual walk, when we say we trust God, we learn that we have to trust Him through the pain, hurts, deaths, losses, yeses, maybe's, and even the no's.

During this test my favorite scripture became "The Joy of the Lord is My Strength." Nehemiah 8:10 (KJV) This scripture carries me through life's encounters and encourages me in my spiritual walk with God. When I consider the character of God, who is sovereign, powerful, loving kind, just and compassionate, I become strong, bold and confident knowing, I serve a God who controls all things.

HIS PROTECTION

Elizabeth Rose

My name is Elizabeth. I was living in Columbus, Ohio, in the fall of 2017 and was asked by a church member to consider becoming a pen pal. It would be for her stepson, who was incarcerated. After thinking it over for a while, I decided to do so. We wrote back and forth, and I visited him.

Fast forward to 2000, we were married. He was still incarcerated, but we had a small ceremony. His cousin, also incarcerated, was his best man. My girlfriend was my maid of honor. After several months, he was given early release. I didn't want to be in a cohabitation relationship. I thought he was mature and ready to change his lifestyle. I didn't tell my family that I had gotten married until after the facts became so obvious. They were surprised, but thankfully to say the least; things went well for a little while. I was happy and he seemed happy also.

Unfortunately, he was having trouble finding and maintaining employment. I was working in my regular position that had varying work hour shifts. He started coming home late or not at all. Eventually, he was reincarnated at a local jail for probation violation. I didn't accept his phone calls or make visits, because I told him that if he ever returned to prison, I wouldn't go to see him.

After a few weeks, he returned home. Things were so-so. Still, he wasn't working full time. His father and stepmother moved out of town. We would visit his birth mother and family locally from time to time and travel to my family in another state. His mother and I talked on the phone often.

After a while, he started staying away from home. My mother said, "maybe that was a good thing." His mother would call to tell me about women he would bring to her house. Sometimes, I would get calls on my landline from other women. Some of my jewelry and money came up missing.

In a new apartment, I had the locks changed but he came by and broke the key in the door. I changed to a cell phone to discontinue communication. However, there were many other events, but he never touched or cussed me. Later I found out he was incarcerated again.

After four years of a dysfunctional marriage, I received divorce papers in the mail, and I signed them. I didn't hear from him for a long time. I would go out of my way not to be near him or speak to him. Now, we do speak to each other using just short sentences and a few words.

Then, he started attending 8:30 a.m. worship service at the same congregation, while I attended at a later time. I was very hurt and depressed because I thought he wanted a better life. I know God didn't put me in this marriage, but His grace and mercy protected me while in it. Someone could have been hurt or killed. He also brought me out mentally, emotionally, and spiritually stronger. I'm truly wiser. I know my hope is truly in Christ Jesus, and my family support has been valuable. They never put me down for what I did. I know God is my helper.

ARE YOU MAD AT ME?

Paulette Jewell

Yes, Jesus Loves me; I know this because He has shown me in so many different times and situations. I was diagnosed with Type 1 juvenile diabetes, my first life-altering disease, at the tender age of 8 years old. I was forced into taking care of myself by injecting myself with insulin and learning to clean the glass syringes weekly. This responsibility prompted me into thinking of becoming a medical professional.

Times were extremely difficult for me as child. I didn't understand what diabetes was; therefore, I stayed sick from high blood sugars a lot. I will always remember my uncle James saying, "This baby always has a smile on her face." He must have seen God's Grace. I recall learning a song as a child that said, "This Little Light of Mine. I'm gonna let it shine." Had it not been for the grace of God and the understanding of medical staff, I could not have made it.

In the 1950s, I was brought into the hospital in a diabetic coma. The medical doctors told my parents that my life expectancy was approximately 15 years based on the fact that I was a Black child, with no insurance and parents who didn't understand diabetes.

Today with technology, I'm using an insulin pump with CGM (continuous glucose monitoring). I'm capable of controlling my diabetes and not allowing it to control me with complications. Thank God for providing me an opportunity to shout out to anyone who will listen how important it is to take care of your diabetes.

Look where God has brought me from! In October 2010, I was diagnosed with thyroid cancer. Then, I had a left knee replacement the next year while feeling weak and sick. Next, my doctors diagnosed me with leukemia. I battled to survive. During the treatment of leukemia, I learned that I was allergic to most chemo medications and had severe reactions. All I could do was pray to God. This scripture provided Joy to my soul:

"Daughter, your faith has made you well. Go in peace, and be healed of your affliction." Mark 5:34 (NKJV)

God blessed me again as I took radiation treatment for the thyroid cancer. The treatment affected my voice. As a health education specialist, I served as a consultant on HIV/AIDS. I was without my voice for almost 8 months. God is good! The team I worked with had videos of my past presentations and helped until I was able to speak clearly. Six months later, I was diagnosed with leukemia. I asked, "Okay God, are you mad at me?" I'm not gonna say this has been easy. Still, I stay steadfast in my faith. "I have learned to be satisfied with the things I have and with everything that happens." Philippians 4:11 (NCV)

In January 2018, I had a knee replacement of my right knee The replacement was not successful, and I had a second knee replacement. My right knee was operated on three times from January through April and remained infected for two years. I just thank God to be alive. From the medicines that I received to control the Red Man's Disease (a skin rash that affects faces, neck, and upper torso), I had congestive heart failure, fluid around my lungs, temporary blindness, and renal failure. I was probably out of my mind because of my temperament at the time. However, I still kept my faith in God and prayed that I and my husband were going to make it through all right. Every day is a day of Thanksgiving. God is so good to me. I will praise the Lord at all times!

While working as a case manager with persons infected and affected with HIV/AIDS virus, I learned that you have to put yourself into your patient's shoes. I kept God first, in my mouth and heart. I spoke with respect and kindness and shared my dedication and beliefs in God to others. Faith means being sure of the hope and knowing that something is real even if we do not see it. Hebrews 11:1 (paraphrased)

My parents were in a car accident. My dad was killed. For 12 years, my mother has lived in an assisted living facility. For me to see my mom grieve the loss of my dad is difficult to see. I know he is with our Father in Heaven, but I still can't talk about it. Sometimes it hurts. I miss my dad.

LeRoy, my husband had been complaining for a few months about heartburn. Finally, he had to go to the hospital. After surgery, he was diagnosed with gall bladder cancer. Additional test showed he had liver cancer and colon cancer. All I could say was, "Lord, have mercy! You have my attention." Eight months earlier, my husband had just finished radiation for prostate cancer. I felt like I was gonna lose my mind! For several days, this news was totally overwhelming. I couldn't talk to anyone. I had to hold it in and be strong for my husband. I sat on my porch swing, walked my dog, and cried in silence. I turn to what I knew, the church and giving praise.

Every day is a day of thanksgiving. LeRoy, my Boo bear, and I are enjoying spending time together, when visitors come pray or to just share memories from the past.

So, I leave you with these thoughts from scripture:

"I leave you peace; my peace I give you. I do not give it to you as the world does. So don't let your heart be troubled or afraid." John14:27 (NCV)

"Is any thing too hard for the Lord…?" Genesis 18:14 (KJV)

NEW KIDNEY

James Harrell

My tribulations with serious health issues began in 2016, and they lasted until March 30, 2022. I almost died; I had amputation of toes, lost sight in one eye, became septic, and had kidney failure and seizures. After bloodwork results in 2019, my kidneys started shutting down. During COVID (2020), I began dialysis at home and became very ill in the mornings. As a result, I had to quit my remote job. I remained unemployed until July 2022. For seven years, physical challenges continued, back-to-back, and mentally many times, I wanted to give up. I was angry with God for a while, because of these multiple tribulations. At one point, there did not seem to be an end in sight. Everything was completely stripped from me, but I continued to stay in prayer and knew His will for me. Then, things started to fall into place.

I posted on Facebook that I needed a kidney. Through the Kidney Chain Program, I received a kidney on March 30, 2022, from my friend, who volunteered. She was the first person I met in high school, when I moved to Louisville in 1998. She became my kidney donor.

The night before surgery I was not in the best place. I was scared and didn't want to tell anyone. I kept the fear to myself because I didn't want to bother my brother or mother. My mother was already worried about me because we almost lost my father during his double transplant surgery. I struggled with this thought in the back of my mind. I decided that I was going to just pray about my situation. When I prayed before going into surgery, I was at peace, because I turned my cares over to the Lord.

Praise God, I did not have any problems with surgery and recovered quickly post-op. Afterwards, I was so happy and excited to be on the other side of this experience. I was so thankful to God and prayed that everything would move forward with medications and other after-surgery procedures. Everything went fine, because as I knew before, everything was in God's hands. I continued to trust God.

After my surgery, people began coming to me. God has put people in my path to make this happen and placed them on my heart. They feel comfortable talking to me about getting a new kidney. I know they are struggling, so if there is anything I can do to help somebody I'm more than willing. I will do whatever it takes to give them peace of mind, pray with them, or talk with them. God has turned this experience into a major positive.

Two weeks ago, I talked with a young lady struggling with getting a transplant; she was just nervous about having it done. We talked for a while and now she has decided to go ahead and go through the process. A lot of good things have come from my experience. The surgery has given me another purpose. I will continue to use Facebook to encourage people to donate a kidney and help those struggling with kidney failure figure out what to do. My help puts people's minds at ease, even if they don't have a blood match.

Over the years, I always knew I was a strong person, and this experience confirmed this even more. I also realized that you must always help others, because you never know when someone may have to help you. Through it all, I learned that God carried me through with everything that was going on during the past seven years. I am now able to return to church and work in the security ministry once a month.

I want the world to know there is a program called the Donor Chain Program for people who need a kidney. If you have someone who wants to donate a kidney to you, they can, even though their kidney does not match yours. Their kidney will go to someone whom they match, and immediately they will find a kidney for the person you wanted to give a kidney to. This process blesses two people instead of one. The highest ethnic group in need of kidney transplants is African-Americans. Unfortunately, African-Americans are the least likely to donate a kidney due to myths. Only education and screening will decrease the need for kidney donors.

A REFLECTION

Loretta Gillenwater

As a young girl, I grew up in church, attending Sunday school and Vacation Bible School on a regular basis. I accepted Christ early in life and was baptized at age 11. During my childhood and in high school, my church life was quite structured, learning about Christ through various Bible stories. Life was simple: I felt close to the Lord and was active in several organizations. God blessed my life.

After going to college, I turned away from my church life, rarely attending church, with the exception of when I went home for the weekend. I was headed in the wrong direction, "knowing" I was an adult and could do whatever I wanted to do, within reason. This included staying out late and going to parties. Through all of these, so called "good times," something was missing in my life. In my senior year, I couldn't wait to get out and start earning my own money. I graduated in four years and was ready to begin my life as a working adult, not realizing how good I had it as a student in college.

After college, I had several short-term jobs, including copier sales representative, team leader of a crime stopper crew, and personnel recruiter. These jobs were barely paying minimum wage. In reality, I was losing money and could barely pay my bills, even though I was living at home. At that time, I did get back into church, all the while praying for a good job. The Lord blessed me with a position as an insurance underwriter. The company offered training and a good paying position.

After working in my new career for two years, while still in training, the company closed the Louisville office, and I was asked to move to Cincinnati. I got married while there and once again found myself falling away from the right path. Within my marriage, we seemed to be going our own separate ways, with little thought of God. The marriage ended after 10 years. After my marriage ended, I felt despair. One Sunday morning, while listening to a Christian network, I heard a message of "hope." God's message of hope was one I needed to hear at that time. So, after being separated from God and trying to things my way, I got back in church.

Over the years, I have had a good career with the same company. There have been difficult job situations at work, and, sometimes, I've felt that I was not prepared to meet the situation. Without fail, the Lord would bring me through. At this phase in my life, I am retired, active in the church, and still have not remarried. I know the Lord is in control of my life, and I will wait on Him to send the right person.

Now, I find Joy in the time I spend with my nieces and nephew, cherishing the sparkle in their eyes and enthusiasm from playing simple games. Teaching line dancing brings me Joy and is one of the ways the Lord has allowed me to share my talents with others. I am at a good place in my life, even though this was not always the case. I understand that all things work for the good to those who believe in the Lord, and I consider it all Joy.

JUST MY STORY

Mildred James

When I turned my life over to God, it changed me forever. As I grew older, I began to depend on God through good and bad times. That thought brings me great Joy. When my parents got sick, I was faced with the fact that they might, at any time, leave me. After they passed, I prayed to the Lord for strength, and He was my comforter.

Today in my life, I recently lost my son, and that really was something. Once again, I had to go to the Lord, and ask Him to give me the strength to get through his passing. As the days went by, I began to find Joy every day. As I grow older, I find Joy in my everyday life, because the Lord allows me to wake up. These acts of the Lord put a smile on my face and warmth in my heart and give me Joy.

I recently had cancer surgery and faced a life-altering situation. Once again, I prayed for strength to go through the surgery and chemo treatments. Every day, I found Joy because God was going to heal my body, and the days became brighter and brighter. So now, I can look back and say only God has given me joy. God brought me through the cancer surgery and chemo treatments. Now I can say that I am cancer free: that brings me the greatest Joy.

Through my trials and tribulations, I have learned that no matter what you are going through that is a part of life (sickness, death, trials, tribulations, etc.), know that God's got you in His hands and you are going to be just fine.

God Has the Final Say

Dr. Anthony Sanders

The premise of this publication speaks volumes so often, even right now, in this tedious journey of life. It was difficult to choose only one, but here is my contribution.

During the early 1990s, I had obtained certification to become a building principal. There was an undercurrent in the Western Kentucky locale that did not value diversity in the educational workforce, especially because there was not much diversity in the leadership component of the school district. In 1992, the district had no people of color in a leadership role and seemed to have no concern that this was an issue.

The only principal of color had just retired. I applied for the principal position of an elementary school, but did not receive the position. As a result, there was community interest that led to a state-level investigation. In addition, the building where I taught and had applied for the position caught fire on the last day of school (after my notification of non-selection). So, after the low-key accusation (never public), of involvement in the fire, the school moved into a large convention center. The makeshift classrooms had to be dismantled weekly, due to other events scheduled for that building. It was one of the most tedious recollections of my teaching career — which is another count it all Joy moment. So, many staff members still have horror stories about that part of being employed at that school.

A new principal had been hired to transition from the alternate location to the renewed location. The former building was one of the oldest schools in the district and was on schedule for replacement at that time. However, it was determined that since it had been brought up to code, it would not be next in line to be replaced.

Not being selected obviously stung, but I persevered and continued teaching in that building and under the selected leadership. There were no battles as a result of not being selected. There was one incident about scheduling on which I was consulted. I had specific knowledge and background but felt that I did not need to be involved, if I was not "qualified" for the position.

I prayed, trusted, and survived with God's help and the support of persons who knew the situation, both internal and external, even though, we could not effect change in the situation.

Interestingly enough and quite unexpectedly, after *one year*, the person in the principal role decided not to continue in the position. I have no idea as to why the decision was made, but the position became open again. I applied and received the principal position (most likely only the third Black male elementary principal in that district since the 1960s) four days before the school year began, in a renewed school building!

The one-year designation is significant in this instance, because often when I am faced with situations in which I do not know which way to move, I will get the Bible and just open it, which is what occurred when dealing with not being selected. Wherever the pages open, I will study the words on that page and notice how it speaks to the situation at hand. In this case, it opened into the Old Testament in Daniel, where it talked about the kings of the north and the kings of the south, and all the things that occurred during those years. These scripture passages spoke to me then, because they taught me continued patience and about all of the events that can occur over years. Now that I am older and more experienced in revelatory study, this prophetic word in Daniel has increasing significance for world events today!

In conclusion, I was able to complete a nine-year stint as principal with all of its ups and downs, but so many successes in many ways. After moving ahead from that position, my faith and trust continues to strengthen, attaining more and more opportunities and experiences in leadership. Presently, I can mentor others toward success, while trusting God. I am critically more attuned that God has it all under control through every test, trial, and tribulation. Being a "church kid," I can hear the elders say, "I have experience with Him and I'm not going to turn back — I've come too far!"

In my life, through no merits of my own, God continues to manifest His love, mercy, grace, and moreover, His right hand of righteousness as a consistent and continuous covering.

Whatever you may be going through as you read this, realize that no one is immune to levels of life's storms — that is not even a promise of God's Word. We serve a great God, who through His Son, Jesus Christ, gives us a victorious outcome, even for situations in which we are ill prepared to handle. God gave the increase! Count it all joy! God has the final say!

SECOND CHANCE

Abe Drake

I raised my family and took care of everything including all my responsibilities. My life was pretty good, but my wife went to church every day — and I didn't go. In Memphis, Tennessee, while at a basketball game, about 20 years ago, I got sick and stayed down there for eight days trying to recover. When I returned home, the doctors found that I had 20% renal failure for four years.

I went on dialysis for 36 months, and during that time God took everything away from me. Previously, I had the best of life. In my opinion, I have had everything including a good job and everything was going the way I needed it to go. After going on dialysis, I no longer had a job.

During the months of dialysis, I asked God if He would give me another chance; I wouldn't become a preacher or sing in the choir, but I would change my ways and begin to go to church every day. So, I began to spend time in church helping everybody including the homeless, cooking for the church, doing men's ministry and all the things I thought I should do that I wasn't doing.

Everything was not going well for me, and then all of a sudden God gave me my life back. He gave me a kidney transplant of a 16-year-old person from Lexington, Kentucky. It's been 13 years since the transplant and now I feel that I made it because of the promise I made to God.

I wasn't a bad person and didn't have bad ways. The big difference was that I just changed my ways, got back into church, and started doing the right things. So, I say the moral of this story is that God will allow you to do good but He wants you to do good for Him. To get my attention, God showed me he could take everything away. When I decided to worship Him and do the things I was supposed to do, He gave me back my life. God gave me a kidney and a second chance at life for 13 years.

I am saying, if you do right by putting God in your life, no matter what happens, He provides a second chance. God gave me a second chance and I've done well ever since. I have never looked back.

SUCCESS THROUGH PERSERVERANCE

Robert Byrd, III

Becoming a Christian at an early age put me in a good position because I learned how to treat others with respect and to treat others the way you want them to treat you. My family went to church daily when I was about 5 years old. I learned a lot of teachings, sang in the choir, and served as a reader. These teachings continue to be used for how I act today. The biggest thing I remember is to love each other equally.

My biggest tribulation was playing football in high school and getting to where I am today. Previously, I wasn't in a good position to be where I am now, but I made the best of everything. From my freshman year until my junior year in high school, I did not start on the field. The coach only let me play on special teams. In my senior year, things changed because I started playing defense. I worked hard every day and was willing to learn new plays. All my strength and an effort put me in a great position because I grew as a football player. As a result, I received a college scholarship to play football. A bad situation was turned into a good one.

Hard work always pays off, no matter how long it takes. Just be patient and put your trust in God's hands; that will get you where you need to be. I would ask God during my tribulation if this was the sport for me. I said, "God, if I could be successful in this sport, I would have a chance. God, do I look somewhere else, follow another path?"

God showed me a few signs, sometimes during a weekly game or at practice. He revealed to me, if I continued doing the right things, my chance to play Friday Night Football would come.

I would say never stop pushing toward your goals and do what you believe in. Believe in yourself. Always do what you like to do; then, you will push harder toward your goal. It takes hard work.

God will let you know if you are going in the right direction. He reassures me and keeps my head straight from bad negative thoughts. Most of all, He gives me the strength to play this physical game.

AND YET…

Sue Terdan

My marriage vows were sacred to me, as a young woman of 22 years. I loved my husband, being married, and everything about making a home together. And yet… I ended up seeking a divorce 11 years later. We had a beautiful child who bought us Joy beyond measure. And Yet…he was caught in the middle of a long and hard custody battle. I had many friends and a loving family. And Yet…most did not know how to help or what to say or do to support me. At age 33 along with my son who is 2½ years old, marked the beginning of my most painful trial. In the midst of my trauma, I felt that nothing would ever be right again. And Yet…through my faith, I am a survivor, I love life, and I live life in peace and happiness.

The process of divorce is a very difficult time in one's life: socially, mentally, physically, and emotionally. Compound that with custody issues, and, for me, that has been the most difficult and traumatic period of my life. I was devastated, mad, and always sad. I was scared and traumatized. And Yet…in my public life, I was working full time, raising my son, appearing strong and focused.

We are God's children, so when I yelled at God (yes, I did!), He understood. When I was angry with Him (yes, I was!), He understood. When I couldn't stop crying, He understood. And Yet…God remained a rock for me. He put His arms around me and let His love surround me. There was no one else I could bare my hurt, embarrassed, crushed, and damaged soul to…but God! Releasing everything to God kept me sane. He kept me. Oh, He Kept me. My sanity was in God's hands. I knew it, believed it, and counted on it. My faith in Him, conversations with Him, prayers to Him, and His unconditional, patient love for me are the roots of my sanity. I continually prayed to God to protect and guide my son always, and, to help me to not come out of this trauma a bitter and angry old lady. God answers prayers…albeit…in His way and on His time!

God is my Confidant. I have been on my faith journey since I was 5 years old. I am always learning, asking questions, and in awe when I discover answers that God has revealed to me, through earth angels, church life, my Sunday School family, and music. I know and understand that God works in His time, He hears us, and He desires a relationship with us. He gives us 365 "promises" and 365 "fear nots" in the Bible. These are two Blessings given to us every day of the year! And Yet…we have a role in this. It is up to me to seek Him, praise Him, thank Him, and ask Him for the counsel I need.

In my Faith journey I have learned that God teaches us patience, understanding, pain, trials, forgiveness, Joy, and love. I have also learned three simple facts of life: you are either 1) in a storm, 2) coming out of a storm, or 3) going into a storm. And Yet…in the midst of our storms, our Blessings always outnumber our trials and tribulations. Therefore, I THANK God every single day for my many Blessings, my trials, His presence in my life, and for guiding me and keeping me a loving, optimistic, kind, and happy 70-year-old lady!

My Career Testimony: The Real Estate Promise

Diane Ulmer

During my corporate career, I have been laid off *four* times from *four* different companies. I hated this fact, because I always worked really hard throughout my career and had a strong work ethic. But circumstances beyond my control can happen.

The first layoff occurred in my mid-20s when, after completing a manager trainee program, the company decided that there was no permanent position at the company for me and they laid me off with very little notice. I was devastated because I really loved the banking industry. I had a college degree and positive feedback in the trainee program. I walked into work one morning and was told that I would be allowed to "collect unemployment benefits as soon as possible."

The next three layoffs at three companies occurred for various reasons:

- The next two companies I worked for were merging with another company and my position was being eliminated.
- The client I worked with terminated the contract with the company which meant that my position was no longer needed.

Bottom line: It appeared that I was always in the wrong department (marketing) at the wrong time. It felt like a target was on my back. I was always losing my job and having to start over again financially. By the time the third layoff happened, I was tired of having a career in corporate America. I felt a lack of control of my own destiny, and I needed something I could manage — and control. The job market was such that I could only land a minimum-wage job. I could barely pay my monthly bills.

I decided that I wanted to talk with my brother, who had recently started a property management business. After a few phone calls with him and further investigation of the Louisville real estate market, I decided to start my own company. This undertaking was a big step, so, as was my custom, I asked God for His opinion. "Lord, would you anoint my new entrepreneurial effort?" "Would you bless the business of purchasing foreclosed houses, the renovations I would need to do on them, and the tenants I would have?" "Would you bless me, Lord, I who do not know anything about property management?"

My answer from God was, "YES, I will!" I believed the Lord, and so, for the next 16 years, along with my having a corporate job, my new side hustle allowed me to purchase seven battered houses below market value. I obtained funding to work with contractors to renovate the houses and set up a vendor relationship with the Louisville Housing Authority to find Section 8 tenants. God assigned my brother as my mentor to guide me. Suddenly, I was meeting with contractors to complete renovations. God allowed me to purchase one house after another. He blessed me with project management skills to handle the budget for each house. Over a 16-year period, I eventually re-sold (flipped) each house for a profit, while still juggling my day job.

God provided for my every need. There were many struggles while managing my business as a sole proprietor. I had many incidents with terrible tenants, major house repairs to pay for, bad housing inspection reports to deal with, and numerous cash flow (money) problems. But each time I prayed to God with a question, the Lord provided a response. He sent angels to protect my houses from burglary, and a real estate agent who helped me sell the houses. He sent money to pay the bills and the right contractors who gave me reasonable prices on repairs.

I could go on and on about how I saw the mighty hand of God moving on my behalf. I remember the many times I got down on my knees to talk to God in my prayer closet. Specifically, I remember the night that God told me that I was going to sell all seven of my houses. I was sitting on the edge of my bed at the end of a tough day. God said to me, "You know, you are going to sell each one of your houses." ***Just like that***!

God kept his promise to me. Sure, there were many challenges, but I was determined and relentless to get to the finish line, to get to the last closing for the sale of my last rental house. After all, I had a green light from God to move forward to accomplish my dream.

In hindsight, looking back over my corporate career, I would not have changed anything. I would not have changed the number of layoffs and my venture into an entrepreneurial career. I now see blessings that evolved from experiencing a turbulent corporate career at several companies that finally ended in real estate.

My relationship with God catapulted exponentially. Each layoff was always a surprise to me. I quickly prayed to God about my circumstance and guidance for my future. I trusted God to help me, to keep his promises to me. I was dependent on Him in each scenario. He never failed me.

I learned to trust his timing as the answer to my prayers. Realizing that He is always Sovereign, caused me to wait on Him to see what He decided to do. The answers He provided for me were not "cookie-cutter." The responses to my prayers were not always the same.

These experiences developed my faith in the Almighty God. They were a threshing floor, a classroom for me to mature in my relationship with Him. God showed me talents that I did not know I had. God gave me a voice I did not know I had.

The continuous loss of my jobs was no fault of my own. However, God used these situations to increase my spiritual connection to Him, pivoting me into new insights, and teaching me about the guidance of the Holy Spirit. What I know for sure is, like many of us, I have been chosen to complete a life's work that, back then, was only the beginning.

A Five-Year Walk of Faith

Beverly Barbour

It's safe to say that life can be challenging! We can easily get distracted and let circumstances take over our emotions and even rattle our faith. We tend to operate in this manner: when life is good, we are happy; when times are tough, we are frustrated; and when hardships come pouring down on us, we are miserable. Trusting God is easy when life is good, and we are feeling competent and in control. I ask myself, is that genuine faith or simply a form of our own self-reliance?

Over the past five years, I have agonized over this question. Is it my faith or is it me that I rely on most? Being a "Type A" personality, I usually find myself in situations where I struggle with learning how to trust and rely more on God versus taking matters into my hands and implementing my own plans of action. Quite honestly, it is difficult for me to slow down — let go — and just wait for God to speak and lead me.

I am sharing a testimony of my latest walk of faith spanning the past five years. It includes what I learned and am still learning about the importance of maintaining a steadfast faith and reliance on God.

With a job promotion in 2013, my husband and I relocated from Illinois to Virginia. What should have been a celebratory period in our lives turned out to be a costly experience. The housing markets had bottomed out and offers were not coming in as expected on the sale of our Illinois home, which meant we were paying housing costs in two different states. After a lot of prayers, we eventually took a loss on the Illinois property resulting in a significant financial setback. Bless the name of the Lord! After two years, we finally settled into a home in the Virginia suburbs and got our finances back on track.

In 2018, my spirit began growing weary and anxious for another change. Although things were going well professionally — I was managing the #1 sales team in the company and earned a trip to Cancun — the job expectations and long hours were starting to take their toll on me. I continually prayed for God to reveal a different plan for my life, but nothing seemed to be happening — or was it? My mother and grandmother often said that God works in mysterious ways.

In April 2018, my husband was unexpectedly admitted to the hospital and had to undergo an emergency triple bypass. What was God preparing me for? Because I had personally experienced bypass surgery in 2009, I felt better prepared and had the patience and understanding to support him through this ordeal. All thanks to God! He made a full recovery, and my job afforded me the flexibility to get him to all of his physical therapy sessions and follow-up doctor appointments. What was God trying to reveal to me? Was this His way of answering my prayers for change?

Then in 2019, we faced even more health challenges. I never envisioned myself as a caregiver, but I soon found myself fulfilling this role when my husband experienced a series of mild strokes. Once again, I gave praises and thanks to the Father! Although my husband had some memory loss, he did not suffer any debilitating effects from the strokes. I was still able to work full time and could arrange my work schedule to ensure I got him back and forth to doctor appointments.

The COVID-19 pandemic changed life for everybody in 2020! In March, my company mandated that everyone work from home. Since several of my sales reps already worked from their home offices, this was not a major adjustment. The biggest change came in April when after eight years, I lost my job due to the COVID impacts on our business. Immediately, my six-figure income and a large life insurance policy were gone! Our finances were impacted even more when the company filed for bankruptcy in July, and I lost my portion of company ownership plus all shares of stock. How would we now live on merely 30% of our former income? How could we still afford to pay bills and eat? I was worried and needed to find a new sense of purpose to refocus my attention. So, I began volunteering as an online tutor/mentor for middle school students; I worked on COVID campaigns in under-served communities to help residents get registered for vaccines. This change was very rewarding. Thank You, Lord, for these opportunities!

The year 2021 brought about the beginning of yet another major change and new start. After the sudden death of my husband's brother, we decided to move again to be closer to our families and friends; we packed up and relocated from Virginia back to my hometown of Louisville, Kentucky in July. I had been gone for over 30 years, so it was challenging to get re-acclimated to the city and find suitable living conditions. Since being back, I remain prayerful while still seeking and waiting for God to reveal a new purpose for my life.

My patience has grown thin, and I struggle with mild depression. But I walked into the new year of 2022 with a renewed faith and prayerful spirit, still trusting and believing that God will reveal His plan for my life. While putting the finishing touches on this testimony, God answered that prayer when I received a call confirming a job interview. Should this opportunity pan out, I will be able to transfer 30+ years of professional work experience in helping high school students to bridge the gap between education and the business world.

It continues to be a long faith journey, but one major lesson learned so far is: FAITH WORKS!! Everything is in God's Time — and He's Still Got Me!

A CRY OF JOY

Alphonsa Fowler

I often wonder how Jesus could love us when sometimes we are so unlovable. Even though we are not deserving of His love, He still loves us unconditionally. Just to know that He loves us this way should make our heart cry with Joy. He is so worthy of our love and praise. The turmoil of 2019–2022 has been insurmountable, but God has kept us safe and He will continue to bless us in the future.

During the COVID epidemic of 2019/2022, my wife and I were blessed not to be infected with the virus. But June 19, 2022, my wife and I tested positive for the COVID virus. I had very mild symptoms, but my wife's symptoms were very severe and life threatening because she was taking medicine for sarcoidosis, and her immune system was weakened. Her pain was so excruciating, she would cry out in anguish, "Lord, please come and relieve me of this pain and suffering." We thanked all our many relatives and friends for the many prayers that they prayed daily for our healing and recovery. Yes, it is true that "the effectual fervent prayer of [the righteous] availeth much." James 5:16 (KJV) The COVID virus was running rampant in our home, but we were confident that Jesus would bring us out victoriously, and He did. If it had not been for His permissible will to deliver us from this illness, we would have still counted it all Joy, for we know He knows what's best for us. All the problems that have prevailed and still are prevailing in the world will not tarnish the Joy that He has given us.

I count it all Joy even when Jesus corrects me when I do things that are not pleasing to Him. One day, I had an encounter with Jesus. I know it was no one else but Him with His awesome passion and infinite wisdom. He showed me a mirror of my life that revealed to me that whatever I had accomplished was not the result of my own doing but only because of His permissible will that these accomplishments became a reality. I found Joy in knowing that this encounter with Jesus has strengthened me in my

Christian faith and my willingness to always put Him first in all my endeavors.

Also, it gives me pleasure to know that I have someone who is always capable and willing to sustain me in my weakest condition. Someone who knows me better than I know myself. Yes, when I am weak, He makes me strong, and reminds me that all things are possible with Him.

I thank Him for His assurances to me of His faithfulness, His blessings, His grace, and His mercy toward me. I thank Him for His abounding love that He demonstrates daily, which strengthens my relationship with Him as well as with other people. I thank Him for the Joy and peace that surpasses all understanding that only He can give and which the world can't take away.

THE ENEMY

Richard McKnight

What the enemy meant for evil God will turn it around for your good.

I came to the United States in February 2000 on a visitors' Visa wanting to see my uncle and other family that had migrated here many years before that I hadn't seen in years. My stay was supposed to be for only a month, but after many discussions with family members, who saw potential in me, I decided to stay. I could do so much more here for myself and for my family back home. This is where my journey began.

The fastest and easiest way for me to maintain legal status in the United States was for me to marry a U.S. citizen and so I did, not fully understanding the immigration laws and the consequences that may follow. Before getting married, my then-wife and I had discussed our living arrangements as we both lived in different states. The plan was that she would live with me for five years and if she didn't like the state where I lived then we would move back to her state to live but that all changed when we got married.

The reason why we had made that living arrangement is because I was employed with my family's construction and restaurant business, and so I had income. I was also very engaged in church ministries as the church musician and held other functions and was very committed to what I was doing, and my ex-wife was very aware of these things and agreed to it, even visiting to see what I did.

After several months of no indication of my ex-wife's intention of moving to my state and me having to fly out to see her all the time I asked her what was going on, what was her plan, and she said that she changed her mind and that she didn't want to move anymore. Adding to that decision, I found out that we were pregnant but also found out via emails that there was infidelity in the marriage. I was devastated. I had many questions with the main one being, "Is the child mine?" I confronted her about what I found out about the infidelity in the marriage and asked her if the child was mine. She was enraged and denied it, even though the emails were confessions about what she did.

My (future) ex-wife wasn't happy about my finding and that I confronted her about it, so to punish me she withdrew her application for my green card, and I was placed in deportation status. Isaiah 54:17 (KJV) says that no weapon formed against you shall prevail. Despite all that was going on, I held on to the promises of God and He made way like no one else could have. God placed a pro bono attorney in my path that got me out of deportation status. I did a DNA test and found out the child was indeed mine and fought through the courts for custody of my son. God granted me victory in every situation.

Today I'm a senior engineer at my job of 10-plus years; I have a great relationship with my son who's soon to be an adult; the relationship with my son's mother and me is better than it was when we first met; God has allowed us to peacefully and respectfully raise our son together with no drama; and I am able to help my family back in my home country much more than I could have ever imagined. Nothing I have now, nothing I've been through, nothing I've accomplished, and nothing I'm able to do now for others, could I have done in my own strength, but it's by the power of God, by prayer, and by the presence and leadership of God's Holy Spirit in my life. There's a Joy of knowing God for yourself and a peace that only He, God, can give that makes you know that whatever is going on in your life, He has it under control.

UNDER CONTROL

Anthony Lamb

I grew up in a Christian household. Attending worship service with my family was always the highlight of my week. Accepting Jesus as Lord and Savior was expected from my parents. So, like many children, I professed Christ to the church and was baptized. However, my personal relationship with Jesus became real and tangible when I became a husband and father. My relationship with God deepened even more when I was diagnosed with a debilitating neuromuscular disease at the very young age of 26. The prognosis was devastating. The doctors reported that by the age of 30, I would be in a wheelchair without the use of my extremities and eventually become a full quadriplegic. This type of tragedy leaves you with only two choices: God is either everything or nothing. God became my everything.

By faith, I was able to become the primary caregiver to my five children (one girl and four boys) and loyal, loving mate to my wife. By faith, I was able to raise my children in the church and provide a solid foundation of faith in Jesus Christ. By faith, I was able to see them all grow into successful adults with families of their own. By faith and God's amazing grace, over 30 years have passed since the initial medical prognosis, and I am still mobile without the use of a wheelchair, able to still drive a car, and although somewhat limited, I still have good use of my arms and legs. To God be all glory, honor, and power! I am a walking miracle.

Unbeknown to me, the most difficult trial I would ever face would happen in January 2022. My first born, one and only baby girl, the apple of my eye, was stricken with a terrible case of COVID. She lay lifeless, in the ICU, in a medically induced coma, on a ventilator, for 23 heart-wrenching days. God prepared my heart for His plan to call her home. He placed this truth deep in my soul. Yet, I continued to plead for His mercy to restore her health. On February 9, 2022, I watched as my wife held our 32-year-old baby girl's hand and sang her into God's Heaven. Once more, I made the decision to declare God as my everything. There was one question I told God I would never ask: Why? To me, to ask why would question His goodness, love, and sovereignty — none of which were ever in question in my soul. On February 19, 2022, we laid our sweet baby girl to rest with a pain so profound it can only be interrupted by God's Mighty Hand of love and power. He did just that.

The very next day, on Sunday, February 20, He brought forth my third grandchild, the first-born grandson, Anthony Geovelle Lamb, III. This little man has managed to capture a large portion of my heart. I can honestly say, he is the happiest baby I've ever met — so full of Joy! He represents the next generation of males to carry on the Lamb family name. However, God would take this Joy to even greater heights when it was made apparent that He wanted me and my wife to have the honor, and incredible privilege, to raise our oldest granddaughter, our daughter's only child, 14-year-old Damariah. We were overjoyed to invite this sweet girl into our home. To have God entrust this tender, grieving, precious child to our care is beyond Joy. He has given us the honor to complete the job our daughter so wonderfully started by raising our granddaughter with much love, tenderness, and grace as we closely follow God's loving direction.

BEST FRIEND

Lena Lewis-Harrell

As a little girl, I always felt alone. I was the second oldest child out of four who had the most responsibilities. I remember when I was in kindergarten my mother had me walk to the store with a note and money to buy items. Once a German shepherd bit me on the way home from the store, I was not injured. Why? Because God was watching over me.

My father was an alcoholic, and my oldest sibling was seven years older than I was. Neither had much responsibility in the home. When I was 9 years old, I had to go to the bank, laundromat, and grocery store all the time. When walking in the streets, men would whistle and say things to me. I would pray and ask God to help me. God directed me in a soft voice to walk on the other side of the street. My mother prayed all the time, and I could not understand why. She struggled to hold the family together, and she would say, "God will take care of us." I knew God was powerful, but did not realize how powerful He was until I was about 10 years old. I went to a visiting church and on that day, I could feel God in my spirit. It was a feeling I never experienced. It was like a peaceful out of body experience. That moment I realized how powerful God was. I knew then He was my best friend and loved me. In addition, I knew he would guide and protect me.

I left New York at 16 years to attend a Methodist college in Georgia. I was lonely occasionally, far from my family, and surrounded by a different culture. I continued to pray, and it was required that we attended church services one to two times on Sunday. Once while in school, a stranger approached me and said that a person I thought was my friend would come with several people and rape me. Nothing but God prevented that from happening. He not only sent that person, but he also guided me to listen to what he said. Later that individual did come with a car full of men. God protected me. What an awesome God we serve.

After graduating from college, I joined the Army and rededicated my life to Jesus while in Korea. At that time, I began spending more time with

God, praying, reading his Word and fasting. I now understand that he loves me and is always with me. What a calming and warm feeling, no longer loneliness feeling. "The Lord himself goes before you and will be with you; he will never leave you nor forsake you. Do not be afraid; do not be discouraged." Deuteronomy 31:8 (NIV)

ALWAYS LOOKING

Cynthia Lusco

As far back as I can recall, I have believed. I have known that there was a God, a presence, that watched over and cared for me at all times. That presence manifested itself as a porcelain figurine of an artist's image of Jesus that sat in the center of my grandmother's living room mantle. The eyes of that figurine would follow my every move as I twirled and cartwheeled around the room. No matter where I was, in the middle of the room or in the corner, standing on the furniture or lying on the floor, those gentle eyes were fixed on me.

My 3-year-old mind wasn't frightened by Grandmama's Jesus figurine. I was fascinated. I spent many moments moving around in what seemed to me to be a massive room, always checking to see if those eyes were still watching me. And they were — they always were. Grandmama told us grandchildren that God was like that. He is always looking out for us, is always with us. Of course, I didn't understand what she meant, but her words were reassuring, just like it was reassuring to have my grandmama always near, day and night.

When Grandmama passed, her open casket was placed in front of her living room mantle with the Jesus figurine keeping vigil. People came and sat in the room, had chicken and potato salad and all the sweet treats my aunties had cooked. We little ones flitted in and out of the room in play. Periodically, I'd check to see if Jesus was still watching me even though the room was filled with other people. He was.

Each night, I insisted on sleeping on the couch with my grandmother sleeping in her casket and Jesus watching over both of us.

Too soon, Grandmama was taken away in a black shiny car and the Jesus figurine along with other keepsakes of hers were packed away.

I grew up with my early impressions of Jesus strong in my mind, so tenderly entwined with my sweet memories of my loving grandmother and her figurine with the soft brown eyes that looked over me wherever I was.

They comforted me and I have continuously felt the presence of God and my grandmother all of my days.

I and my faith have evolved. It has been bittersweet. Life as a believer has been good, but it has been mighty hard in some places. I learned in troubles and loss, particularly the death of my son, that some things are far too big to endure on one's own. Early on, I believed that if I lived right and served God, that all would be well, that no problems or sorrow would come my way. And I believed that if any bad things headed in my direction, I could just pray them away. Well, that certainly was not true. In fact, those notions aren't even biblical.

The day my son died was a beautiful sunny spring day, cool and breezy. He, as I do, loved springtime, and he had spent much of his day outside with friends. He and I laughed and chatted with one another as he came in and out of the house for one thing or the other. At one point, he planted one of his annoying but wonderful wet kisses on my forehead, just like his grandmother often did to him. He told me he'd be right back. He was going to take one of his jackets to a friend who was cold, who didn't want to go all the way back home to get a coat.

That moment, that kiss was the last time I saw my precious son until I viewed his body on a cold hard table in a local hospital. He had been killed by a hit and run driver.

I'd like to say that in the shocking aftermath of Chris' death that I felt comforted by my faith and my loving God. I didn't. I reeled in shock, sorrow, and anger, so much anger. How, God, could you let this happen to **my** child? I have been faithful, I have served you, why didn't you protect him? I thought you promised to be with me. My questions and accusations of the Lord continued day after day after day. The good life I thought He'd given me had ended, and I was at the lowest place I'd ever experienced.

As time went on, I relearned how to get up and put one foot in front of the other. My prayers changed from demanding answers from God to prayers of simplicity. In the morning, I prayed for the Lord to help me get through the day and to show me something I could do for another. In the evening, I thanked him for seeing me through the day and to be with me through the night.

I can't imagine how, but I had some amazingly peaceful moments during that period of horrific traumatic suffering. In the stillest times of the night and early morning, the Lord gave me the ability to actually sense Him speaking to me. How awesome. And in the midst of my grief, I knew that He was with me, comforting me, listening to me cry out, and continuing to pick me up out of my darkness.

Today, I am wiser, and my faith is stronger. I know that my God is not some genie in a bottle who grants wishes and keeps the realities of the world away. However, He is Ever Present, Ever Loving, Ever Sustaining, and a marvelous Comforter. He, for me, has and continues to be always watching over me wherever I go.

SMALL BEGINNINGS

Rebehak Dow

Earlier this year, I quit my job.

I can't believe I just typed that. I'm staring at the words and asking myself, "YOU DID WHAT?!?" But...

Yeah. I quit my job. The last few months have been the hardest, most pain-filled months of my life. I was fighting an injury, illness, and time. Worry and anxiety crept in, and I began to wonder if I made the right decision.

During this process, I began to listen to the voice that I'd been running away from. That dreaded, awful voice of truth telling me: maybe I am the problem.

The truth of that stung a little... and then a lot. I began to understand and cope with new diagnoses, and recognized that I needed to change bad habits that were causing me to stumble in order to move forward in a different direction. It was time for me to take inventory and work on myself.

I had a lot working against me. Attention Deficit Hyperactivity Disorder is a hellish nightmare that robs its victims of the ability to push through a wall labeled "Already defeated." Despite my best efforts, the traits of my disability kept showing up in the most inopportune moments and I was drifting further and further away from what I really wanted for myself and my family. I was making stupid mistakes that were unnecessary and beneath my full capabilities to perform.

That level of truth came with a high price: my pride, vulnerability, and scariest of all, my trust.

Everything was not ok, and I couldn't keep pretending that it was fine. I needed help, as I was seeing all that I worked hard for come to an end.

Then, a voice whispered to me Zechariah 4:10 (NLT): "Do not despise these small beginnings, for the Lord rejoices to see the work begin, to see the plumb line in Zerubbabel's hand."

That word "beginnings" felt like a contradiction in my heart. Everything for me was ending, but the Lord sent a word to tell me things were beginning? That wasn't what I wanted to hear. I wanted to hear he was going to fix it, not destroy it!

Therein, the Lord showed me what my problem was:

"I WANT."

The Lord was revealing to me that I was driving myself off a cliff with my wants.

Isaiah 55:8–9 (NIV) says, "'For my thoughts are not your thoughts, neither are your ways my ways,' declares the Lord. 'As the heavens are higher than the earth, so are my ways higher than your ways and my thoughts than your thoughts.'"

When I began submitting to what His Thoughts were, I learned more about who I was and who He IS. He began showing me through His word how off course I was, but He would always follow up with words of encouragement, love, peace, and Joy. My deeper understanding of how full of mercy and grace our Lord is has caused me to count it all Joy indeed!

COUNT IT ALL JOY

Candace Johnson

In 2012, I was diagnosed with ovarian cancer. After surgery, they told me it was stage 2 cancer. I must admit that was one of the most difficult times in my life. I was told by the doctor that the cancer hadn't spread, but that she wanted me to have six rounds of chemo therapy over the next six months. This was more frightening than the diagnosis itself, because it never made sense to me that such a toxic process could help or heal a person's cancer. I seriously thought about not getting the chemotherapy; after all the cancer hadn't spread.

But with God's help, my husband's, my family and friends, I started the chemotherapy. My family and friends were praying, and I was seeking God and praying, also.

After two rounds of chemo here in Cincinnati, I decided I couldn't take chemo any more. I cried out to God. He reminded me of a book that a doctor I had consulted recommended, a book called *Life Over Cancer* by Keith Block and Andrew Weil M.D. The author of the book was an integrative oncologist at the "Block Center," who incorporates nutrition and other wellness treatments into the therapy process. I called the Block Center and found out that my insurance was accepted. I was so happy and thankful that God/Jesus had already made a way for me to complete my journey to wellness. Mike and I started making this trip to Skokie, Illinois, every six weeks and I finished my last four chemo treatments there. I am healed. It has been ten years as of August 2022. I loved going to the Block Center; the people there are super friendly. The founder of the center is my oncologist. He loves talking to Mike and me. There were times when the nurse would come in and tell him it's time to move on. I was not just a number with Dr. Block, as he took his time talking to us. We would talk about interesting and fun things. I'm still in contact with the Block Center, and I continue to have wellness visits there.

As I look back on this trial in my life, I can better understand what James 1:2 means. It says, "Count it all joy brothers and sisters when trouble comes your way, consider it an opportunity for great joy." James 1:3 (paraphrased) says, "For you know when your faith is tested, your endurance has a chance to grow." I can say that this trial has worked for my good. I have grown closer to God. I'm stronger and healthier than I was in my 40s. I have more peace in the trials that come into my life; I trust God more. I know Jesus as my Healer, Deliverer, Protector, and Joy! I also have a passion for helping people who want to live a healthy lifestyle to prevent cancers and other preventable diseases. God has blessed me tremendously since this trial and I give Him all the Glory!!

DEFYING THE ODDS!

Evangelist Hatcher

On September 11, 2015, a day that should be one of the happiest times in life, my sixth grandchild was due to make his entrance into the world. My daughter was in labor for 41 hours before he made his entrance into the world. When Judah arrived, he was pale blue, and the doctors took him before we could even realize what was occurring. We did not know it then, but our grandson had four blood clots and had experienced a right posterior cerebral artery stroke in utero. As a result, he was having seizures one right after the other. As his life hung in the balance, we began to call on the Name of Jesus and tighten our hold on faith. We went to the throne of grace, our source, and refuge. The prognosis for our grandson was grim, and we were told that there could be possible brain damage or cerebral palsy due to the 26 seizures he experienced in one night, but our faith in God persevered.

Seven years later, our grandson Judah Jacion, whose name means praise and healed, is a living testimony to the wonder-working power of God. The doctors said that Judah had three kidneys, and today he has two. The doctors gave him a prognosis of autism spectrum disorder, but through prayer, faith, and counting it all Joy, Judah has confounded even the wisdom of the doctors. Whenever we face trials of ANY kind, we know the distinguishing characteristics between being happy and experiencing real Joy.

The real Joy in this case came through watching our grandson defy the odds. He is healthy, and thriving wonderfully! There is no brain damage, no diagnosis of cerebral palsy, or autism, and he is flourishing. The trying of our faith for Judah is a continuous reminder that even in the most challenging of circumstances, we can still experience Joy, for the Joy of the Lord is our strength.

HOW TO BE JOYFUL DURING TRIALS

Dawnene Byrd

I have relied on my trust in God throughout my entire adult life — mostly dealing with relationships. One of the most recent times was when I found out I was pregnant with my third child — at 41 years old. I had been feeling anxious all morning, for no real reason I could pinpoint. My sister and nephew came downtown to go shopping, so I met them for a quick lunch while on my break from work. I could barely concentrate on the conversations and my heart was racing. I figured I must be coming down with something.

On the walk back to the office, my stomach churned that familiar feeling and suddenly the thought popped in my head: *You're pregnant. No. There is no way, Is there? But this is that feeling. No, I can't be.* I passed a Walgreen's and quickly turned around and told myself I'd just buy a cheap test to get the thought out of my head. I headed straight for the bathroom when I got back into the office. I gasped when the pink line appeared clear as day within seconds. *How can this be? No. I'm too old. We don't have enough space in our apartment. Will my marriage survive this new addition? How can we afford this? And childcare?* All of my fears crept into my mind. But then: *A new baby. A life. Please keep us safe, God. Make this work out somehow. I don't know how, and I cannot do this without You. You have to help me. I love this baby already.* I turned to the prayers my parents had instilled in me ever since I was a child: Trust in the Lord with all your heart. Do not be afraid.

My entire pregnancy was a balance of my fears versus my need to trust that God would work all things out for His good. And mine. I had really bad anemia and had to have weekly iron transfusions. They set me up for a possible blood transfusion after the baby was born, which thankfully I didn't need. The baby was born healthy, happy, and loud. I was so thankful. Joyful. This new blessing to love. Then, three weeks after his birth, I woke up one morning with a headache like I'd never experienced before. I could not move my head to even nod without the sharp stabbing pain. I literally started seeing stars and flashing lights. My legs were swollen so much I looked like I had cartoon feet. I called my husband in the room and told him something was wrong. I called my sister. I tried to reason maybe it was just exhaustion from having three little ones under the age of 5. My sister came down right away and looked at me and insisted I go to the doctor. She and my husband watched the kids while I took a cab downtown. I prayed the whole way: *Please let me be OK. I want to live for these children. Whatever this is, let me be OK.*

I was seen right away. The nurse took my blood pressure and turned out the lights and rushed out of the room. The doctor came in moments later and said in a low, quiet voice "Dawn, I'm so glad you came in when you did. Now you're not going to like to hear this, but you need to listen. You are not well, and you cannot go home today. I need to send you to the emergency room to be admitted. You have post-partum eclampsia, and it's very serious. I'm afraid if you go home, something even worse will happen." I was so confused. I was just coming in to get checked out. *Please keep me safe, God. Let me live.* I was in the hospital for a little over a week. The doctor said if I hadn't come in when I did, I would have certainly had a stroke or worse at home. One doctor said it was a miracle I was alive. It took a few months to recover fully, but I did recover. I thank God for keeping me safe during these trials, and I continue to be Joyful that he has given me more time to be here with my loved ones.

IT CAN'T BE REAL!

Linda Pope

Why would they misdiagnose my sister? Why wouldn't she listen to my advice when I told her to find another doctor? How could she have cancer all along and the doctor not know beforehand. So much unnecessary anguish, sorrow, and sleepless nights! We were from a family of three. She was my only sister and the youngest of the three. In fact, she was eight years younger than I. Her life seemed to have mirrored my life. We graduated from the same college. Both of us graduated with a degree in nursing. We each had one son. Both belonged to a professional nursing sorority. Our homes were even purchased in the same neighborhood. We had so many similar things in our life. Then, the unthinkable happened.

She was diagnosed with cancer. Why would this happen — no one in our immediate family had cancer. Prior to my being diagnosed with cancer, the doctor had given her another non-related to cancer diagnosis. Then, I became very angry with the doctor and knew that it was time to seek another doctor's opinion. However, my sister wouldn't. It appeared to me she was satisfied with this doctor.

My days and late into the nights were spent with my sister. We shared growing up experiences, laughs, sad moments, and prayers. I wanted to make sure she was comfortable, fed, and without pain.

The night before she passed, I knew something was different. So, I kept asking the Lord, "Is she gonna pass? If so, I don't want to be here alone and I don't want her son to be alone either." Her son and I were at her bedside making her comfortable when she took her last breath.

The scene continues to play in my mind. I ask myself, could I have done something different?

A few days before she passed, she forgave the doctor for misdiagnosis. I couldn't understand her feelings then, but now I believe she had reached an inner peace. She, also, had been angry with the diagnosis. No one in the family knew she had cancer except me and my brother because she didn't want people to feel sorry for her.

The experience was really hard for me as well as dealing with the emotional struggles of her 19-year-old son. What comforts me most is to know that my sister knew God and is resting in peace.

Her son is still living in the house, and we work together making decisions about it. He completed college and is working in the business world.

This trial made me realize that when things happen, God is in control, orchestrating all the events of our lives. Your timing is not God's timing. I have grown stronger in my faith and do not sweat the small stuff anymore. We allow unimportant things to take up our time and space. Allow God to direct you with your choices that also include relationships with people. More importantly, just put your trust in God.

I HAD FALLEN BUT GOD LIFTED ME UP!

Jerry Jim James Thomas

I had fallen, but God lifted me up. I have had three episodes of falling out, but this was the very first episode, so it was brand new to me.

How did I get in a supine condition, falling down on the floor in my kitchen? I thought, Good question. I started to run through my mind to investigate my situation. How did I get here? How long have I been here? Am I injured? I can't find my cell phone. I'm trying to get up, but I can't. No matter how hard I try, I cannot get up. What is going on? These were questions in my head. *I see no blood. I feel no bumps that I can feel. I have no bruises that I can feel. Okay, Jerry. What happened to you?*

As I tried to assess my predicament, I had to go to the boys' room. But now, I can't get up off the floor. *I bet I'm not more than 35 feet from the boy's room. What now? What now? What now?* When you gotta go, you got to go. Life is rough, sometimes. *Why today?* I have another problem. *I can't stand being wet with urine,* I'm thinking.

Louise, call! Louise, call me! No Louise. And I guess I drifted off to sleep because it was morning when I was aware of myself, again. *So, what—? I've been here all night? I haven't taken my pills?* The phone was close, but I couldn't reach it. Water is close. I'm on the floor in front of the sink and I can't reach it. The refrigerator is behind me, and I can't reach it. I can't eat. *What is going on? Ohhh — What is going on?* I'm not talking about the song, "What's Going On?" I'm talking about myself. Internally.

    Then, I realized, *I have an Alexa.* So, I called out, "Alexa!" And that thing answered.
    Good, I thought. *Now I can get out of here.*
    I said, "Call 911."
    And this automated service said, "I can't do that."
    I said, "Call the police."
    "I can't do that," replied Alexa.
    "Call the fire department."
    "I can't do that," Alexa repeated.
    So, I'm thinking, *What good are you?*

So, Alexa says, "You want me to play some good mood music?"

I kinda chuckled to myself and said, "I'm in dire straits— and you want to play me some mood music?" I want to scream!

So, there it is again. This time, I thought it was #2. But it was only urine. I can't stand the wet clothing on me, so I come out of my pants and my shorts, lying naked and thinking, *God, I hope I don't have any rodents*, as I chuckled to myself, but that wouldn't be funny. So, when I saw the sun go down, I went off to sleep. My second day without my pills. I'm diabetic. Not only am I wet, — *Ahh! And this is November! I hope we don't get a freeze,* I think to myself. *I will freeze my* — Oh, well.

So, now I'm losing count. Another day has dawned, and I am still here. I can't get up, and I've tried every way I can to pull myself up, but I can't get up. Here I am, retired military. Retired from Louisville Gas & Electric, and I can't get off the floor. *Oh wow!* And one of the things you learn in the military is to look at your surroundings and think what I can do. I wished I had some military pills that turn urine into purified drinking water when you're in a battle zone. Then, my next thought was, *I don't have anything to put the urine in.* Although I'm on the floor in the kitchen, and the faucets are above me, I can't get to anything above me. I can't get water. It takes water to live, but I'm not gonna give up! I'm not gonna give up! And then, I hear a familiar voice.

She's saying, "Jerry, Jerry, Jerry!"

And I called out, "Louise, Louise, Louise! Don't go away, please, please help! I need help! Oh Lord Jesus, have I prayed for help. I'm lying in — I'm wet from head to toe. I'm lying in it. I'm hungry. I need water. I need my medicine."

Then, there's a bam, bam, bam at the door. I can't get up and answer the door. I can't get up and answer the door. *Don't go away. Please call for help to get in the door.* I didn't drift off, but I thought I heard many voices banging on windows and doors. Oh Lord! Have mercy! God evidently heard my cry! Then, I heard smashing. Then, sirens. Then, all of a sudden, the door was kicked in and there was a stretcher coming in and medics. Then I saw Louise. Then I saw my sisters —

Oh Lord, my sister is going to see my naked body, I thought. That was my modesty coming out. Then, I realized, "put that in your past." Then, I saw her: Louise.

"Why haven't I heard from you in three days?!" she asked.

"Well, I've been lying on the floor for three days," I replied.

Looking around, I saw my sister. I saw my brother-in-law. Yeah, there's Darrick! I say, "Wow! She's called everybody!" Then I asked one of the EMS workers, "Can you put something over me please?"

As the medics wheeled me through my front door, I thought, *It could have been worse.* I didn't have to poop! Wow!! And I didn't die! During those three days of torture, I said goodbye to my daughter and my son. I said bye to my sisters and my brothers, and I prayed.

Two lessons came away from this experience. One, I have a family who checks. And two, where I might have given up, God didn't. God is in control, and that's why I'm so joyful.

MY SAVIOR, MY HEALER, MY DELIVERER

Ann Elliott

You can never be prepared for the unexpected, but if you live long enough, trouble and trials will come your way. Just because you're a Christian doesn't make you exempt. I've encountered many trials and tribulations as a believer in Christ.

In 1996 on Mother's Day, I lost my son who was 21 years of age in an automobile accident. I was devastated! I didn't know how I would make it, but I knew I had to be there for my husband and daughter. My faith in God had always been strong; however, this time seemed different. While attempting to pray, I was struggling with what to say, and two passages of scripture came to mind. "The Spirit intercedes for the saints according to the will of God." Romans 8:27 (ESV) and "Nothing will ever be able to separate us from the love of God demonstrated by our Lord Jesus Christ when he died for us." Romans 8:39 (TLB) This was my saving grace! God had allowed us to have our son for 21 years. He had accepted Christ prior to entering college. Later after his passing, we discovered that he had touched so many lives along the way. **To God be the Glory!**

In August of 2006, 10 years later, I started experiencing excruciating headaches. I was 54, and I thought in fairly good health except for being diagnosed with rheumatoid arthritis. I had never had high blood pressure or many headaches. The headaches I assumed were allergy related. God was trying to tell me something, but I didn't listen! We had scheduled vacations over the next three weeks. The first was in Colorado Springs where I first became ill with stomach issues and headaches. I assumed it was a virus! We made it back home and I was feeling somewhat better, so we headed to Las Vegas. On the plane, my symptoms grew worse. I was having pain in the center of my back, along with the headaches. We landed, checked into our hotel, and I rested after taking some ibuprofen. The following morning, I awoke not feeling much better, and my husband took me to an immediate care center. My blood pressure was in stroke range! They immediately gave me meds through an IV. An hour or so passed, and they thought it had stabilized; they were going to release me. When I stood up to go to the bathroom, I felt faint. They rechecked my blood pressure and I had bottomed out at 60/40. They immediately rushed me by ambulance to the ER! After eight hours of running tests and getting my blood pressure under control, they released me with no explanation for the cause. We canceled our remaining vacation and headed back to Louisville the next morning.

Upon returning home, I saw my primary doctor who scheduled a series of tests, which revealed no explanation for the high blood pressure. About a week later, at around 4:30 a.m., I awoke to go to the bathroom. When I tried to reach for the toilet paper, I had no control of my right hand, I couldn't speak, and the room was spinning. I immediately thought, "you're having a stroke!" This lasted for what seemed a few minutes and I was able to make it back to the bed and dial 911. The ambulance took me to the hospital where I spent the next 21 days in the ICU and Open-Heart Unit. I had a total of five TIAs (transient ischemic attacks) or mini-strokes. I would pass out and couldn't use my right hand or speak. In the ER, I told the doctors they had to save me because my husband and daughter couldn't go through another death so soon. I was putting my trust in them rather than in God. My surgery revealed that I had a dissection of my left carotid artery, which was preventing blood flow to the brain, thus causing the TIAs. My surgeon apologized for cutting my neck because he originally thought a plaque buildup was causing my problems. As a result, I will have a scar for life. The fact that I have a scar, when I could have had a major stroke, is a reminder that I serve a great and merciful God!

Following the first surgery, I developed a hematoma in the blood vessel of my neck. That meant I was going to have to have surgery again. I was getting better but not well enough to go home, but afraid to go back to surgery. The morning of the scheduled surgery, I awoke early (if I had any sleep at all) before staff came into my room. I started praying! You know the saying goes, "just a little talk with Jesus makes everything all right!" I apologized to God for putting my hope, trust, and faith in the doctors with tears running down my cheek. When I finished my prayer, an unexplainable peace came over me, and I was ready for surgery. "For the joy of the Lord is [my] strength." Nehemiah 8:10 (ESV) With all of this behind me, the doctors told my husband, "She's one in a million," that something like this happens to someone and they live to tell the story without any side effects.

I try to live each day as if it were my last, for tomorrow isn't promised to anyone. I serve a God who is sovereign, and He knows what's best for me. Many times, the Holy Spirit will give you a sign or a warning, but you must be willing to take the time to listen and act. The beauty of what I went through is that God has allowed me to tell my story, and I know that it is only by His Grace that I'm still here.

I am truly GRATEFUL, and I have JOY! "Trust in the Lord with all your heart and lean not on your own understanding." Proverbs 3:5 (NIV)

JOY IN SUFFERING REFLECTIONS

Not only so, but we also glory in our sufferings, because we know that suffering produces perseverance; perseverance, character; and character, hope. And hope does not put us to shame, because God's love has been poured out into our hearts through the Holy Spirit, who has been given to us.

Romans 5:3–5 (NIV)

1. What messages do you have about suffering in life?

2. Why do we have suffering in our lives?

3. How do you respond to suffering?

4. What will you do differently this week when you encounter a suffering/trial/tribulation?

5. What does Romans 5:4 tell you about "counting it all joy"?

FROM THE HEART

As you review Philippians 1:1–30, the author considers these points for your review:

- During your trials/tribulations, there will be people to support, encourage, and provide your needs, and Paul wishes them the best of God's grace and peace.
- Highest honor is to be a servant of God. Remember Paul, formerly known as Saul, persecuted the Christians, and now he is zealously working with them to spread the Gospel.
- Paul prays for the people to gain more knowledge and insight and be blameless and pure for the day of Christ.
- Paul sees his suffering as advancing the Gospel because he is in chains, and the people notice this and become more confident in proclaiming the Gospel.
- Those who preach Christ out of good will do it out of love for Christ. Paul rejoices when the Gospel is preached.
- Paul believes his suffering will lead to deliverance.
- Paul is torn between two issues that are as follows: 1. If he lives, he preaches the Gospel that he loves and 2. If he dies, he will be with Christ that is much better. He is convinced that if he lives, he will continue to see them progress and experience true Joy in their faith.
- Paul advises believers to stay together, stand firm in the faith because the adversary will try to destroy you, but you will be saved.
- Count yourself in a manner that represents Christ.

God will never leave or forsake you. He is with us in the good times and the bad times. Paul testifies to this truth during his ministry. He suffered greatly for sharing the Word of God, but God had people who comforted him. Through his enormous trials and tribulations, Paul's mindset was on what God wanted. Paul wanted all people to experience the Joy that comes from God and was willing to suffer any persecution to meet that goal. He believed that suffering leads to deliverance because it gets us back on track with what God wants us to do. Deliverance takes the focus off of self and places it on Jesus Christ. Paul advises believers to stay together, stand firm in their faith because the enemy will try to devour them. As a representative of Christ, carry yourself in a manner that represents Him. The world cannot deliver you from sin, only Jesus Christ can.

PRAYER

God thank you for your word. Sometimes, I just don't understand why the world is in such turmoil with you as Lord and Savior, but I am going to trust anyway because you have the power to do all things. Thank you for your grace and mercy that sustain us. During my times of suffering, you always send someone to comfort and reassure me that you love me. Because of your love, I am strengthened and continue to grow in the knowledge of the Lord and Savior Jesus Christ. There is nothing like knowing that you are always with me during not only the darkest moments, but the joyful times as well. So, I will praise you in all times. Amen!

GOD'S PROCESS

Robert L. Byrd, Jr.

Consider it a blessing when we go through a lesson.
It's refreshing, to look past the surface to see the message.
How can your faith grow without testing?
Your life is on the ropes, sometimes you're pinned down like wrestling.
You should never question God's methods,
Worried about right now, he's looking at long-term investments.
Before the count of "three" you managed to get a shoulder loose,
Everyone is watching you thinking nobody noticed you.
Then out of nowhere you are getting a lot of energy,
Something in your spirit got you pinning the enemy.
Steady with your faith keep your problems under your feet,
Walking with belief God makes your journey complete.
We are all God's children on the throne we got a seat.
Which means we'll always win and never be in defeat!

Chapter 2

JOY OF BELIEVING

Though you have not seen him, you love him; and even though you have not seen him now, you believe in him and are filled with an inexpressible and glorious joy.

1 Peter 1:8 (NIV)

THE JOY OF BELIEVING

Mary and Joseph were engaged to be married; however, an angel appeared to Joseph and told him Mary would have a baby even though she did not know a man intimately. Mary did not understand how this could happen. As Joseph considered leaving her, he was instructed not to be afraid but to marry her. The baby was named Jesus because he would take away the sins of the world (Matthew 1: 18–24).

Then, there was a man named Job, wealthy, well respected, and an upright man of God. Satan wanted to see if he would curse God if he lost all his possessions. God says in Job 1:1 (NIV), "there is no one on earth like him; he is blameless and upright, a man who fears God and shuns evil." However, Satan wants to prove that Job only serves God because of his possessions and great wealth. Once these possessions are removed, Satan felt that Job would curse God. Satan asked God to remove the hedge of protection that he had around Job.

Believing matters! In the Merriam-Webster dictionary, "believe" is defined as to accept or regard something as truth. Christians believe that God sent his son, Jesus, to provide everlasting life for those who believe in Him. Sending His Son through the virgin Mary, who knew no man, took a lot of courage for Mary to accept. Mary could have been stoned and/or ostracized for having a baby out of wedlock.

> Now faith is confidence in what we hope for and assurance about what we do not see.
>
> Hebrews 11: 1–2 (NIV)

Who was always obedient to the Lord, lost so much during his test with Satan, but he never wavered in his belief? Job. In the midst of his trials, he, too, exhibited courage, confidence, and faith. In the end, Job received twice as much as he had in the beginning because he persevered and walked by faith in the Lord. In Hebrews 11: 1–2 (NIV), the scripture reads: *"Now faith is confidence in what we hope for and assurance about what we do not see. This is what the ancients were commended for."*

We commend Mary and Job for their faith walk. However, the Bible is filled with other examples for you to discover. Walking by faith means you know that God is going to do what He says, and His Word is truth. Christians don't have to know the entire story from the beginning to the end because God is forever with them working things out.

My grandmother was a minister, who fervently preached the Word of God. She loved her grandchildren and supported their efforts. One day, I swallowed a bean that lodged in my windpipe. I couldn't breathe and was rushed to the Negro hospital. They were not able to remove the object and suggested we go to a white hospital. Arriving at the hospital, they said, "We can't help Negroes." The doctor suggested my parents drive 88 miles to Duke University for help.

According to my grandmother, who held me and was praying, my situation was dire. As I turned purple, she pleaded with God to restore me and allow me to continue to live. My parents were crying and praying as well. Finally, we arrived at Duke University. The bean was removed. Here I am now sharing this story with you. God answers prayer. When you walk by faith and not by sight, the impossible becomes possible. When I go home to visit family, neighbors still share my survival story and recall how my grandmother held me, prayed, sang, and praised the Lord the whole time.

This walk by faith not only impacted me and my family, but also the entire neighborhood. When you see God perform wonders, miracles, and signs in the lives of others, you are encouraged and will ask Him to do the same for you.

In Kyle Idleman's book *Don't Give Up: Faith That Gives You the Confidence to Keep Believing and the Courage to Keep Going* (2019), he mentions questions that he wrestles with regarding faith. They are as follows:

> Am I following God in a way that requires faith?

> Do I do anything at all in my life that requires courage and confidence?

Idleman further states, "a story of faith is a 'don't give up' story." Testimonies in this section of the book are "don't give up stories" of how we can have the courage and confidence in the Lord Jesus Christ to get us through the good times as well as the bad.

God gives us the faith to "keep on keeping on" (my parents would say). Only God has the entire picture; therefore, we place our trust in him.

Believing in the Lord is a day-by-day journey that requires an open and receptive heart. The scripture says:

"And without faith it is impossible to please him, for whoever would draw near to God must believe that he exists and that he rewards those who seek him." Hebrews 11:6 (ESV)

So, I ask you the following questions:

Do you want to please the world or God? Hebrew 11:6

Do you prefer a life of turmoil, unrest, destruction, and no peace?

For Mary, who chose to believe, said, "I am the Lord's servant. May it happen to me according to your word." Luke 1:38 (many versions) When Elizabeth, mother of John the Baptist, found out about Mary's pregnancy, she proclaimed, "blessed art thou among women and blessed is the fruit of the womb. [Jesus]." Luke 1:42 (KJV) The role Elizabeth plays in this scenario shows how God always has someone to come forward to bless, encourage, comfort, support, and reassure you that He is in the plan during those challenging times of life.

Job's belief in the Lord was so strong that he stated:

"The Lord giveth the Lord taketh away, blessed be the name of the Lord." Job 1:21 (paraphrased)

May words of praise forever be on your lips as you go through life. Job did not curse the Lord and was able to persevere the scrutiny of his friends, family, and the curses Satan placed upon him. In the end, Job was restored and blessed with abundantly more than he had in the beginning. God blessed him and increased his territory.

This section of testimonials reflects how Christians have experienced Joy during trials/tribulations because they believe all things are possible with the Lord.

> **Joy is a gift from God, who assures us that He has total control of our lives. We are confident that all things will work for the good and make the decision to praise and worship Him at all times.**

Chapter 2

JOY OF BELIEVING TESTIMONIES

> "Joy is a net of love…."
> Mother Teresa

ALL JOY

Sandy Miller Jones

"Well Baby, let's just go as far as we can see, and then we can see further". That's the very wise advice that my father, Robert Miller, gave to my 16-year-old self when I was worried about how on earth we would be able to afford to pay the expenses to Howard University which my scholarship did not cover. He also assured me that as always, God would have my back.

Of course, my father was right, and I have continued to make those my guiding principles throughout my 76 years in this life. I spent four wonderful years at Howard, making many lifelong friends like Melba Watson (now Dr. Melba Swafford, MD) and Jackie Jackson (now Dr. Jacqueline Fleming, PhD).

After I graduated from Howard in 1968, I found that I had to go as far as I could see once more, with God as my shepherd. I was offered a spot in Northwestern University's MBA program (whatever that was), but I did not even have the money to get me to the University, located in Chicago at that time. So, by His grace, the University agreed to hold my spot for one year while I worked to make the funds to get there.

It was providential that I had that year of transition, because I learned so much about "real life" during that time. I was 22 years old and working as a dormitory head and counselor for Job Corp residents who were 18 to 21 years old. And boy did they give me some life lessons! Perhaps the best example of this is the "dormitory queer smell event". I kept smelling a funny odor in the dormitory at night, and the girls assured me that it was a malfunction in the furnace. When a friend from New York visited me overnight, she was alarmed that I allowed the girls to smoke pot!

After working for a year at the Job Corp, I saved enough money to get to Chicago and cover my basic expenses, but of course I did not have enough to pay Northwestern 's exorbitant tuition. I went to Chicago anyway, and God provided a way forward once more. I got a scholarship and a job from the First National Bank of Chicago and graduated in 1971 as the first African-American woman to receive an MBA from Northwestern University.

I now still head a national marketing services company, which I founded over 42 years ago. I am married to my business partner. Lafayette Jones and we have a beautiful daughter Dr. Bridgette Jones Brooks who lives with her husband and son in Atlanta. As an entrepreneur, wife and mother, I have had to overcome many challenges throughout these years, but that 16-year-old advice from my father has never failed me. Whenever I cannot see my way through, I just go as far as I can see, knowing that God has my back.

JOURNEY TO JOY

Leisa Martin

I'm excited to share reflections of joy in my life. I am from a large family of eleven in rural Alabama. My parents emphasized the importance of God, love, family and education. Church played a major role in my family's life and I joined at an early age. My love and trust in my parents guided me throughout my Christian walk. During this time, I did not know the importance of having a personal relationship with God. All I knew was there was a God, who loves me and He is in charge of the whole world.

As a teen and young adult, I was naïve about life. Marriage happened immediately after college and Christ was not included in our relationship. Needless to say, it was a rocky 4 years of marriage. Finally, we decided to go our separate ways.

After living a disobedient life without God, I realized that something important was missing. So, I returned to church. At first, a lot of hit and misses occurred because I still wanted to be in charge of my life. I learned more about Christ and wanted to do the right things in His eyes. The Holy Spirit continually convicted me of my wrongdoings and I was helpless without God. So, I finally said, "Yes, Lord" and accepted Him as my Lord and Savior. Studying the Word provided me a different outlook on life.

For examples, I learned:

> I am not alone;
>
> In my weakest moment, I can draw strength from Him;
>
> To Pray, listen and patiently wait on God;
>
> To Keep your eyes focused on Him and
>
> To Stand on the truth of God's Word or you will fall for anything.

While in Sunday School, I met my shining armor (I thought). His knowledge of the scriptures impressed me. We moved too quickly and rushed into a marriage, ignoring any red flags. When you take your eyes off of Jesus, sometimes lust is confused with the word love. After marriage, the atmosphere between us changed due to abuse. Seemed as if I was trapped, afraid and stripped of who I was as a person. I was walking on egg shells to maintain peace in the relationship. The best thing that happened was that we became parents of two beautiful children. I know what you wondering and you are right. My rationale was to maintain a family life for the children. So, I stayed. However, the children could see and hear the brokenness. I just didn't want to face the reality a broken family and marriage. When you stay in a marriage for the wrong reasons, life may get worse before it gets better.

As the abuse continued, I sought marriage help from a mother in the church, who dismissed what I shared. She couldn't understand or believe what I was sharing was a reality. The reason is an abusive narcissist is a master of deception. Power drives them and a victim's silence fuels their need. For me to survive, I had to very carefully calculate a plan to avoid being a statistic.

Why am I sharing this story? Someone needs to hear this message. Without God's love, mercy and grace, I would not be here to share with you. After 21 years and 6 months of persevering, I was able to walk away from my biggest storm and remain alive. Experiencing the pain of abuse may have been avoided if I was obedient to God. He would have shown me, through His Holy Spirit, who to marry.

No longer am I a child in Christ. My relationship with Him has grown. We spend a lot of time together in prayer, study, meditation and conversations throughout the day. Our relationship now is for eternity. In my adult relationship with Him, I learned:

>He has forgiven me for my disobedience (sin);

>He continues to show me mercy, love and grace;

>He rescues me from struggling times in my life;

>The Holy Spirit convicts and guides me;

>I thirst to seek His will;

  He gives me love, peace, hope and joy that comes only from Him; and

  He will never leave me alone.

During your times of helplessness, I pray that you will focus on God. He will direct you in the right way. Say, yes to Him. You will know for yourself what a relationship filled joy and peace provides.

Joy Comes In The Morning

Diana L. Mott

"Sing to the Lord, all you godly ones! Praise his holy name. For his anger lasts only a moment, but his favor lasts a lifetime! Weeping may last through the night, but joy comes with the morning" Psalm 30: 4-6, NLT. When I think of JOY, the verse "joy comes with the morning" comes to mind. How true this can be. I praise God for his great love and the favor He has shown me since I came to know Christ as a young child. But it's also true that we all go through difficult times in our life. I've known my share.

A few years ago, I went through a terrible time of depression. Out of nowhere, fear would descend and grip me tightly. Sometimes I would take a drive to escape the darkness, and scream out "God where are you?!" Looking back, I realize that He was right there beside me, lifting me up. In 2017, I developed a condition called sarcoidosis, an inflammatory disease that attacks multiple organs. In me, it invaded my lungs and spread to my heart, causing my already damaged mitral valve to close.

After a heart catheterization failed to restore blood flow that December, my doctors informed me I needed a new mitral valve. And so, open heart surgery was scheduled in January. Fear again took over my life, and thoughts of dying nearly consumed me. As I began to pray, God slowly began to penetrate my soul. He brought to mind a song, an old favorite by Phil Leager, "I'm In His Hands". Day after day, I would listen to that song for inspiration. One of the verses says, "I will not fear, tho' darkened clouds may gather 'round me; I trust the One who whispers, "Peace". What peace He brought to me! Further it says, "Although the winds and waves would threaten to confound me, He walked upon the ancient seas, He still can calm the storm in me."

True to His word, the Lord brought calmness to my life. On the morning of my surgery, all I wanted was for people to pray for me. When I walked into the hospital waiting room that morning, there was such a peace surrounding me. All fear vanished. My spirit was so calm as I went to sleep on the operating table, trusting that whether I went to be with Him or I lived, I was in His hands. Praise be to God, the surgery was successful, and I awakened to a better quality of life than I thought possible. One of my most precious joy, is my husband Art. What an incredible man that God brought to me 50 years ago, when we were just 15. In our life journey we have had many ups and downs, "in sickness and in health". His strength and steadfast love for God, his love for me, and our children have brought more joy than I can express. God used him every step of the way for me and our family.

So, when I think of JOY, His comfort comes over me. I know without a doubt Christ is always with me. Has everyday been perfect? No! After the valve replacement came seven heart ablations, and now I have a pacemaker as well. Still, every step of the way is filled with joy, because He is with me. God never stops loving us. He blesses me daily, and his presence brings unspeakable JOY to my life

SECOND ANGEL

Joseph Wiley

I have always been a man of faith, since entering my adult years. My faith has grown over the years, especially when faced with challenges in my life. I will share an incident, in which I experienced a challenge unlike any that I had known before. It all started when my wife of 47 years (my angel sent from God), was diagnosed with breast cancer. We accepted the fact and prayed that the condition would be resolved. To us, the resolution we wanted was for her to be cured. We believed that God was in control, and He would make everything all right. We prayed and prayed, and God answered our prayers by sending us a competent physician, who performed a surgical procedure that provided us with a resolution that took care of the cancer, but not in the manner we had hoped.

A few months later, we learned that the cancer was no longer attacking her breast, but that a new cancer had appeared and was attacking other parts of her body. Past experience, with the previous cancer scare, led us to address this illness much the same way we had approached the first illness. This phase of the illness was not identical to our first experience fighting cancer. This time the cancer was more aggressive and brought with it a great deal of pain. It was during one of the painful experiences that our faith was sorely tested. My wife had been admitted to the hospital and was placed on pain medicine. She was in so much pain that the nurse called the doctor, at home, to request that my wife be put on a stronger pain medicine. The doctor approved the stronger medication, but it could not be started for another two hours. The pain did not let up; in fact, it seemed to intensify. What were we going to do? We did the only thing we knew to do, which was to continue to put our trust in God, a God that we believed was in control and a God that would make everything all right.

We prayed as we held on to each other. I could feel the tenseness in my wife's grasp as she held on to me. Then something happened: her grasp loosened, and she raised her head from my chest. She whispered, "The pain's gone." It was at that time that I knew God had stepped in and made everything all right, just as we knew He would. It was an awesome experience watching God move right before our very eyes. God is real and can do anything but fail. I've known this for years. The incident only drew me closer to Him and strengthened my relationship with Him.

I've told and retold this story many times, as a way of praising God and witnessing to others, to let them know just how good God is, even in my darkest hours. It's been 10 years since my wife and I shared that life-changing experience in the hospital. That same year, God saw fit to take her home.

My life has changed and so has my faith. Life has not been all "peaches and cream;" I did not expect it to be. Due to my uncompromising faith, I find myself leaning on God at all times and anticipating Joy, even in the midst of adversity. This feeling of assurance that God is in control and will make everything all right allows me to continue to praise Him daily, through my contact with people, in all walks of life, and especially in the work I do in my church's ministries. God also sent me another "Angel," with whom to share my life as we live out our faith in God together and seek Joy regardless of whatever we're going through.

DOWN IN MY HEART

Barbara Lyons

According to Webster, "Joy is an emotion evoked by well-being, success or good fortune." I think of the chorus we used to sing in Bible School, "I've got joy, joy, joy, joy down in my heart'…and that describes what Joy means to me. I consider Joy, a "down in my heart" kind of feeling. I consider it a state of being rather than an emotion. Emotions are temporary — Joy is lasting. If you are sad, angry, disappointed, jealous, these are temporary. They will eventually go away, but Joy will sustain you.

I had a wonderful childhood, great parents, grandparents, aunts, and uncles. My parents made sure that I had a variety of rich experiences, that I had a work ethic, valued education, and that I had a relationship with God and His church. My marriage was just as blessed. I had a wonderful husband, two outstanding, healthy children and a life filled with wonderful memories and very few regrets. I had happiness, but more importantly, I had Joy "down in my heart."

Then, the unthinkable happened. Rodney was diagnosed with lung cancer and was given only a short time to live. He was only 66 years old, and I was 61. He had always been so healthy and active. I watched him deteriorate slowly and nothing I could do could stop it. Those things that made me smile and laugh were temporary and tainted with the realization that it was just a fleeing moment of happiness. I had lost my Joy. My heart was empty. I had prayed unceasingly for three months for his healing and victory over the cancer — I felt that none of my prayers was answered.

A friend shared a book with me *Why Bad Things Happen to Good People* (by Harold S. Kushner). It explained that we are physical creations just like the trees in the forests, the fish of the ocean, insects, plants, animals, etc. Some live long lives; some only exist for a short time until something brings their life to an end. From God's perspective, the important thing is our soul, not our physical being. He allows our physical world to function independently as He has created it. He can make things happen, but we have the gift of free will to make decisions and manage our own lives.

This idea was comforting to me and made sense. I stopped praying for Rodney's healing and began praying for the fruits of the Spirit, especially Joy, peace, faithfulness, self-control. God answered my prayers. During Rodney's final days and after his death, I found myself facing life alone, making important decisions with confidence and experiencing a feeling of peace. I had emotional strength that I never dreamed I could have. Even though I didn't have Joy down in my heart, I had most of the fruits that I had prayed for. As time goes, we become accustomed to the emptiness that lost Joy leaves. But what we must understand is that eventually Joy will come back into our heart to stay. After a few months, one day, I realized I had my Joy back.

MY AMAZING EXPERIENCE

Tacia Lyman

My amazing experience and journey are filled with mercy and grace, to the testimony of the Father, Son and the Holy Spirit. The Trinity leads us to faith, hope, and love 1 Corinthians 13:13 (KJV), with the greatest of these being love.

I count it all Joy James 1: 2–4 (KJV), as my experience began with me leaving Detroit, Michigan, on August 10 headed to Cincinnati, Ohio. I was attending the annual Honkie Classic bowling tournament for a three-day competition. Once the tournament members arrived, we checked in because we had to be on the lanes by 6 p.m. Friday night. Once the tournament ended for the evening, our group headed back to the motel where we played cards, listened to music, and of course, were drinking.

The next day, Saturday morning, we had to be on the lanes by 9 a.m. to complete two tournaments that day. After the second tournament, the group decided to eat. My bowling partner and I asked for water, and it took a long time for us to get it. Once we finally received it, the taste was tainted and affected our stomachs immediately. My partner suggested Pepto-Bismol, which helped enough for us to bowl Sunday morning.

As we headed back home, a virus began to take over my organs. Fever arose, body ached, chills (hot and cold) continued; by August 16, I was in an emergency room. The pain was unbearable. The doctor was trying to determine the severity of my pain and asked me to allow my chin to touch my chest. Tears began to flow as I tried and tried again, but just could not do it. Immediately, the doctor ordered a spinal tap, because he'd diagnosed that I had meningitis and recommended a viral doctor to treat me. This diagnosis was concerning to me because a lot of college students were dying from it.

With a temperature of 106 degrees, my eyesight, sense of smell, taste, and legs were not functioning normally. Regardless of what was going on around me, I did not give up hope. Even though I was going to miss my baby brother's wedding. The doctors ordered another spinal tap with my temperature still 106 degrees, and finally the doctors proclaimed, "We have done all we can do." I continued to pray.

Then a door opened to my room, and I asked, "Who are you?"

She answered, "I'm the Chaplain. I came to pray."

I replied, "Do you have faith?"

She answered, "Yes!"

I responded, "I do not want you to pray me down in the ground." So, I prayed, "Lord put me on the whole armor of God and Satan you might as well get back because I am going to get out of this bed."

Later in the evening, a nurse came in to take my temperature. My fever had gone down to 99.8 degrees. She was excited, and tears ran down my face with Joy in my heart. All I could do was kick my legs. Doctors visited and were shocked as well. They gathered around my bed asking a lot of questions. As the brain swelling decreased, I regained my sense of smell, taste, and sight, and my legs got stronger with rehab.

During my 11 days in the hospital, my mother never missed a day comforting me, taking care of me, bathing and feeding me. Each day, I focused on Jesus and knew victory was near. Thank you, God, for granting me your grace and mercy. The recovery process was long and tedious; but God had someone there to comfort me — my mother (who is now in glory with God).

The doctors told me I would not be able to work. After 25 years of work, I am ready for retirement. I'm going to always keep praying, trusting, and believing in Jesus.

Trusting as the moments fly,

Trusting as the days go by,

Trusting Him whatever befall,

Trusting Jesus that is all!

Remember God loves us. Never give up on God. Your response to Him is to allow His will to be done in your life. So, whatever you are going through, count it as all Joy!

COUNTING IT ALL JOY DURING TRIALS AND TRIBULATIONS

Dr. Jewelene Richards

My desire to get a college education and become a schoolteacher was strongly encouraged during my high school years. I was supported and encouraged to participate in various programs and activities that would enhance the opportunity for that to happen. In 1955, when I graduated from high school, I received a $200 scholarship to Kentucky State College. Initially, I was so excited to know that I had met the requirements and been awarded the scholarship. My desires and dreams were becoming a reality, to which I gave thanks to the Lord.

I would be the first one in my immediate family to attend college, so I had no knowledge of the financial burden college could be on a family such as mine that wasn't prepared for additional expenses. I guess that I assumed it would be just another bill they would pay monthly, as they did with our other bills. Both of my parents worked, and my mother managed the finances. Also, I worked the summer after high school graduation, which I thought was a significant contribution.

My mother and I calculated that the $200 scholarship, the money she had saved since my graduation and a small allowance she would send me weekly would be sufficient for the first semester. Going forward she was going to save for the second semester from her earnings and economize wherever she could.

It was a well-laid plan. Yet at registration I was informed that only half of the scholarship could be used the first semester. The testing of our faith followed that revelation. My mother managed to pay the balance of the bill for that semester by working a weekend job. My father was off on weekends; he and my younger sister managed the home. When I returned to the campus at the beginning of the second semester, I immediately went to the office of the Dean of Students, to apply for a campus job, to supplement the balance of my scholarship. I was informed that all student jobs had already been assigned. The disappointment and fear that followed must have been evident because the Dean of Students offered me a job in her home preparing lunch and dinner for her and her mother. She also invited me to eat my meals with them.

This was, in fact, a student job, and it eliminated the need for me to pay for a student meal card for the semester. I kept that job for my remaining three and a half years of college, and gained much support and guidance from the Dean. Who but God could have made that all happen? How could I not fully understand that the disappointments, lack of adequate funding, and ignorance of how that system worked were all designed to help me become more mature and complete, and to increase my faith.

At the end of the first year, I realized that I would also need to work during my time away from school. So, I cleaned houses during short vacation breaks and worked the following jobs during the summers:
- kitchen help at a drive-in restaurant
- house cleaning for private families
- cooking for a woman at her summer home in East Hampton, Long Island, New York
- camp counselor

Money, or lack thereof, remained a critical issue for me as I continued to pursue my college education. Tuition, housing, books, and other fees still needed to be paid and paid on time, and additional family trials and challenges occurred during those four years. Among the obstacles were my mother's pregnancy with her sixth and last child, my father undergoing major surgery, and a house fire.

Our perseverance and faith were really put to the test. Yet, we stayed the course, held on and watched the Lord work. I graduated in four years with no debt, which was completely God working in us to help us become mature and complete.

Job 10:12 (KJV): Thou hast granted me life and favor, and thy visitation hath preserved my spirit.

Truly I can say, I count it all Joy!

WORKING WEIGHTS

Daniel Byrd

When I was very young, I became a Christian. I was born into a Christian family and got baptized at an early age. In Sunday school and the Sunday messages, I learned a lot, including the proverbs at Saint Martin de Porres. I loved it.

Every though I am in high school, I go through many trials and tribulations. The biggest was when I weighed 240 pounds and struggled with my weight for a long time. For a year and 11 months, I kept going through trying to lose weight. So, I said to myself, that I was going to focus on myself, and I really did.

One day I just started; it was rough trying to reach my goal. I refused to give up. Within three months, something just snapped for me. I just started working out every day and began losing weight. My workout consisted of doing 3,000 push-ups a month, working on cardio, playing football, and joining track and field (which really helped to get me where I am now). At 220 pounds, I had muscles. I looked as if I was 180 pounds. Today, I am 200 pounds.

My weight was a trial because people would announce to others that I was trying to lose weight, so that I would not be enticed to eat, or they would not give me something that was not good for me. What made it hard for me was staying motivated to stay on the plan because it is hard work for anyone who is trying to lose weight.

Of course, there were fake and negative people who didn't treat me well. I took that negativity and built on the positive which made it better for me to embrace all that was going on around me. Now the negativity toward me has changed over time. I am an overcomer because I didn't allow the negative influence of others to dominate my thoughts.

The reason that I was able to handle all this struggle is because I always prayed to God, asking Him to lead me on the right path, so that I could lose weight and get muscles to get stronger. I talked out loud to Him constantly about it because I had many allergies and colds that required me to go to the doctor a lot. I learned from watching my family, grandparents, and relatives who continued to stay in prayer during all situations.

I count this all Joy because the ending was very good, and I had a challenge that was great for me. I learned that if you put your mind to something, no matter what it is, you can inevitably do it. Together with God leading me, it came to pass. I had an opportunity to share my experience on a radio sports show. God lifts you up. Never give up.

A WAY OUT OF NO WAY

David Byrd

When my father passed, I was 9 years old, and it affected me a lot. My mother had to bring me up. We moved to Chicago, stayed awhile, then moved back down to Alabama, for a year and a half. I don't know what was wrong with my grandfather, but he would take things out on me. He would whip me all the time. Mama decided to move back to Chicago in 1949 and we've been here ever since.

After marrying and having four children, my wife passed, and life was hard for me. I stayed off from work for two months to get things settled with the kids because they were all in college. The death hurt my youngest son so badly that he went away for six or seven years. I had to learn to adjust without my wife, because she did everything for me. Finally, I went back to work. On the job, I had a pretty bad stroke that paralyzed my whole right side. After eight to nine months, I came out of that tragedy. The only problem left from it is my right eye. I can't see out of it now, but everything else works fine on the right side of my body. Therapy helped me to learn to write again using my right hand.

Fortunately, my wife introduced me to Christ. I was hesitant at first, but I kept following her instructions and went to church. Before I joined the church and was baptized, things in my life were not going in the right directions. I didn't like the way things were headed, so I followed a different direction that was a life-saving direction.

God has brought me a long way from where I have been. There are occasional setbacks, but I go to God and tell him all about them, even though He knows anyway. I ask Him for forgiveness because we all have committed some kind of sin and need His forgiveness.

I have learned a lot from my trials and tribulations. The number one thing that I have learned is to be patient with my family and everything else. Sometimes, I would get really angry about little things that came up, but I don't do that anymore, because I learned to listen. When you are listening to someone who is having a problem, those are times that you can understand what they are going through. There are no two people on earth that are alike; so, you have to listen to them and see what their problem is so that you can try to help them along the way.

To experience what real Joy is I think that people should first believe in the Lord God Almighty. Put your trust in Him always and go to Him when problems arise. He always makes a way when there seems as if there is no way! Just relax!

I MADE IT THROUGH

Dennis Prince

I became a Christian at an early age. My mom and dad brought me up in the church since I was a kid. I remember being in the pre-Sunday School at 9 a.m. service before regular Sunday school started. The teacher would actually give a preview of what the Sunday school lesson was.
I remember being in Sunday school from when I was in training (3–4 years old) up to an adult. Sunday School was fun, and it taught me a lot about what a Christian does. The different stories in the Bible created life-changing experiences because I learned how powerful, loving, kind, trustworthy, patience, understanding, and who God really is. Many of the stories taught you how important it is to make Godly decisions. When I was around 12 or 13 years old, I made the most important decision of my life and that was to become a Christian.

There are many tribulations I have encountered but the one that is very personal to me is my experience as a minster of music at a church that had an outstanding minister of music for 30 years who died. As the deceased's replacement, I was expected to be an exact example of who he was. I don't mind being held at a high standard but find it unreasonable to be like the person I am replacing because God gave both of us some uniqueness that still allows the Lord to be praised and glorified. Therefore, I was judged with extremely high and specific standards. I tried to meet their expectations and at the same time walk in a way that was pleasing to God. My lifestyle was scrutinized to see if I was living a life that represented what I was playing or teaching. They wanted to know if I was living under Godly laws; if not their reactions toward me would show in the things that they would say. If I was in a relationship, the number of people observing me increased.

I am a believer in the Word. My favorite scripture is Romans 8:28 where it says, "All things work together for the good for those who love God, who are called according to his purpose." (CSB) In order for that to happen, you must have a relationship with God. As a result, I can always go to Him first because He knows my name and my voice, and I know His name and His voice. Therefore, we communicate directly on a daily or moment-by-moment basis.

Every time I think about what God has brought me out of; what he as pulled me through; and what He has delivered me from, I just say, "thank you, God, for all you have done for me," and I count it all for Joy. I definitely don't look or feel like what I've been through. I just know for a fact that if it had not been for the Lord on my side, I don't know where I would be. I can't stop thanking him for grace and mercy. I can't afford not to give him a lot of praise.

I would advise you to get in the Word of God. Whatever you are going through never forget the God factor. A lot of times, we have all kinds of uncertainties in our lives, and we go to other people, social media, friends, beauticians or even a barber for advice. At the end of the day, God is the only one that I know that can make a way out of no way. He is the only one who matters, and his track record is proven!

Proverbs 3:5–6 (KJV): "Trust in the Lord with all thine heart; and lean not unto thine own understanding. In all thy ways acknowledge Him, and He shall direct thy paths."

RETURNING TO THE WORD AND THE AWAKENING OF MY FAITH

LeDoan C. Smith

One morning, two or maybe three days after Christmas of 2010, I decided to turn on the television. I began flipping through the channels and stopped on a channel that showed a little blonde girl, who couldn't have been more than 9 years old, adjusted her microphone and began to sing. I can't remember the song or even the tune. Listening to the tone of her voice and the words to the song hit me like a ton of bricks. I just remember sitting down on the couch and crying to the point where I was weeping. Once she finished the song, she walked off the stage, exposing in the background a tall dark-haired man who identified himself as the little girl's father, Pastor Mel Blackaby. He headed the First Baptist Church of Jonesboro, Georgia. His sermon was quick and to the point. At that moment, I decided that I had to find this church and learn more about why I felt the way that I had felt on that Sunday morning. I sat in my living room and begin going back in time with my thoughts that spanned almost 28 years from the time I entered the military until that Sunday morning. It was a trial of an Awaking of my Faith.

I received Christ as my personal Savior and was baptized at 10 years old. Weekly, I attended church until I entered the military at 17 years old. During the summer of 1995, I rededicated my life to Christ while stationed in Heidelberg, Germany, at the age of 30. However, I never really had a personal relationship with God.

I have had many trials in my life, over a 28-year span, and I wouldn't be honest with myself if I only narrowed it down to one or maybe two trials. Collectively, I led an irresponsible life. Let's just say that my trials had one common theme that led me to this point to search for the ultimate prize of Joy!

At the age of 18, I decided to get married and one year later my wife packed up her belongings and left me. While in the military, after my second marriage, I had to decide if I really wanted to be a soldier, a father and husband, or a full-time student. During this situation, I prayed, on a snowy night on 25 December 1995, while stationed in Heidelberg, Germany. I realized patience is my best friend and to turn the other cheek, no matter how hard it may be. There is a reason for everything. Prayer solves problems and we become stronger at our most challenging moments.

Toward the end of my 23-year military career and three failed marriages, I really had to decide to love myself, or to choose between loving the world or loving Christ. There was also the question of whether I could find Joy to fulfill my life. The following scripture comes to my thoughts:

> "Love not the world, neither the things that are in the world. If any man love the world, the love of the Father is not in him. For all that is in the world, the lust of the flesh, and the lust of the eyes, and the pride of life, is not of the Father, but is of the world." (1 John 2:15–16)

Again, my response to my trial that Sunday morning in 2010 was to desire the Word. I think of the words of Peter, who wrote in his epistle of joyful hope to provide believers with a divine and eternal perspective on their earthly life:

> "Therefore, laying aside all malice, all deceit, hypocrisy, envy, and all evil speaking, as newborn babes, desire the pure milk of the word, that you may grow thereby, if indeed you have tasted that the Lord is gracious." (1 Peter 2:1–3)

Months later, on Easter Sunday, my wife, stepson, and I decided to attend the church where I heard the little girl sing. Her song made me cry. I attended Sunday School and the Easter Sunrise Service. We immediately felt loved and accepted. Then I noticed in the church program the mission statement:

"To glorify God by making disciples who invest in other people and impact the nations."

What a powerful statement of Joy for others and so fitting!

Shortly after attending the Easter service, I felt the Holy Spirit guiding me and a sense of Joy overwhelmed me daily. But the next task was to witness to both my wife and stepson about the Joy of Jesus. Both were enculturated and practiced Hinduism since birth. A passage from the book of 2 Corinthians 6:14 says the following: *"Be ye not unequally yoked with unbelievers...."*

Days after witnessing to both of them, a mission group from the church visited our home and talked to both my wife and stepson about God.

Within a blink of an eye, they were both Saved in our living room, and on 22 August 2010 both were baptized. To my surprise, my sister and brother-in-law came to visit me in Atlanta that weekend and attended the baptism, as well as my stepson's father. It was a wonderful day to share that experience with my best friend and sister — a Joyous day!

To begin, there was a protocol that we as a family had to take to strengthen our faith. It started with weekly Bible study. We decided that we would select a verse and a topic and discuss how it pertained to our daily lives and how we could apply it to strengthen our faith as a family. Whoever had it on their heart to facilitate the discussion would lead the Bible study.

Secondly, we practiced obedience through tithing. The Bible says in 2 Corinthians 9:7, "God loves a cheerful giver, not one who gives grudgingly." (paraphrased) I explained to both my wife and my stepson that God wants us to tithe (to give 10 percent of what we earn) to show obedience. We figured that we would include our annual income to strengthen our faith, to control our lifestyle, and to establish a Christian foundation. The benefit of giving is huge. Tithing not only taught a lesson of obedience by giving to the Lord, but we also discovered that we had more disposable income when it came to participating in family activities and managing our finances.

Next, participating in church activities furthered our commitment and Joy. The Bible says in 1 Corinthians 2:5 to rest on the power of God, not the wisdom of men. By gathering with other Christians, we increased our wisdom, dispelled fear, uncovered truth, avoided incompetence of the Word, and suppressed greed. Church activities included attending Sunday services, participating in the Lord's Supper, and participating in other ministries.

Lastly, unlike my previous marriages, this marriage has a stronger Christian foundation. I found that I experienced more Joy with God as the center of my life, because it gave me direction as a husband and as a father.

I would like to add, since my awakening, my relationship with God has become personal and complete. My faith has increased by reading a verse out of the Bible and spending my early morning moments with God in scripture and meditation. In addition, I attend church weekly and tithe without hesitation.

Through my experience of returning to the Word, I feel complete and more focused. The riches and possessions of the world aren't important. I don't feel as though I have to please friends or family to the point of acceptance. My relationship with God is more important and my spirit is humbled.

Think of this testimony as "a Work in Progress." We are all broken and shouldn't be ashamed to admit it. Joy and grace are offered to us. To admit that we need God, shows that we are willing to humble ourselves and to leave our rebellious nature behind because His Grace is there for us to receive. If we want to have the gift of Joy, just stand still and believe the Lord when he says, "I am with you always."

CANCER, CHILDREN, AND CHRIST

Durell Hall

Cancer, children, and Christ will expose you to what "time" it is in your life! The entrance of any of these three can make you stop to appreciate the moment, and/or make you move in spite of circumstances.

I would like to briefly share with you how cancer has strengthened my Christian walk and appreciation of time. I was diagnosed with an early-stage prostate cancer 16 years ago. I was in my late 40s. For those who are familiar with this type of cancer, I had a Gleason Score of 3+3. Cancer cells were discovered in several of the nine biopsy cores taken from my normal size prostate. The positive cores were taken from my lower prostate — the worst place to treat.

I was at work and over an hour drive from home when the doctor's office called to inform me of this life-changing news. "Hello Mr. Hall, this is Dr. Hardy's office. The doctor would like to speak with you, just a moment please." The harsh-speaking urologist quickly stated, "You have cancer. What do you want to do?" I became extremely nervous. Yet, I softly told him I would get back with him.

I said to myself, "what now?" as thoughts of mortality and fear filled my mind. I quietly went to God in prayer in my car, "Lord, help me get home." Sadly, my home was in peril as well. My wife had filed for divorce, left the house, and taken our two children. The Lord guided me home safely that day.

Somehow God would not give up on me.

I remember distinctly one night pulling into the garage and yelling out loud to God, "WHERE ARE YOU?" I said to myself: "I did all the right things. I stopped running around. I got married. I work hard to provide my family a new home and a car for my wife. I teach Sunday school, am chairman of the Church Trustee Board, helped my neighbors," and on I went. Why Lord?

Somehow God would not give up on me.

These points were important to me as I processed my situation. In researching the various treatments for prostate cancer, I quickly learned — enjoy today! Do not let people move you into sorrow with their "help" of pity. In other words, don't feel bad when God — even for a moment — allows you to feel good. With the aid of the Holy Spirit, I reminded myself, "today I feel good. And I'm not going to feel bad about what I don't know about my cancer — period!" I know what the harsh speaking doctor said; but right now, I can walk, I can talk, I am in no physical pain, and I can feed myself. When God blesses you to feel good physically and emotionally — go ahead and feel good! God does not give sorrow with blessings Proverbs 10:22 (KJV).

During the outset of this difficult time, I made up in my mind that I emotionally wanted to own nothing. I intrinsically realized I am only a steward of God's blessings — which includes my health. The pressure of relentlessly holding on to things robs you of peace and lessens your ability to hear God's voice. Yes, I wanted to be without cancer. Yes, I wanted my wife and children home. Yes, I wanted longevity and peace on my job as a photojournalist for the state's largest newspaper. Yes, I wanted my cousin to share equally with me the inheritance of my grandfather's farm. I learned from my quadriplegic sister that being HEALED does not always include being well.

My cancer: I came to accept once I did all that I could humanly do, I was either going to get well or go home to be with the Lord. I became at peace with whatever God decided. I was emotionally healed at that point, but not physically well.

As you know, the devil is a roaring lion seeking whom he may consume physically and emotionally. The enemy was moving in to totally destroy me. In roughly a year, my divorce was finalized, I lost my job of 26 years, and my Federal Judge cousin "maneuvered" me out of most of my inheritance in my grandfather's farm in South Georgia. However, it was during this dark time, I had a successful nerve-sparing prostate cancer surgery (radical prostatectomy).

Somehow God would not give up on me.

I paid my child support with unemployment and continued teaching Sunday school. Strangely, if you don't give up on God, He will not give up on you. In not abandoning my commitment to my children, my Sunday school class and the teachings of Christ — the Holy Spirit sustained me. I now realized God was pouring revelation and understanding into me via illness, loneliness, and loss.

I have found it to be true: "…He who has begun a good work in you will complete it until the day of Jesus Christ." Philippians 1:6 (NKJV)

However, the cancer attempted to come back 10 years ago. But God allowed 39 treatments of precision radiation to stop it. For over two months, I went daily to treatments. I clearly remember as the radiation techs positioned me under a machine the size of my pickup truck; I would recite what God told Isaiah in chapter 43:2 (NET), "I am with you." God's cancer-free grace continues in my life today! My marriage: this time, I allowed God to direct me to a loving wife. She turned our house into a home and helped me build a business with dedicated employees. My grandfather's farm: well, we had our first family reunion this summer in Louisville. It's a start…

In closing: I better understand Psalms 119:71 (KJV) that states, "It is good for me that I have been afflicted; that I might learn thy statutes." I am a man of grey hair and God's grace — healed by HIS blood. After I was called to the ministry Easter Sunday over a few years ago, God moved me from my church of 35 years. I and my wife joined Burnett Avenue Baptist Church in Louisville, Kentucky, desiring to further fulfill God's calling in our lives.

HE MAKES THE FINAL DECISION

Frank Thomas

I was called to go to Vietnam and asked God to protect me, and He did because I came back home unscathed. I have always had a relationship with God, but at that particular time I needed to call on Him for a special covering. As a result, I never went into Vietnam. I was stationed on the outskirts with a special unit called Special Ops, back at that time.

On November 11, 2020, I died and came back to life. I am not making light of it, but I just simply tell people that I was on my way up and He said, "No, I ain't ready for you yet. Go back down!" I had contracted COVID-19 and it impacted one fifth of my heart; therefore, I have heart problems. At the hospital, I couldn't breathe. So, I said to myself, "this is it."

Well, I am back to work in the educational field and it's all due to the Master allowing me to stay here. Secondly, the medical professions took care of me and helped to straighten out the problem. It's hard for me to say it because so many people don't survive when they get terminally ill

My family was very concerned when I went through COVID-19. My sister, a nurse for 45 years, acted as an extra doctor to make sure that I spoke with a doctor and understood the medical lingo. Most people who had COVID-19 were up and running around in two weeks — but not me. I had a heart condition. This trial has been really hard for me to endure, but I am still recovering.

My grandson and daughter were happy about my recovery. My youngest grandson, 12 years old, would say, "glad to have you here, Papa. I am around to help take care of you Papa." My oldest grandson, 20 years old, was really concerned and tried to put me on a strenuous diet. He said, "I want to keep you around, man." I just simply say, "you have to have trust and faith, and then the Almighty Master determines if it's your time or not to remain here on earth."

TRUST HIM

Susie Grady

I was working at a job that I thought was a good job, at that time. I had just purchased my first new car and all of a sudden in December 1989, I took sick and really thought it was nothing but just back pains. I went to the doctor, and it turned out to be a herniated disc in my back. So, I prayed about it. I have four children and couldn't afford to lose my job. Therefore, I went to therapy and returned to work. A few days later, I ended up having my first back surgery. I came through the surgery fine. Then I went back to work a second time.

During the entire time, I thanked God for his healing power and for saving my job. One year to the date of my first surgery, I went to work in excruciating pain. I couldn't even get off the elevator. My employer sent me to the hospital that night, and this situation was the end of my job. But God! I had a second back surgery, then, two months later cervical cancer. The doctors told me I could not return to my job.

I was bed-ridden for quite some time. After losing my home, my children and I moved in with my mother. I prayed and asked God where I was going next. I felt like I had lost everything and had no place to go with four children. I held on to my faith with much prayer. God is so amazing. If you just trust Him, no matter how the situation may look, and if you are faithful, He will see you through.

I have been on disability from my job since 1990 and took an early retirement until I reached 65 (full retirement age). I am now 70 and my early retirement started at age 32. God will make a way if you just trust Him. It wasn't easy, but God. Every day, I read Psalms 121 and still do it today. It says:

Psalms 121

(NIV)

A song of ascents.

¹ I lift up my eyes to the mountains —
where does my help come from?
² My help comes from the L ORD,
the Maker of heaven and earth.

³ He will not let your foot slip —
he who watches over you will not slumber;
⁴ indeed, he who watches over Israel
will neither slumber nor sleep.

⁵ The L ORD watches over you —
the L ORD is your shade at your right hand;
⁶ the sun will not harm you by day,
nor the moon by night.

⁷ The L ORD will keep you from all harm—
he will watch over your life;
⁸ the L ORD will watch over your coming and going
both now and forevermore.

Amen!

INVISIBLE

Niyetta Williams-Hill, Ed.D.

My story is not one of overcoming a death-defying experience only to emerge on the other side, unscathed. It is not a tale of rags to riches or the unimaginable impact of enduring homelessness or extreme poverty. This is not a story of my incredible journey to defy the odds when faced with certain death. Instead, this is a simple reflection of my seemingly small, observably insignificant, yet potentially debilitating daily battle.

The room was crowded and warm. There was a hum circulating the auditorium. The overlapping sound of conversations shared among families, as they waited, filled the space. My hands were shaking. I steadied them. I walked with my mother through the double doors. Eyes spotted me and a hush slowly blanketed the room. I swallowed. My mother led me to the piano where I took a seat. My dress was neatly pressed, and my patent leather shoes shone over frilly white socks. I inhaled. My hands lifted to the keyboard, and I began to play *Für Elise*.

A Beethoven classic. I had played it dozens of times. I knew it by heart. Memorized the piece. I froze. "Momma!" I yelled. Startled and concerned, she swiftly came to my side. "I can't do it," I cried. "Yes, you can. Now, go ahead and try," she comforted. "I can't." The words hovered above me like an impending rain cloud. Hands, shaking uncontrollably, left the keyboard and fell upon my lap. I pushed myself away from the piano. Smoothed my dress, and walked out with my mother. The silence lingered as the double doors slammed behind us.

The Lord has blessed me with many gifts. I grew up playing classical piano. As a Black girl in a lower middle-class neighborhood, my skill set was quite a novelty. Often, I was asked to perform for church, community, and school events. The highlight of my piano career occurred when the conductor of our local symphony orchestra invited me to christen the symphony's new grand piano, at a distinguished ceremony, with a performance of a Bach *Gigue*. I was fifteen.

I wish this were a story detailing how I came from humble beginnings to become a world-renowned concert pianist. Sadly, it is not. This is the true story of how anxiety has tried to steal my dreams and rob me of my God-given talents.

Like many people with high-functioning anxiety, my condition is not obvious to most. I have donned many labels: introvert, quiet, cold, enigmatic, kind, optimist…but "anxious" never makes the list. For the most part, I have successfully hidden my anxiety. Onlookers are unaware of the battle that never ceases to rage within me.

In college, piano performance became more of a hobby than a career goal. I would only play during my lessons and allowed stage fright to extinguish any and all public performances. Determined not to let anxiety crush my other dreams, I set my sights on international travel. My first flight was 22 hours across the Pacific to the beautiful island of New Zealand. I knew little about the culture, but was excited to have an immersive experience. Studying at the University of Otago, my best friends hailed from New Zealand, Hong Kong, and Japan. Eventually, my travels took me to Pardubice, Czech Republic (where I taught English), Mexico, Jamaica, the Bahamas, and various states within the U.S.

As a natural goal-setter, I acquired my doctorate shortly after turning thirty. I've worked hard to be a good mother, wife, and educator. Although my anxiety has attempted to thwart all of these achievements, I turn to Christ for comfort and strength.

My favorite story is that of the woman with the condition of blood. Determined to let her faith lead her to healing, she merely wanted to touch the hem of Jesus' garment. Her goal was not to be noticed or make a scene. Her goal was a silent, private healing. Yet Christ would not allow her to remain invisible. "Who touched me?" he asked. Such a simple question, with a profound implication. As dozens of people pushed against Christ as he made his way through the crowd, he knew that one person, a faithful woman, had touched him seeking lifelong healing. It was for her faithfulness that she was healed.

In many ways, I see myself in that woman. Anxiety can be a silent and crippling condition. It is invisible to many, but a true healing is always desired by those who suffer from its torment. Countless times, I have reached out and touched the hem of Christ's garment through prayer and thanksgiving. He has touched my heart, given me strength, and led me into the future He's promised. For that, I give Him praise.

As I conclude this piece, my glance drifts toward the window. The sun is shining, leaves gently rustle through the fall breeze, and a joyous anticipation fills the air. My hand gently falls from the keyboard as I turn toward the corner of the living room. My piano. The same one I had as a child. The one my parents bought for me as a wonderful gift. It sits. A nearly abandoned relic of my past. I walk across the room, pull out the bench and hear its legs squeak across the hardwood floor. I sit and place my hands neatly on the keyboard. The music comes to me. My fingers have it memorized, still. I begin to play *Für Elise*.

MY 3 P'S THAT LEAD TO JOY (PRAYER, PATIENCE, & PEACE)

Karen Mize

Early in my adult life, even though in my professional life I worked with young children, I lacked patience. Thankfully, I was patient with children. Although in other areas of my life, family, friends, and in some situations, my patience was absent. I was snappy, short tempered, and fast to jump to conclusions and responses. Lack of patience did not contribute well to relationship-building in my personal or professional life.

After living through numerous, often difficult experiences caused by my impatience, I earnestly, prayed that God would grant me patience in my life. My t-e-s-t was that I had to wait for those prayers to be answered. This in itself was not easy. I KNOW that God absolutely answers prayers. He has granted me the SPIRIT of patience in all aspects of my life. My family notes, "Mom, you're not the same. Something has changed." Co-workers have noticed a "calmness" in my interactions. I've gotten comments from others indicating that in a crisis they would turn to me, in all confidence that things would be handled properly.

Having my prayer for patience answered has led to a PEACE in my life that I didn't even have the sense to know existed or could be granted.

My experience of PRAYING for PATIENCE, that God granted, has led to a PEACE in my life, that absolutely exceeds my ability to explain. When I have to deal with difficult situations or trauma, I now know from within that my daily living is pure JOY, because my prayer for patience has been granted, and peace was extended as a bonus.

GOD'S JOY

Rev. Keith Williams

There is a street in Western Kentucky where you can place your right foot in Kentucky and your left foot in Tennessee. It is close to my grandfather's home, "cotton country."

As a young Black man, my grandfather had wanted to see other kinfolk in Nebraska, but fortunate for me, he ended up in Henderson, Kentucky. There he got a farming job on my grandmother's tobacco farm. My grandmother always addressed him as "Mister Carr" because he was sixteen years older than she was.

All of this family history brings me to the "Ties That Binds." Both of my grandparents believed in God, and attended an old country church where people both Black and white would turn out for "Basket Meeting." People would bring food and come together to celebrate the Lord.

The church was near the train tracks and the train would drown out the service because it was so close to the building. Some came in cars, while others were drawn by horses. That was 60 years ago, and I thank God for the Joy it brings to my heart to remember those times.

Joy is something that does not need a warranty. Those who have been called by Christ know it by its traits: love, peace, long suffering, gentleness, goodness, faith, meekness and temperance. Each of these traits come from God's Holy Spirit.

When trials come, I keep reminding myself what God did the last time I needed him. A lesson I learned from Rev. Anthony Brooks, who married my wife, Linda, and me, 54 years ago at my home church on a snowy night in December. Although I came to know Rev. Charles Stanley rather late in my life, I am thankful to the Lord for his words of encouragement for eight years or longer. His words remain with me to this day.

As a young man, I moved to Louisville for a job. My wife and I had three children. My oldest daughter, when she was quite young, started to show signs around her shoulders and neck that caused us great concern. We couldn't figure out what it was. Upon visiting the doctor, my wife informed me that our daughter had scoliosis. The best doctor for treating scoliosis was in Louisville, Kentucky. Little did we know about her illness five years before we moved to Louisville, to work at the *Courier Journal*, while also acquiring good health insurance. God brought us through this trial, and my daughter is now past 50 years old. He has been with us all those years and it's a marvelous story that I tell quite often. God prepared a place (Louisville) with a nationwide scoliosis specialist for children and adults (Dr. Leatherman) and excellent company health insurance.

People go through many trials and tribulations, but I keep remembering what God did for me the last time I needed him.

THE RIPPLE EFFECT

Charmaine Ward

It's amazing how a fall changed my life. It caused me to have a different perspective on life and God. Interestingly, I had just matriculated to the Louisville Presbyterian Theological Seminary. I was pursuing a Master of Divinity Degree and had just begun the journey September 2020. On November 7, 2020, during the first semester of my first year, I experienced a fall, hitting the back of my head. I was shocked, but I did not pass out. When I returned home, I had my niece look at my head. She said that it was red, but it was not swollen or bleeding, so I placed a wet cloth on it and continued my day. I have always felt like God would protect and strengthen me through any trial or tribulation. I had in 2012 been diagnosed with breast cancer, which God contained in one spot, making it easy to remove. He took me through six weeks of radiation with no damage to my skin and allows me to be cancer-free today. What a wonderful, powerful, and faithful God we serve! I feel such Joy, just to know He loves me enough to heal me and creates a ripping effect through people who provide awareness and assistance when needed. Let's see how God worked through people to take care of one of His children.

After the fall, I never experienced any pain or headaches that would indicate problems. On Thanksgiving night, I had a very enjoyable conversation with my son, who lives in California. Upon completion of the call, he phoned my niece, who lives with me and asked her to check on me. The conversation we had was disjointed and my responses were not aligned with his questions. My son's request heightened and confirmed Tiffany's earlier observations of me dropping items or forgetting things. She tried to go to sleep and address the concern the next morning, but the Lord urged her to react now! She came to my room and said, "Aunt Charmaine, we need to go to the hospital." I immediately dressed and prepared to go.

Once we arrived at the emergency room, I kept telling myself, "Nothing is too hard for God." As the nurse was checking my vitals, my hands began to tremble. I was told that those were seizure behaviors. I received a brain scan and was told I would have to have brain surgery because my brain was bleeding in my skull, and it had pushed my brain from the left to the right side of my skull. Dr. Williams talked to my niece while they were prepping me for surgery. I was in the process of praying and reminding God that I was His and that I was confident that He would guide the doctor's hands to repair the problem. I told Him how much I loved Him and would continue in His work upon recovery. Little did I know what lay ahead, but I went under anesthesia believing that God would allow me to be victorious. I fell into a deep sleep, trusting in God, and slept in peace.

That night I had three surgeries. The first surgery consisted of inserting a tube to drain the blood; it didn't work. The blood was so congealed that it would not move, so Dr. Williams had to perform a second surgery to remove the blood. After removal of the blood, I was in recovery, not aware of any of the two surgeries. An assistant checked me during recovery and found that my pupils indicated that I was not coming out of the anesthesia, and she immediately alerted the doctor. He informed my niece that he would have to perform a third surgery to repair the bleeding. I lovingly tell people that I had one surgery in the name of the Father, another surgery in the name of the Son, and another in the name of the Holy Ghost — three surgeries for the Trinity.

Upon being awakened the next morning by someone calling my name, I opened my eyes and felt so overjoyed that I was alive. I said, "Thank you Jesus, I knew you would look out for me." The nurse therapist came in and had me do several exercises and walk down the corridor. She made the statement that I was a walking miracle, that with three surgeries in one night many others couldn't perform half of the exercises I had completed. Hallelujah, thank you Jesus!

The next semester began in January. I took two classes and 19 months later, I am still occasionally working with Jefferson County Public Schools. I am close to finishing course work at the Louisville Presbyterian Theological Seminary. Life is good, and my Joy has not been blemished, for I know where my help comes from — Jesus!

THIS JOY

Sandra Malone

Years ago, Shirley Caesar wrote the song *"This Joy I Have."* One stanza goes like this, "This joy I have the world didn't give to me…the world can't take it away." Joy is rooted in God, and in having a genuine relationship with Him through Jesus Christ. On the other hand, people and external things can bring momentary happiness; happiness is what the world can give, and the world can and will take it away.

For more years than I care to mention, I focused on being happy. As long as life was going well, I was on top of the world, yet the moment my world turned, and life was not so good, there went my happiness.

Can I get a witness? Have you ever had a life-altering experience that nearly took your breath away, or am I the only one? Well, 24 years ago, God allowed a situation to occur in my life that I literally did not think I could live through.

I was living life, so happy. Then suddenly, along came a decision beyond my control that immediately turned my world upside down. My circumstance felt like a tornado registering about an F5 on a Fujita scale. Completely devastated, I felt shattered. My world appeared dark and grim; nevertheless, I was able to cling to my faith, and my relationship with God remained intact. He did not forsake me, as He so faithfully promises in His Word (Deuteronomy 31:8). In fact, His presence was so pronounced throughout this trying time.

While my prayers were reduced to moans and groans, the Lord reassured me that He heard my faintest cry (Romans 8:26-28). I could hear Him say, "What you are going through will only make you stronger. I will teach you to surrender your all to me, to trust me completely, and to believe that I am with you always, no matter what, because I am able." God continued saying to me, "Happiness is based on external circumstances, but Joy come from within. The great *'I AM,'* is the only one who provides unspeakable Joy."

God reminded me that Joy is not absent of heartache, pain, sickness, sorrow, sadness, or disappointment. Joy and suffering can co-exist, no matter what you go through in life.

Yes, I outlived that challenging episode of my life. God made sure of it. His amazing grace and mercy kept me. He brought me through much stronger, wiser, and better. It was life changing for me. The Joy of the Lord remains in me. This Joy was and still is my strength!

The last stanza of the song "*This Joy I Have*" is, "Who gave it (joy) to you, nobody but Jesus, Jesus." Remember, Joy finds its roots in God, which comes from having a genuine relationship with Him through His Son, Jesus Christ.

I pray your heart, mind, and soul can receive the blessing found in these words from Romans 15:13 (NIV), "May the God of hope fill you with all *JOY* and peace as you trust in Him, so that you may overflow with hope by the power of the Holy Spirit." Let His Joy remain in you!

UNSPEAKABLE JOY

Toni Byrd

I was saved when I was 12 years old. I remember when the church bus would come to our project housing and pick kids up and take them to Southern Baptist Church in Cincinnati, Ohio. I loved going to church at a young age — and how it made me feel. I loved God, and I soon learned about how much he loved me.

A trial that I experienced was having an abortion at 18 years old (actually, I had 2 abortions). In my mind, I did not want to be a statistic "of another teenage unwed mother." But little did I know, I would be another statistic of "a young woman who had an abortion." I thought if I killed/got rid of the baby it would make it all go away. No, that was not true. I was still a mother of two children — but they were just dead.

After choosing to do this (free choice Roe vs. Wade), I later found out it was the worst decision I could have ever made. My behaviors changed, I became more moody, sad, withdrawn and insecure. I did not know I was grieving the loss of my children. But thanks to God I met a woman (unnamed) who told me about the Pregnancy Crisis Center, that provided counseling for post-abortive women. I soon joined the group and was on my road to deliverance. During the classes, we did many things to heal. We named our children (Titus and Tamara) along with other things, like asking for God's forgiveness and learning to forgive ourselves. As God continues to heal me, I learned that my previous behavior was linked to the trauma and grief I was experiencing from the loss of my children.

How can I count those countless nights of crying, yelling, screaming in regret as **Joy**? Well first of all, I thank God, that in the midst of it all, He never left me or forsook me; His grace was still there. The counseling helped me to be honest with myself and learn about being confident in who I was. It showed me how to be grateful for the small things in life. Most of all, I learned how much God loves me and how to share His love with others. He will forgive you if you ask. Later, I joined the counseling team at the Pregnancy Crisis Center and was able to be used by God to lead many other women to Christ.

If you ask me if I am pro-choice, I would say, "No, I am Pro-Life." Once the egg and the sperm meet in the fallopian tubes, if you leave it alone, it will produce a fetus. The choice is only to have sex or not. As my dad said, "The sin is not in the child; the sin was to commit fornication" (having sex without being married) and also, "Only God can give life." Thousands of people have sex every day; not everyone gets pregnant.

Through these experiences, I have changed and have Great JOY. I now know that God loves people who make mistakes and bad choices. I trust and believe that God can take something bad and turn it into something good. I am secure that God has forgiven me, and I have forgiven myself. I am a living testimony of God's love and unconditional grace. God has given me a peace that I can't explain and Joy that is unspeakable.

BLESSED, ANYWAY!

Veronica McGill

Joy for me is "Peace of Mind." For many years I lived a life of trying to keep the peace in my household. I was trying to keep my kids and myself safe. My life was in a state of confusion, and I was just trying to hold it all together.

God brought people into my life that help me make decisions that I never would have made on my own. After a conversation with an old friend at the grocery store, I realized it was time for me to retire. My father helped me realize that it was time to end my marriage. A friend at work helped me with financial decisions about my house. Several people helped me make decisions about other work opportunities that I had never considered. God was helping me get my life together, and I didn't even realize it until I looked back and saw what he had provided, and I hadn't even asked.

I learned even though there are people who may be causing all the disruptions, that He loves them also. I understood this one Sunday, when I was in Sunday school. I cannot remember the scripture that we were studying that morning, but it changed the way I was thinking about what was going on in my life.

After that Sunday School lesson, I started thinking differently about my life. It was up to me to create my life and not be so mad about what was happening. God started providing opportunities for me. It was up to me to act on these opportunities if things in my life were going to change. He keeps providing these opportunities and I keep thanking him for them.

God has given me new friends, new jobs, new activities, so many things to help me get to this state of "Peace of Mind," which is real Joy. I live my life knowing that He is blessing me, despite my sins, because He loves me as well as everybody. I am not rich. But, because of God's blessing I am living my life like I am.

That old saying that "God is good all the time" is so true. He has never let me down, even when I didn't know it. He is always helping and blessing me. Stress, no, no, I am "Too Blessed to Be Stressed."

WHO'S IN CHARGE!

Wanda Mitchell-Smith

I have given up on the illusion of being in control of my life. When things are going well, it is so very easy to feel as though I am in charge — and truly, I'm not — and understand that I cannot perceive myself as my master. It is my belief that the more comfortable I might become in this role, the harder I will fall.

God wants us to enjoy the times of smooth sailing and to be thankful for them, but we should not become addicted to this logic of being master over your life and do not consider the norm. In your life, storms will come and uncertainties will materialize for sure. How audacious for me to cling to control and feel entitled to having things to go my way, because I would drown in self-pity when difficulties come, and things don't go my way.

I always consider myself to be in training to trust in Him, for He is my refuge and strength. I realize that the use of adversity God uses toward me, He uses it to also free me from the illusion of being in control. So, when my circumstances and my future are full of uncertainties, I look to Him! It is in those moments that I feel secure in knowing who He is in my life. He is my Master, who is sovereign and absolute over any storm, that I may have encountered in my life. I AM SO BLESSED! PRAISE GOD!

> "Now listen, you who say, 'Today or tomorrow we will go to this or that city, spend a year there, carry on business and make money.' Why, you do not even know what will happen tomorrow." James 4:13–14 (NIV)

YOUR JOY IS RETURNING

Nancy E. Hall, MSW, LCSW

Holy Spirit whispered this to me about a year ago. He whispered it at a time when I didn't even remember what true Joy felt like. I was confident that it was my Abba Father who was speaking to my aching heart. How could Joy return in the midst of this kind of pain? How could I trust Him to restore and make sense out of what I was currently experiencing? These were only some of my questions in prayer.

"Let it grow, daughter. I am still building the foundation."
I had written the above statement in my Bible many months ago next to our focal verse, James 1:2–4, before I knew about this book's creation — much less being asked to participate in it. Our sweet and compassionate God truly does know the end from the beginning. I believe He gave me these sentiments to use in my life in many ways, and I now know that one of the reasons is for them to be used for the encouragement of His people.

When God told me to "let it grow, daughter," He was speaking specifically to verse 4. Our faith as Believers not only WILL be tested, but in fact it also HAS to be tested. How do you know if what you have is real if you've never had to use it? If I told you that I have an amazing, luxury car that can be driven for hundreds of miles at a time with great gas mileage, but never let you see it or ride in it, you might begin to question the validity of my statement. You might even wonder if I have a car at all! God has to allow our faith to be tested to do two things; strengthen it and let us see what we have in Him is real and true. One of the beautiful things about our God is that He is so full of gentleness, and He will walk right beside us in our faith-strengthening process. We never have to do it alone. He is the God of Covenant. To the Believer, that is so reassuring because He is committed to us forever. He, who is committed to us, will teach and support us through our life's journey when "troubles of any kind come our way." (verse 2)

When I chose to truly believe my Abba Father, what He spoke over me about my Joy returning was true, He allowed me to start seeing His perspective. Kingdom perspective is filled with so much wisdom. God tells us in Proverbs 8:11, that wisdom is more valuable than rubies. My faith in Christ began to rise up slowly, but surely. Being filled with His wisdom allowed me to see what I had never seen before. Our Savior speaks over His children. He rejoices over us with singing Zephaniah 3:17 (KJV). Stop and think about that. The Creator of the universe rejoices and sings over what He made! Come into alignment with what He has spoken over you! Choose to believe Him above your feelings, your frustration, and your confusion. Bring Him all of what you are feeling; I promise He can handle it. He wants your endurance to have a chance to grow, so that when it is fully developed, you will be perfect and complete, needing nothing (verse 4).

As I reflect on verse 2, there's a final point God wants me to highlight. In the NLT translation, it reads "...when troubles of any kind come your way, consider it an opportunity for great joy." God does not waste absolutely anything. He doesn't give up on what He made, and He will take advantage of every opportunity to bring you closer to Him. It's His heart's desire for His children to be close. He wants to build your trust in who He really is. Again, I present another *food for thought* moment; How do you know He's the lily of the valley if you've never been in the valley (dark moments, troubling times)? How do you know He's the bright and morning star if you've never been lost and needed direction? How do you know the Holy Spirit is one of His primary roles as the Great Comforter if you've never had an aching heart?

He says to consider all of these as opportunities for the God of Heaven and Earth to reveal more and more of Himself to you! The verse is not saying that what you will experience in this life will always be joyous, but what He is saying is to surrender these experiences to Him, so that He can create an opportunity to show you His hopeful and joyous plans for your life! Be encouraged today and let it grow!

SELF-DISCOVERY

Felicia Smyzer

Self-discovery brings to mind the song by Michael Jackson. I must begin with "Man in the Mirror." It is truly about the beginning of my own self-awareness. God stated in scripture as described in Jeremiah 1:5 (KJV), "Before I formed thee in the belly I knew thee; and before thou camest forth out of the womb, I sanctified thee, and I ordained thee prophet unto the nations." God lets us know that before we were even thought of, or a twinkle in the eyes of our parents, He knew our abilities and capabilities to be great.

However, situations sometimes have to arise for us to know what discoveries they are. We must figure that these discoveries will come about often rather than not at all. God demonstrates His faith and belief in us. He implanted dreams of what we can be. The dreams He had already preordered/preordained within us to be that which He designed for his glory.

I discovered a lot about myself, in some ways; I already knew what path that I wanted to take to continue my journey as I grew into adulthood. Even as a young 6-year-old girl, teaching was my first love, although I did not start my career in teaching, I started it in healthcare. God goes on further to state in the Jeremiah 29:11 (KJV), "For I know the thoughts that I think toward you, saith the lord, thoughts of peace, and not of evil, to give you an expected end." God wants great and good things for us.

I am into 14½ years of patient care, still in training and teaching mode, and helping people have a healthier life. Then falling into higher education in the midst of those 14½ years, to know my final destination would be just as it was at six years old. I started at 46 years of age, 40 years later to be with my first love, teaching. It is not until we are prepared to do self-inventory that we learn and grasp who we are and whose we are will we accomplish that which he has for us: "I knew you BEFORE." We have to grow to be comfortable in our own skin. To know and recognize that God has my back in order to move forward. God told Joshua in the contemporary English Version Joshua 1:5b (CEB), "I will be with you in the same way I was with Moses; I won't desert you or leave you." God reminded Joshua that "He had his back" and to "be brave and strong." Joshua 1:6 (KJV)

We go through life knowing that there will be situations that are going to be life changing. Some situations we are able to handle, but not handle in the way we think best. In the midst of it all there is something we can discover about ourselves. We discover ow we handle certain situations with personality. The pathway that led me to the life that I deserve and wanted to have is simply me believing in myself, just as someone else believed in me. We have to know that in this life and journey to our destination God has set aside/prepared for us, "I can do all things through Christ who strengthens me." Philippians 4:13 (NKJV)

JOY OF BELIEVING REFLECTIONS

The people who don't give up are the people who find a way to believe in abundance rather than scarcity. They've taken into their hearts the idea that there is enough for all of us, that success will manifest itself in different ways for different people, that keeping the faith is more important than cashing the check.

Cheryl Strayed

1. Why does believing matter to you?

2. What Mary-like or Job-like experiences have you had? How were you blessed in the process?

3. When did you first believe in the Lord Jesus Christ? What were your responses?

4. Philippians 3:4 says to "Rejoice in the Lord always." What does this acclamation mean to you?

5. How do you demonstrate belief in God in situations you do/did not understand?

6. How do you find Joy in believing?

7. Describe how these testimonials demonstrate believing matters in the lives of Christians.

FROM THE HEART

Philippians 3:1–4

- Believing means that you rejoice in the Lord because He is in control of your life, and you can trust him. He is truth and life.
- Our rejoicing is not in external, outside enjoyments but in the Holy Spirit who dwells within us.
- As believers, we are aware that there are people/evildoers who will mislead and misinform us; therefore, we must know the Word for ourselves.
- True knowledge of Jesus Christ changes behaviors.
- Paul was willing to go through any trial or tribulation so that the world (the saints) would know of the Lord Jesus Christ, His birth, death, and resurrection.

Believing in Jesus Christ causes believers to approach life differently. Things you used to do, you no longer want to do. You have a new attitude that is focused on pleasing the Father. Satan, who comes to rob, steal, and destroy our lives, will try to take away the Joy that comes from the Holy Spirit. Remember, Satan is not in control of this world: God is. All power is in God's hand. Be not afraid as you walk with Him. He goes before you protecting and guiding, like a shepherd. Your joyful life should be shared with others, so they, too, may experience everlasting Joy.

PRAYER

Thank you, Lord God, for coming into the world to provide everlasting life. For with you, Lord, all things are possible because we believe that there is none other like you. Lord, you have shown us through your earthly journey that you love us and will not forsake us. Because we believe in you, we need not fear, for you are a spirit of power, love, and a sound mind. Thank you for leading and guiding our footsteps in your precious name. Only you are worthy to be praised! Amen!

> Joy is a gift from God, who assures us that He has total control of our lives. We are confident that all things will work for the good and make the decision to praise and worship Him at all times.

A REASON TO REJOICE

Rev. Bob Byrd

Luke 10:1–3; 17–20 (KJV)

Often, I am asked, "Why do you smile so much? Are you really that happy?"

I have learned to smile from the inside. There is a Joy within me that provides continuous happiness. I have a reason to rejoice and be happy.

Today, we have many reasons that we claim are reasons to rejoice (e.g.., Christmas, New Year's, anniversary, birthday). What is the motive behind our celebration and rejoicing? How can we rejoice, when born in a world of sin and a world of decay? Some people say we should rejoice because we are another day older.

If your motive is to rejoice because God has chosen to create a new expression of His love through your life, maybe that is a true and a good reason to rejoice. In the scripture above, Jesus gives his disciples a true reason to rejoice. The same reason given to the disciples is a valid reason to rejoice even today.

Jesus in this scripture had just finished teaching His disciples about their commitment and need to follow him. The disciples must be willing to give up everything for the cost of following him. Jesus set his face steadfastly toward Jerusalem. He knew what would await him there, the cross and Calvary, which would be a low point in the lives of his disciples. They would need a reason to rejoice.

When Jesus chose his disciples, He explained that the task would not be easy. Before sending them out two by two to cities to spread the Word, they learned from Him, as they had lived with Him for more than three years. The disciples were able to sit at His feet and learn.

Have you ever come face to face with Jesus? Have you ever been in the presence of our Lord and Savior? Have you heard Him say go? Paul, Thomas, and I heard him with no place to run or hide.

There are so few laborers because "straight is the gate; narrow is the way to life that few ever find it." Only a few are willing to meet these requirements. Few people are committed to the cause of saving others. We must be willing to perform against these visible, unbalanced odds with Joy. The disciples talked about how devils were subjected to them. Only Jesus can bring you to this new awareness. You want to rejoice about this good cause. As disciples, you have been given great power over all the enemies' power. So, rejoice in the Lord always!

Again, I say rejoice, because disciples' names are written in heaven in the Lamb's book of life (Revelation13:8). Is your name written in this book? I know the author of this book. I know the publisher of this book. My name is written there, so I rejoice and am exceedingly glad to be called to witness in the uttermost parts of the world, knowing that He is with me even to the end of the age.

"Joy does not simply happen to us.
We have to choose Joy and keep choosing it every day."
Henri J.M. Nouwen

Chapter 3

THE JOY OF GIVING

"No one has ever become poor by giving."
Anne Frank

THE JOY OF GIVING

God gives Christians/believers everything they need to pull their lives together. His provisions serve as roadmaps or guidelines to a life of Joy that are found in his Word. His laws and precepts guide us to truths and an everlasting relationship with him that causes our hearts to rejoice. The author desires that believers experience this Joy that only comes when we are close to God. He wants us to give our lives to Him, and when we do we become concerned about others and share what has been given unto you.

For example, Paul writes to the Philippians thanking them for how the church gave him more than what he needed. Giving within the church or to serve a mission helps pay salaries and provide resources for outreach, evangelism, and discipleship (David Murray, *The Happy Christian: Ten Ways to Be A Joyful Believer in a Gloomy World,* p.144).

Giving is more than money. In the book titled *Giving—The Sacred Art: Creating a Lifestyle of Generosity (The Art of Spiritual Living)* (2008), Lauren Tyler Wright writes that there are various ways to give, for example:

1. Volunteering your time to nonprofit organizations;
2. Opening your home to show hospitality;
3. Praying and interceding on behalf of others;
4. Forgiving others;
5. Giving possessions to others for redistribution in a thrift store or other human resource organizations;
6. Donating organs and/or blood to help in times of emergency; and
7. Being gracious and courteous by giving up your seat or place to sit.

Unfortunately, the world has more takers than givers. The scripture tells us that our reward is great when we give without expecting anything in return. "…God loves a cheerful giver." 2 Corinthians 9:7 (NIV) The idea that we please God brings Joy to our hearts. The fundamental essence of this scripture is sacrificial giving. A giver with an open heart, just as God has given freely to us, demonstrates trust and faith.

> When the world sees a cheerful giver, they see you are more like Jesus.

Giving involves more than monetary gifts; it also includes time, talents, and service to others. Have you noticed the Joy you experience deep inside when you give unconditionally? Giving brings Joy to your heart as well as the receiver's. I know of no one who has ever gone broke from giving because, as Luke 6:38 (KJV) states:

Give, and it shall be given unto you; good measure, pressed down, and shaken together, and running over, shall men give into your bosom. For with the same measure that ye mete withal it shall be measured to you again.

More importantly, God held back nothing from us by giving his only begotten Son so that we may have life everlasting. God's love gift to us goes on, and on, and on — never ceasing and never ending. God's generous giving should bring Joy into our hearts so much so that we would share this Joy with the world (friends, family, neighbors, coworkers, etc.). The world needs to know this truth.

Let us always remember that He gave full forgiveness on the cross. Christ cried out, "Father, forgive them they know not what they do," Luke 23:34 (KJV) as the soldiers divided up His clothes by casting lots. Forgiveness that glories God involves repentance and reconciliation (Murray, *The Happy Christian: Ten Ways to Be A Joyful Believer in a Gloomy World*, p.159).

> Forgiveness that glorifies God involves repentance and reconciliation.
>
> Murray

The scripture Matthew 18:15-17 (NIV) provides the following instructions:

"If your brother or sister sins, go and point out their fault, just between the two of you. If they listen to you, you have won them over. [16] But if they will not listen, take one or two others along, so that 'every matter may be established by the testimony of two or three witnesses.' [17] If they still refuse to listen, tell it to the church; and if they refuse to listen even to the church, treat them as you would a pagan or a tax collector."

Everything you have belongs to God, for he has entrusted us with these belongings as stewards to use them wisely for his glory. When we give cheerfully and generously, the world begins to see how you are more like Jesus Christ.

Generosity brings God's blessings to others. I have a friend who gives and gives and gives. He is willing to help anyone and always empathizes with others. He is not a rich person, but he gives abundantly. People marvel at his benevolent spirit. He is never without and is a great example of how God blesses His people. Even though my friend is not exempt from the trials and tribulations of the world, God's grace and mercy are sufficient. God always provides and protects him. This benevolent gentleman has a series of health issues. When he encounters a challenging trial, God miraculously delivers him. God has given him a powerful testimony through giving. My friend has been in the Vietnam War, survived cancer, and is experiencing heart conditions, as well as knee and hip pain. Through his trials, he continues to rejoice in the Lord.

My late husband donated his kidney to a truck driver 38 years ago. The gentleman is doing well and enjoying a new life. This gift changed his family. Thinking of this experience brings Joy to my heart. For me, a part of my husband lives on in the truck driver.

The testimonials, in this section of the book, are about giving in a special way and how it brings Joy to both the giver and receiver. I have included a few testimonies because no one is exempt from trials and tribulations.

> **Joy is a gift from God, who assures us that He has total control of our lives. We are confident that all things will work for the good and make the decision to praise and worship Him at all times.**

GIVING TESTIMONIES

"Think of giving not as a duty but as a privilege."

John D. Rockefeller, Jr.

GOD'S BLESSING

Linda Kennedy

On June 14, 1972, my husband and I received the devastating news that our newborn daughter, who was 6 1/2 pounds with dark curly hair, was breech (entering her new world bottom first). As she grew, clinical signs of brain damage began to appear. My family, husband and I prepared ourselves to manage our daughter's disability with expert medical care, prayers, faith, and hope. Disability is virtuous suffering and should be accepted as God's Blessing. Scripture says, "My grace is sufficient for you, for my power is made perfect in weakness, therefore, I will boast all the more gladly of my weakness, so that the power of Christ may rest upon me." 2 Corinthians 12:9 NIV

The weekend I went into labor, my obstetrician, who I saw during the 9 months of prenatal care, was off duty. Therefore, I was seen by the staff doctor. In the delivery room, I immediately told the staff doctor that my baby was breech. He proceeded with the preparation and delivery procedure, by giving me an epidural block, where medication is given through a tube placed in the lower back for labor pain and delivery. Due to the baby's bottom down position in the birth canal, the staff doctor used forceps for the delivery.

When my baby was delivered, I did not hear crying like most babies do. I was in a semi-coma condition from the medications for pain but could hear the nurses rushing around the delivery room. They moved very frantically without saying a word. My newborn daughter was rushed to an incubator for a few days. Meanwhile, my husband waited patiently to hear good news from a doctor or nurse. He was told nothing! I came out of a semi-coma condition and the nurse revealed that I had a baby girl, who was fine and in an incubator. My husband and I assumed the baby was fine. She was a beautiful baby.

When she came home to meet her siblings and family, we loved and spoiled her as if she was our firstborn. Soon, we noticed that her development was not normal. At 3 months, she could not raise her head, roll over, hold small objects in her hand, or focus her eyes on us. So, we knew something was wrong. We took her to a highly recommended pediatrician for regular examinations. My husband and I were told that our baby was fine and that we were being anxious parents, who were rushing her developmental stages.

At 1 years old, she was not sitting up, holding objects, rolling over, crawling, standing up, or trying to walk. She was not going through the normal child's developmental stages. Something was not right with our baby's development but we kept getting the run-around (professionals saying, "she's fine"). Finally at 2 1/2 years old, we were told that she was retarded (abnormally slow in development, especially mental development) with cerebral palsy, (paralysis and inability to control movement due to brain injury).

Why did we have to wait for 2 1/2 years for a diagnosis? I was in totally shock and denial. This diagnosis is too much for a young mother, who did all the right things during pregnancy. I went to the best doctor in town, ate the right foods, got the proper amount of rest and had family support. As my husband and I reflected upon what happened, we believed the reason for the delayed diagnosis was to avoid a negligence lawsuit. Maybe, the stature of limitation expired after 2 years of birth. We were not sure what to do next, so we didn't pursue a lawsuit.

In the doctor's office, I was broken mentally, physically, and emotionally. I fell to my knees and cried until there were no tears left. As I left the doctor's office, I believed money could fix it. Therefore, we took her to specialists and recommended therapy programs, locally or out of state. My husband and I realized that all the money and therapy programs in the world would not help our daughter. We had done everything to help our daughter, except give her to the Lord. Scripture reminded us to "Cast your burdens to the Lord, and he will take care of you. He will sustain you; He will not let the righteous be shaken" Psalm 55:22 NIV. Through faith and prayers, God has been our strength, refuge, and guide. He has given me peace and joy. Today, the smallest of responses from our daughter gives me joy (i.e.; a smile, laughter, the pleasure of watching her eat ice cream, watch us move about the house, and her unspoken love for her family). Daily, I find joy just having her with us.

God's joy has brought her parents closer as husband and wife. This experience has taught us the following things about life: love unconditionally, enjoy the small things of life, understand people better, see God's goodness and Joy through all trials and tribulations. For 50 years, God gave us Joy while taking care of our daughter. There is no fear, no anger, just God's Joy in our daily care for her. His love, joy, grace, and mercy are all you need in life.

BLESSED WITH JOY

Dr. Gail Clark Dickson

Recently, August 2022, I attended a Homegoing Celebration, where many of my friends from my hometown of May's Lick, Kentucky, were in attendance. I arrived at the Church and was greeted by a multitude of friends. Repeatedly I heard, "Do you know who this is, Mr. John Clark's daughter?" "Yes, she looks just like him." Or "This is Mrs. Essie Clark's daughter." They shared stories and memories of my father and mother, stories I've never heard.

Kenneth shared stories of the fun mischief done by my father and his father, Mr. Bill. Discipline at the May's Lick Negro School, a Rosenwald School, was sacred. I asked, "How do you know this?" He said his daddy often shared stories with him. I had no idea that he and my father attended the same school. Of course, May's Lick Negro School was the only school in the May's Lick community allowing Black children to receive an education. The original school opened in 1868. Eventually, a new school was constructed with Rosenwald Funds and dedicated July 17, 1921.

The school remained in operation until the early 1960s. The May's Lick Negro School was added to the National Register of Historic Places in 2018. In 2019, fund-raising events began to restore "OUR SCHOOL."

It brings me great **JOY** in knowing that Daddy's, my, and my siblings' educational foundation was the learning and the teaching by outstanding teachers at the May's Lick Negro School. Mr. Bill's daughter, Linda Sue, and I were classmates and began our early learning at the May's Lick Negro School. She and I remain friends to this day and often reminisce the **JOY** of being a student at Mays's Lick Negro School. This educational foundation established us as successful adults in our careers, our endeavors of outreach and spreading **LOVE**, **PEACE** and **JOY**.

I met Donna at the same Homegoing Celebration. She said, "I know your mother, Mrs. Essie Clark. She made an apron with matching potholders for my grandmother and it was passed down to me." Donna continued to share the **JOY** of wearing the apron at a birthday event as the family prepared the meal. She indicated that all the ladies took turns wearing the apron. I was amazed and filled with **JOY** as I listened to her story. Later, Roberta shared her story of Mama saying, "Mrs. Essie Clark was our seamstress." She made my outfit for an FHA event, and she also made me a stuff donkey which was always made an appearance at our Church Christmas Pageants." My mother was talented and gifted and shared her crafts throughout the community. I smiled and felt the **JOY!**

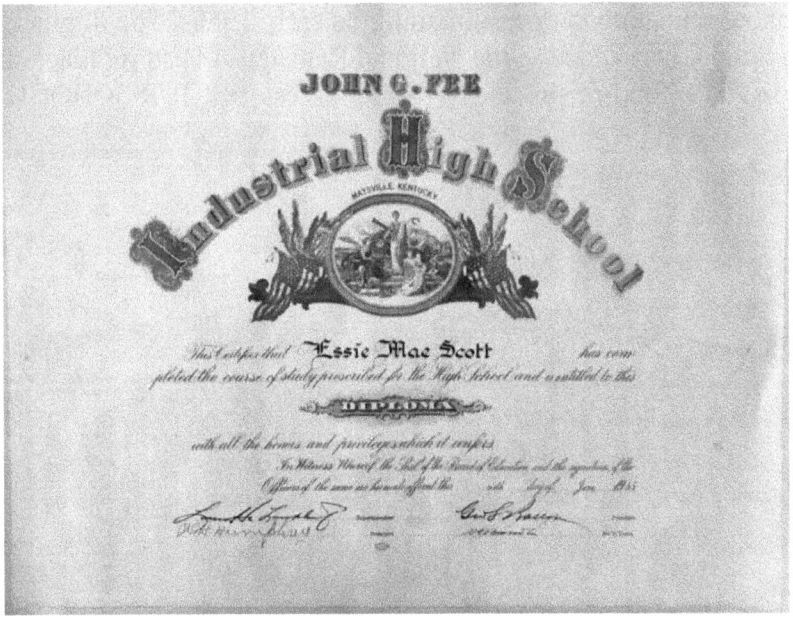

My mother's educational foundation was similar to Daddy's. She attended the John G. Fee School, a Rosenwald School in Maysville, Kentucky. Her teachers were outstanding and loving, contributing to her multiple achievements in the Community Home Makers Club. Mama traveled through the community training others and sharing her crafts.

Our schools back in the day were never inferior. We often heard those untruths of inferiorities. These Rosenwald Schools were staffed with outstanding, caring, and knowledgeable teachers. There were lack resources and inequitable issues: used/marked textbooks, no bathrooms, and no cafeteria. But, in spite of all those inequities, we remained resilient and still we soared. Yes, all were based on **FAITH**. Actually, we could have designated the May's Lick Negro School as a Faith-Based School. We had prayer and marched up the school steps singing, *"Onward Christian Soldiers."* Our Baptist church was next to our school. This church was where most of the students were baptized. The older students were our role models; our teachers were relatable; and, of course, our parents were our first teachers.

My parents left us a legacy of **LOVE** for community, **GIVING** to others, and **FAITH** within. Both Mama and Daddy were wonderful and proud parents. I am **BLESSED** to be the proud daughter of John and Essie Clark. Their **LOVE** and **MEMORIES** will forever bring me JOY!

Recalling the Prayer of Jabez:

> "Oh, that you would bless me indeed and enlarge my territory"! Let your hand be with me, and keep me from harm so that I will be free from pain." I Chronicles, 4:10 (KJV)

Caregiving with Joyful Heart

Dr. Pam Randolph

As long as I can remember, attending church has been a part of my life. As a young child, my mom would take me to church on Sundays and during the week. I loved seeing her fellowship, worship, and praise God. My mom would hear the gospel songs and pastor preaching, and she'd get filled with the Holy Spirit. I watched her and wondered what was happening to her. She would sing, shout, and run around the church. In 2 Samuel 6:14 -22 (KJV), it talks about dancing like David; my mom did just that. So, that's what I did, too. I imitated my mom, and our church family called me her shadow. When I noticed my mom crying, I would immediately rush to her side to comfort her. In our home, I noticed my dad verbally and physically abusing my mom. I jumped into action and was there by her side, defending and comforting her. My mom, siblings, and I found refuge at church. It was our safe haven where we could release our hurt, pain, and sadness. Church was our sanctuary of Joy, love, peace, and freedom. As the middle child, my siblings would look to me for advice, guidance, and support. I realized early, I was the protector and caregiver of our family.

My life of caregiving started to evolve, and I believe it was my mother who planted the caregiver seed. She worked tirelessly serving others. My mom was influential in my spiritual walk and acceptance of God. She is truly a woman of faith; I am forever thankful and grateful she exposed me to a safe, loving, and joyful place called church. During these special times, I acknowledged my salvation, and my love for God manifested. I served in various capacities at church: singing in the choir, usher board, Sunday school, serving meals, whatever was needed to edify the kingdom of God. These great memories were priceless and life changing.

As a retired educator, I always knew my leadership strength was servant leader. It makes my heart glad to care for others bringing them Joy! Reflecting on my life, I truly count it all Joy for the trials and oppositions I have faced in life. Roadblocks and obstacles renewed a sense of urgency to seek God more! I must continue to persevere and share the love of God with those in need. My days are filled with caring for my elderly parents, daughter, grandsons, husband, and other elderly family and friends. God's grace and mercy continue to sustain me.

As my faith in God has strengthened over the years, I've realized self-care and finding a balance are significant to my mental and physical health. It has taken me a long time to fully understand that before I can take care of others, I must take care of myself first. My health and well-being are a priority. This means a daily routine of exercise, eating healthier, more water intake, study and meditation, prayer, fasting, positive affirmations, reducing stress, and eliminating toxic relationships. Carving out more time to do the things I enjoy while loving myself!

I thank God for my husband, Andrew! He supports me and infuses love, Joy, and laughter into those stressful caregiving moments. Author and caregiver Sonia S. Morrison suggests caregivers create a joyful journal that focuses on happy events. I love this idea and plan to create one!
I have embraced God's purpose and plan for my life: caring for others. Daddy and my sweet mommy have passed away. My heart is forever filled with gratitude for all the wonderful years I was their caregiver.

HOW COULD YOU, LORD?

Dr. Louise Byrd

My husband of 38 years died, and I felt numb, mad, scared, shocked and in disbelief that something like this could ever happen to me. How could the Lord take someone who loved Him, family, church, and me? My husband was the person I had prayed for, and now what do you do when he is gone? As the center of the family, he ministered and handled everything. Yes, everything — even cooking, cleaning, and finances. So, you can imagine how I felt when his support and love were removed. How could you do this, Lord?

Alone and confused, I didn't know what to do first. I cried, prayed, and asked God and friends, "What am I to do next?" My friends were so helpful, and I thank God for sending people who were comforters. It is amazing how many people impact your life by showing up in your darkest hour, to confirm how important relationships are. God wants us to build relationships in order to serve others and bring them into a saving relationship with Him. No man or woman is an island; therefore, they cannot stand alone in this world. We need each other to make it daily.

What was most critical, during this time, was to maintain whatever possessions I had and not to make any rash decisions. A trusted friend showed me how to make a ledger of items that needed to be addressed and bills that needed to be paid. I felt that I needed more knowledge about the lists and how to formulate my own ledger.

At church, I emerged myself in Bible groups, service organizations, and Sunday services. A theme that continued to surface was stewardship. So I enrolled in a church-directed study on the importance of stewardship and giving to God your tithes and offerings. I didn't miss a class or an exercise because this class brought Joy to my heart. God spoke to me, and I was convicted. I learned so much about what God has given me compared to what I had given Him. Learning about stewardship got my attention, and I will keep these points in my heart:

- All I have belongs to Him;
- He asks for 10%; I have 90% to do whatever I please (within reason);
- It's all right NOT to keep up with the Joneses. Tell the Joneses they win because you are no longer competing;
- Ask the question, "Would my spending please God?"

Now, I maintain a spending log and intentionally work to wisely become a steward of what God has given me. In fact, less is better for me! Stuff doesn't excite me anymore. In fact, I moved from my home to a condo and gave away so much stuff. You may relate to what I mean, for example: stuff with tags, stuff I forgot I had, stuff that is outdated, and stuff I really didn't need. My actions reminded me of Proverbs 22:7 (NIV), "The rich rule over the poor, and the borrower is slave to the lender." Running up credit charges needlessly has its consequences. My husband told me these things, but I didn't listen. God has a way of finally getting your attention. I hear you now, Lord!

Since completing stewardship classes, I have a good feeling to be at peace about spending wisely. Now, I have a new way of thinking that is not of the world, but pleasing to God. Therefore, I give to God first and help others. This process has been a journey and not an overnight fix. My desire is that these practices are embedded into my life.

I am so glad that I learned how to become a better steward of what God has given me 1 Corinthians 4:2 (KJV). I challenge you to examine what God has given you and how your stewardship aligns with His plan, for we die from lack of knowledge. There are a few scriptures that I use to keep me focused and have committed to memory. May these scriptures bless you. They are as follows:

"Every man according as he purposeth in his heart, so let him **give**; not grudgingly, or of necessity: for God loveth a cheerful giver."
2 Corinthians 9:7 (KJV)

"**Give**, and it shall be given unto you; good measure, pressed down, and shaken together, and running over, shall men **give** into your bosom."
Luke 6:38 (KJV)

Keep your life free from love of money, and be content with what you have, for he has said, "I will never leave you nor forsake you."
Hebrews 13:5 (ESV)

Some people can't find Joy because they are distracted by the woes of the world. Accumulating things does not bring about Joy; only what God has for you brings Joy. Things are temporary, but Joy is everlasting. So, I say, "Thank you, Lord, for teaching me, in this moment of grief, that you are in control of my life, and I need to be obedient to your plan and trust you explicitly!"

GIVING LOVE

Yolanda Farris

I was raised in a Christian home. My Christian direction has been a part of who I am for as long as I have been alive. My belief in God's guidance was never more evident than in 1996.

In April of 1996, my father had a stroke. From that point on, the dynamics of our relationship changed dramatically. This shift of responsibility between my father and me was unexpected. I was a single college student with my main focus on completing my degree. Before his stroke, my father was MY support. My dad prided himself on his independence and making sure that I had all that I needed. Because of the effects of the stroke, his days of independence were somewhat limited. In a blink of an eye, I was the one making sure he had what HE needed. My sister was very aware of the situation, supportive, and helpful, but she lived in another state, hundreds of miles away. She handled the financial aspect of his business.

One of the first things I had to do was to find my dad a facility that would take care of all his needs (and he was very particular). I had no idea where to start. Through constant, continuous, and faithful praying (and a few tears), the Lord directed me to individuals within the health system who helped me find a perfect place for him to live.

I also had to attend care meetings, meetings with state human services, meetings with doctors, and meetings with a bevy of other individuals. I had no idea how to handle what was necessary to take care of my father. I felt like I was drowning. At times, I didn't know where to begin. I had to obtain strength from somewhere.

Again, I went to the Lord in prayer (at any given time or place). This faith gave me the right words to say and questions to ask on the journey of care for my father.

As time went by, my father made health improvements and was comfortable in his new home. I was now more comfortable with navigating my way through the different aspects of his changed life. I graduated from college on time with my bachelor's degree and I was even able to relocate to a neighboring state to continue my career. I moved close enough to visit dad on a regular basis and pick him up to have dinner. There continued to be health issues with my father, but my faith and Joy knowing that the Lord hears and answers prayers will always be my comfort.

I know now that it was nothing but the Lord who brought me through, directed me, gave my father continued improvement with his health, and guided me in my quest to make sure he was taken care of.

When you don't even know where to start, close your eyes and just tell the Lord all your needs. You will receive an answer.

LET'S SEE

Dr. GL Byrd

Going to church and joining a body of believers is a great experience. The more you study the Word of God, the more you grow spiritually. As my pastor says, "The Word does not come back void. It reaches and touches the heart of the believer, and you become a doer versus a hearer of the Word." Going to church is not for entertainment but to worship and praise the Lord Jesus Christ.

Early in my marriage, my husband and I wanted to grow from spiritual babes in Christ to spiritual adults in Christ. In other words, we were on spiritual milk like babies and want to feast on the spiritual meat of the Word. At an early age, we participated in Bible study groups and had heard many times in Sunday School, Baptist Training Union, and Vacation Bible School, that you can't beat God's blessings; the more you give the more you received. We accepted those teachings and thought how wonderful they were.

On a special Sunday morning, I heard Mark 12:41–44 (KJV) clearly for the first time. The message was about Christ observing people placing money in the offering. Rich people gave out of their abundance, but a poor widow woman gave two copper coins worth only a few cents. Jesus called his disciples together and told them that the rich people gave out of their wealth; however, the poor widow gave all she had. Therefore, she had put in more than all the others.

Wow! How powerful to give all that you have and trust God for the rest. Often, I would determine my giving based on what I needed for the month or week ahead. During the offering, my husband leaned over to me and whispered, "Let's try it. If we are going to be Christians, let's move up in our faith walk and see what God will do."

On the way home in the car, we looked at each other and held hands. My husband said, "We are going to be just fine." Here's the amazing part — all of our needs were met: rent, food, clothing, gas, etc. (all the things you need to survive). We didn't have fancy meals or go out shopping for unneeded items, but miraculously God blessed us and kept us. Was I concerned? Did giving away the money create fear? Yes, but we would refocus our thoughts because we knew there would be spiritual warfare. Satan would not want us to have this victory. During this time, we stayed completely silent about what we did for a month.

You know the song, "I Couldn't Wait to Tell Somebody"? Well, we had a testimony, and I am sharing it again with you. When I hear people say that don't have money to give because they are barely making it themselves, I share my story. After all, what we have belongs to Jesus Christ anyway. He created heaven and earth and everything in it, including you.

Here's the rest of the story. I worked part time and my husband had a meager salary compared to what is needed to live in the second-largest city in the world. But God showed us what our eyes have never seen. His wonders never cease. God provided all we needed. You can't just take my word for it; try for yourself. God loves to bless His people. All we need to do is trust Him.

THE GIFT GOES ON!

Rev. Robert Lee Byrd, Sr.

I grew up in a family that believed that you should help each other. If a neighbor needed a cup of sugar or butter, you shared. At church, if there was a family in need, you chipped in to help. At an early age, you knew what the expectations were on Wednesday (Bible Study) and on Sunday (Church all day)!

I loved the socialization at church and finally became a Sunday School teacher. During my adult life, I embraced others totally. I enjoyed talking to people, wishing them a good day, saying, "God Bless You." One time I said it to a lady on an escalation and she continued to talk to me about what was going on in her life. She needed to receive a blessing from God, so I prayed for her and asked her if she had received Christ in her life. She had.

When I was out in the mall where I worked, I would say the same thing and my co-workers noticed, especially the ones who know Christ. A gentleman named Mike invited me to his church at the Salvation Army, where persons who were mostly struggling with the woes of life attended.

I fell in love with the people and felt that I was called to serve in a very special way. I prayed with them; got to know their families; spent a lot of time ministering to them; providing shelter, food, clothing, education; and helping them find jobs.

I gave up an executive position, near retirement time, to work with the Salvation Army full time. Of course, my family had questions, but knew my love for the Lord, family, and others and slowly accepted my choice to be obedient to the calling of the Lord Jesus Christ.

The experience was not a bed of roses, for I was constantly attacked by evil forces; challenged by my skin tone; and thought to be too aggressive vs. full of the Holy Spirit. Regardless, you do not let people try to steal your Joy from you. I know that God wanted me to serve the homeless. I felt that when Jesus was traveling, sharing the Word, He would definitely stop by to teach those who were lost and needed a Savior. When we think of the homeless, we think that they are persons who don't want to work or didn't stay in school. Many of the people I served were professionals who encountered a trial/tribulation of life and just could not cope.

Every evening before meals were served, I shared the love of Jesus Christ and the Joy that He brings to those who will receive Him. My work had no time limit, but I went home after 9 p.m. every night. Sometimes, a person would say, "You are letting them take advantage of you. They don't pay you enough." Quickly, I would respond, "No one can take advantage of me, unless I allow them to. Whatever I have belongs to Christ. He can do with it whatever He pleases to glorify Himself. What I do is done freely and unconditionally. There is nothing that I need that God has not already provided or will not provide. I trust Him to take care of me and my family."

In this world, naysayers will try to discourage, so know who you are in Christ and don't let anyone turn you away from what He wants you to do. I say, it is a test of your faith. If you believe with all your heart that He is in control and is the Savior of the world, don't let anyone turn you around. Don't be afraid for He is not a spirit of fear, but of power, love, and a sound mind.

As a result of this sacrifice, God blessed my family in a different way. Family income doubled; family grew stronger in Christ; and we had women, men, and family Bible studies weekly in our home. There is nothing like opening your home to praise the Lord. I started my life sharing sugar and butter with neighbors; now, I get to share Jesus Christ.

ONLY YOU

Dr. Louise Byrd

"Those who walk with God always reach their destination." — Henry Ford

How could this be, with a person like me, who is afraid of death? I tried to avoid grieving persons and worked harder to avoid funerals, wakes, or visitations, because I grieved more than the family when I attended these functions.

After 35 years of marriage, I had to face death in a profound way. The thing I avoided the most I had no choice but to go through. The pain and agony of death are indescribable emotions. Every bone in my body ached and without God sending people to comfort me, the recovery would have taken even longer than three years.

To survive and maintain my sanity, I stayed in the Word all day. I personalized a few scriptures and recited them constantly. From Matthew 6:11 (KJV), I would say, "Give me this day my daily bread," or "give me this moment or this hour. I need you Lord to help me and give me the strength." I would remind the Lord that in Matthew 6:24–34 (KJV), you told your disciples not to worry about food or clothing. I cried out, "Lord, you know my needs. You feed the birds of the air and clothe the lilies of the field; how much more will You provide for me, your child, your creation, whom You love?"

As I moved through the grieving stages and became stronger, I began to serve others. My pain was lessened when I took the focus off of me and began to help others. How is this possible? My answer is with God's mercy and grace. He had a plan for me all along. God's Word says, "For I know the plans I have for you, declares the Lord, plans for welfare and not for evil, to give you a future and a hope." Jeremiah 29:11 (ESV)

The one thing I avoided I now embrace. Since I have grown in faith and trust in God, I can sit with grieving widows, attend funerals, wakes, visitations and co-facilitate an online grief ministry. So, I count it all Joy, because I can complete the plan God has for me, knowing that He will never leave or forsake me. I trust Him and have learned that He is in control, not I. As a result of my trials and tribulations, I have learned to be more tolerant of others, to understand their concerns, to care for and love them spiritually as brothers and sisters.

Walking with God has given me the confidence to speak boldly about Him. The walk was not always a smooth one because there were a lot of stones and pebbles that caused me to stumble. However, I get back up and try it again knowing that God is working out a plan for my life. Today, I am a better person than I was three years ago and will continue to grow in the Lord. He has turned my mourning into dancing again and has lifted my sorrow Psalms 30:11 (KJV).

GIVING REFLECTIONS

Stop asking yourself what you want, what you desire, what interests you. Ask yourself instead: What has been given to me? Ask: What do I have to give back? Then give it.

Cheryl Strayed

Philippians 4:14–20 (KJV)

1. Describe Paul's Joy in Philippians 4:14–20. How has God met your needs?

2. In what ways do people see Jesus Christ in your giving? How may you become more like Him in giving?

3. In the world there are givers and takers. How do you describe yourself and why?

4. God gives approximately 7,000 promises to us. Find or share a promise that you will make a part of your life.

5. In the testimonials, how did giving differ and which one had the greatest impact on you?

6. How are you witnessing giving in the world (home, family, friends, jobs, etc.)?

FROM THE HEART

- It's good to have something to share/give and/or help others meet their needs.
- Your fragrant offerings are acceptable and pleasing to God. God loves a cheerful giver.
- It is more blessed to give than to receive.
- Giving not only blesses the receiver; it brings Joy into the heart of the giver.
- God will meet your needs according to his riches in glory.
- Give with all your heart, mind, and soul!

With gratitude and worship, we give cheerfully to the Lord. All we have belong to Him anyway. God is gracious to allow us to use what He has given to meet our daily needs and bless others. The more you give, the more you receive. Giving not only blesses the receiver, but it also brings Joy. "Give, and it will be given to you. A good measure, pressed down, shaken together and running over, will be poured into your lap. For with the measure you use, it will be measured to you." Luke 6:38 (NIV)

PRAYER

Our Father, we are so thankful that you gave your son, Jesus Christ, so that we may have an everlasting relationship with you. This good news brings Joy to our hearts, minds, and souls. In our lives today, Father you constantly provide more than we can imagine. We say, "thank you." May we, too, be examples of cheerful givers in a world that does not know how blessed it is to give rather than receive. Above all, let us be willing to forgive as Christ has forgiven us. Forgiveness provides peace and a restored relationship with man and God. Thank you, Father, for continuing to enlighten us through your Word. In Jesus' mighty name, we pray!

Amen.

[14] Notwithstanding ye have well done, that ye did communicate with my affliction. [15] Now ye Philippians know also, that in the beginning of the gospel, when I departed from Macedonia, no church communicated with me as concerning giving and receiving, but ye only. [16] For even in Thessalonica ye sent once and again unto my necessity. [17] Not because I desire a gift: but I desire fruit that may abound to your account. [18] But I have all, and abound: I am full, having received of Epaphroditus the things which were sent from you, an odour of a sweet smell, a sacrifice acceptable, well pleasing to God. [19] But my God shall supply all your need according to his riches in glory by Christ Jesus. [20] Now unto God and our Father be glory for ever and ever. Amen.
Philippians 4:14-20 (KJV)

Chapter 4

THE JOY OF HUMILITY

"Be more joyful is not just about having more fun. We're talking about a more empathic, more empowered, even more spiritual state of mind that is totally engaged with the world."

Archbishop Desmond Tutu, *All Joy*, p. 63

JOY OF HUMILITY

Being humble, forgiving, and putting others before self is not a characteristic that is honored in a world where one seeks to be the top person and have people serve them. Most people are competitive and strive to be #1 and receive kid-glove treatment accompanied by champagne and caviar. Society celebrates confidence, greatness, and pride. In our minds, instant gratification impresses others and puts them in the spotlight. In other words, we want to be the center of the universe. Oftentimes, we are our worst enemy by pursuing worldly things. What do we gain? Most of us are unhappy, worn out, depressed, overextended, and stressed, because we see ourselves in competition with each other.

> We look upward to Christ and outward to other people.

Matthew 16:26 asks the question, "What does it profit a man to gain the whole world and lose his soul?" God wants us to have money and success, but not at the cost or risk of losing your soul or relationship with Him.

Can we celebrate others and their successes versus developing envy, strife, and a contentious spirit? People who show humility derive their self-view from God, not man (Nona Jones, *Killing Comparison* p.125).

Andrew Murray quotes (*Humility*, p.48): "the humble man feels not jealousy or envy. He can praise God, in spite of what is happening around him. He can accept hearing others being praised and himself overlooked. In God's presence, the Apostle Paul learned, 'I am nothing.' 1 Corinthians 13:2 (KJV)

Unfortunately, our interpretation of humility does not align with God's viewpoint. God wants us to submit to His authority because all power is in His hands. God controls all nations. He wants us to realize we need a Savior. He is a righteous and faithful God, whose name is above all names. His authority is to be revered and adored. Therefore, every knee shall bow, and every tongue confess that Jesus Christ is Lord. Philippians 2:10–11 (KJV)

In Isaiah 6:1-4 (KJV), the prophet describes the magnitude and awesomeness of God:

".... I saw also the LORD sitting upon a throne, high and lifted up, and his train filled the temple. Above it stood the seraphims: each one had six wings; with twain he covered his face, and with twain he covered his feet, and with twain he did fly. And one cried unto another, and said, Holy, holy, holy, is the LORD of hosts: the whole earth is full of his glory. And the posts of the door moved at the voice of him that cried, and the house was filled with smoke."

Isaiah was humbled by this experience and repented of his sins. Then, his mission to carry God's message began. Completing this mission would take some time because people's ears and eyes are not attuned to what God has to say. God needs you to deliver His message to a sin-sick world that considers good, evil and evil, good. Your work will last a lifetime as well.

I remember how somber I was when my husband, Bob, announced he was quitting his job to work with the homeless men at the Salvation Army. My first thought was worldly, "How are we going to survive on a minimum salary?" His response was, "God has taken care of us for 15 years, why wouldn't He continue?" I was stunned to say the least. My husband reminded me that he was called by God to serve the homeless at the Salvation Army and he needed to accept the call. His employer was shocked and thought maybe he needed some time off to think about it. With conviction, Bob was determined to follow God's directions.

Bob has always loved sharing God's Word. In fact, he carried a sermon with him in case he needed to speak. Our home was filled daily with Bible study groups. If you stopped by our home for a visit, you engaged in Bible study.

During this time, I was working on a doctorate degree. My teacher made sure no classes occurred on Wednesday night, so I would not miss Bible study classes. Isn't God magnificent?

When Bob was in high school, he had a special gift. He won many debate team awards for his speaking and analytical abilities. People liked talking to him because he gave you his undivided attention. Before you knew it, you would think you were a part of his family.

God used those gifts to make a difference at the Salvation Army. The work was challenging, but saving souls was more important. When I am out shopping or doing errands, I get a chance to see some of the men whose lives he touched. I am glad he was obedient.

When you walk by faith, interesting things happen. What seems impossible becomes possible with God. Earlier, I mentioned how concerned I was about surviving on minimum income. God provided all my needs. The blessing with having less is we became a stronger, committed husband and wife team. As a result, we formed a couple's ministry. During this time, I learned how to submit, not only to God, but to my husband. Walking with the Lord is a lifetime experience that has an eternal impact.

Archbishop Desmond Tutu wrote the following:

"Humility is the recognition that your gifts are from God, and this lets you sit relatively loosely to those gifts. Humility allows us to celebrate the gifts of others, but it does not mean you have to deny your own gifts or shrink from using them." (*All Joy, p.211*)

Experiencing humility requires looking upward to Christ and outward to other people as a servant of God. According to Dr. Charles Stanley, founder of In Touch Ministries, humility is the opposite of arrogance. In other words, an arrogant person's focus is strictly on self. Arrogance is an example of an obnoxious person with a false sense of self-worth. Christ is the example of humility. When the angels announced his arrival they proclaimed, "I bring you tidings of great joy." He came humbly into the world to save us from our sin so that we may have eternal life with the Father. He was crucified, bled, and died, and on the third day arose to testify that we, too, will rise to be with him in eternity.

When Christ chose the disciplines, He said, "If anyone desires to come after me, let him deny himself, take up his cross, and follow me." Matthew 16:24 (NKJV) Christ is the example of humility as He does what the Father asks. He came not to be served, but to serve others. Wouldn't it be great for the world to provide more service to mankind versus to self? Philippians 2:3–4 (NIV) reminds us to: "Do nothing out of selfish ambition or vain conceit. Rather, in humility value others above yourselves, not looking to your own interests but each of you to the interests of the others."

The following testimonials demonstrate how believers gave of themselves unconditionally to bless others.

> **Joy is a gift from God, who assures us that He has total control of our lives. We are confident that all things will work for the good and make the decision to praise and worship Him at all times.**

HUMILITY TESTIMONIES

> "Be completely humble and gentle; be patient, bearing with one another in love."
>
> **Ephesians 4:2 NIV**

CHANGE OF LIFE TO BRING FORTH A BETTER LIFE

Dr. Victoria Felicia Hanchell

"For all of your homeschooling needs, come to the Christian Supply Store!"

That was the tagline blasting on the Christian radio station as I prepared to drop my two children, Zaria (6) and Zion (3), off at their private Christian school for the start of a brand-new day.

Homeschool? Me?

I'm a manager of an organization! I am completing my doctorate! I am about to finish my dissertation and go on to make all of the money that I dreamt about at the start of my doctoral experience!

That was the moment my life took a drastic turn wherein I no longer lived according to my goals and aspirations, but according to the direction of the Lord — except, I was unhappy about this direction because it was not in my grand master plan for MY life.

Being the talk-back natured person that I am, even in my prayer life, I blatantly told the Lord that I would fast and pray about the possibility of homeschooling. However, within seconds, I received a phone call and the person on the receiving end asked, "This may sound weird, but have you considered homeschooling?"

At that moment, I was shaken. The Lord had answered a prayer that I had not yet even uttered.

In that same moment, I was ticked off because I had submitted several other prayers to heaven via the "Express Prayer Lane" that had yet to be answered, yet God had chosen to immediately disperse a response? Excuse me, Jesus, but since you are in the mood to speak, could you also send some additional answers totally unrelated to this matter? I mean, I didn't ask about this!

I still held to my attitude, and I shook my proverbial fist at the Lord by exclaiming, "Well, I will not drive all over town looking for this unknown Christian Supply Store!" Then, I rolled my eyes, typed the store name into Google Maps and *shockingly* the store was only seven minutes away from my current location. I begrudgingly went to the store as I clearly saw that my will nor my way was no longer leading. Upon arrival, I felt prompted to speak to one particular store employee. I told her that I was getting my doctorate (flipped my hair) yet felt completely inept as I embarked upon this homeschool *thing* (rolled my eyes). In my arrogant state of mind, she had mercy on me and promptly brought me three various curriculum guides to select how I should proceed.

Sounds easy? No.

I was getting my doctorate in education, but teaching my own children proved to be the greatest challenge of my life! I exchanged wearing my business suits for T-shirts and shorts. I exchanged my private office with an administrative assistant who answered my calls to sitting on the floor teaching my 3-year-old son how to count nickels. I exchanged my routine lunch meetings to being the lunch lady for my daughter, who favored beans with weenies. All I could see was the loss of my life. All I could see was my will and my wants being taken from me. To make matters worse, when I finished my doctorate and I was ready to toss homeschooling to the side, I couldn't find a job! I was stuck in a career that I did not choose for my life — to teach my children— at home! I was supposed to be Dr. Victoria, but, instead, I was Dr. Mommy.

God had humbled me. I thought that I was getting a doctorate, instead He gave me direction.

Over the course of six additional years of homeschooling, accepting a position in the public school system to keep my family as a priority, the Lord allowed me to see the fruit of my investment. The scales had fallen from my eyes.

What I could not see while I was on the floor teaching my son and daughter, was how my daughter would eventually graduate at the age of 15 with a 4.75 GPA and a full academic scholarship. I could not see how the COVID-19 pandemic was going to close the school doors, and all children were in fact going to be homeschooled. God, in his infinite wisdom, had prepared us, and we knew how to instantly pivot and remain on course even with academic studies, because we had obeyed him years prior. God had to redirect that *"me-my-I"* selfish nature and point my energy toward my children. Psalms 127:4 (KJV) says, "As arrows *are* in the hand of a mighty man; so *are* children of the youth." I was so focused on myself that I could not see what I had in my hands! I had budding scholars in my hand, but God needed to redirect my focus to point them in the right direction. God gave me Zaria and Zion to nurture and point in the right direction, but they were the change agents in my life to set me straight. I was once angry about God's redirection, but now I can count it all Joy in reflection because this was all the Lord's doing. The sacrifice of *"me-my-I,"* was well worth the price!

COUNT IT ALL JOY

Rev. David Dow

I have never been strung out on drugs. I have never lived a life of debauchery and destitution. I can't tell you that I have (hardly) been in a lot of trouble with the law. I have escaped many of the vices some of my peers have experienced. Looking back, this I can count Joy.

I have had to go to a graveyard and rescue my daughter from languishing at the grave of someone she had planned to marry. I have had to drive across the country and stand with my son as he was pronounced guilty for disciplining his stepson. I have been asked to sit outside the pulpit of the church, that not only licensed me to the Gospel ministry, but was my home church, the church that I was raised in. These and many other personal experiences have taught me to still count this as Joy, too.

The Word of God is true. It takes many experiences to learn this. It's not necessary to be a drug addict or an alcoholic to trust in God. [You] don't have to murder someone to speak against murder. When the Word of God says, "…count it all joy when ye fall into divers temptations," James 1:2 (KJV), it isn't merely meant for those taken in the usual vagrancies of life: all — good and bad — are included.

I count it all Joy, whether personal or for those I love and care about. I simply try to deal with whatever comes my way. As the old precept goes,

> "Prepare for the worst.
> Pray for the best.
> Accept whatever God allows in your life."

JOY IN HUMILITY

Pat Richardson

Scripture reference: Hebrews 12:2 (KJV); Looking unto Jesus the author and finisher of our faith; who for the JOY that was set before him endured the cross, despising the shame, and is set down at the right hand of the throne of God.

Humility, according to Webster's dictionary, is freedom from pride or arrogance: the quality of being humble. How can we have Joy when we are facing problems, situations, troubles on every hand? We can count it all Joy. You see Joy is not a feeling, it is a mindset.

When I was going through a dark time in my life, I lost my sister and four months later my mother was diagnosed with terminal cancer. My sister's death was sudden, and my mom's death was a slow process. I was working a full-time demanding job that required me to travel. I had to have someone come in to stay with my mom, as I worked and sometimes had to travel out of town. My dad also required care. My father and mother divorced when I was young. That is two different households, with me running between the two houses. I moved in with my mom to take care of her. The care of my mom was hard because she was grieving the loss of my sister. The grief was extremely hard for her, so she had no real will to live. I knew that I could not stay in grief, because she needed serious care, love and understanding. I gave up my life to be with her. I could have easily gone into self-centeredness, but I knew that the Lord was with me, and it would be all right. I enjoyed the Sundays with my mom, as she could not attend her church anymore and I could not attend my church physically, because I needed to be home with her. My church had online service, so every Sunday while cooking her breakfast, I would turn my computer on, so we could watch my church. This Sunday routine was helping her to move past the grief. It gave me a sense of Joy to see her improve.

My dad had a stroke months later. When the hospital called, I told my mother I needed to leave to go to the hospital. Her reply was "Why are you going to see about him? He never did right by you as a child." I explained to her that the Bible says to honor your mother and father, so your days will be long on the earth. I loved my mom and my dad. She was very agitated about me going, so I explained to her that Jesus died so that we may receive forgiveness. The same way Jesus forgives us is the same way we need to forgive those who have hurt us. Jesus endured the cross for our sins, to give redemption to us so we must also learn to forgive. When thinking about her anger, I had to humble myself, because I did not understand her pain after all these years. My dad hurt her severely. When I returned, I apologized to her for not understanding how she felt. I also let her know that I was staying with her and not him and that I understand her pain. I also know that forgiveness is the key to Joy.

Forgiveness is hard, but in forgiving, you must humble yourself to do so. Yes, I could have stayed mad at my dad as my mom did, or I could have stayed angry at my mom for not understanding why I had to deal with my dad, but I chose to forgive and move on. That is what we must do in life. We must stop being prideful and arrogant. That is the lesson that I learned when I went through other trials and tribulations. Jesus humbled himself to endure the shame, the beatings, mockings, clothes torn from his body, yet — as the scripture says — he counted the Joy in knowing that he died so that we might have life everlasting. Jesus has loved us with an everlasting love for our lifetime and the life thereafter. The Joy of humility helps me to celebrate even when I am facing challenging times, bosses being mean, children not being obedient, marriage falling apart. I can count it all Joy.

LOVING ENERGY

Mary Lou Bryant-Reid

What a comfort to know our Lord told us, once He went back to His Father, we would not be left alone. He promised to send us the Holy Spirit. As we all know, our Triune God is not tangible, but rather a Being with three distinctions: the Father, the Son (as Redeemer), and the Holy Spirit (as Sanctifier). The word spirit in the Hebrew language is "ruah," which is declared as feminine gender. I make this point, because I view the Holy Spirit as showing the feminine attributes of God. This is not to be taken as a sexist statement, but as I view my God. Keeping that in mind, I may refer to the Holy Spirit as She, just as I refer to the Father and Son as He.

As human, most of us find a mixture of joys and trials through our daily lives. I have always been a person who sees "the glass as half full." In a large part, I attribute that to my faith-filled upbringing. I understood and still do, that this Holy Spirit surrounds us with opportunities to grow closer to our God. Once I personally became aware of this, daily trials were easier to handle. Her Loving Energy was always present, I just had to remember to "tap in."

Having taught and worked with adolescents my entire adult life, I could cite many examples of how the Holy Spirit showed Herself as Loving Energy. One experience, outside of the classroom that appeared to be straight out of "Her Playbook," was when I received a phone call one crisp April morning in 1987. A person on the other end identified herself as representing Pregnancy Helpline. She said that someone told her that I would help assist in this immediate need. The urgency was to house a 16-year-old girl, who was five months pregnant, until her delivery. Her family lived two hundred miles away and her parents were embarrassed by the fact that their daughter was pregnant outside of marriage. They created a lie telling others that she needed back surgery in another city. Big life-changing decision to make, especially for me as the primary caregiver for the next four months. After discussing the situation with my former husband, an 11-year-old son, and a 7-year-old daughter, it was a go. I knew I would need Loving Energy for strength and guidance.

Believe it or not, the girl, I will call Anna, and her parents arrived at our home the day after Mother's Day! I couldn't imagine leaving my sixteen-year-old pregnant daughter with people I had never met. Her parents lived two hundred miles away from me. The family made it known that they would make arrangements with a lawyer to place the baby in a private adoption. I told them our conditions were that the father of the baby be informed, and Anna sees a psychologist. Her mother was quite combative. She said no to both. Her father was noncommittal. Finally, she agreed to the counselor, but not to the boy's discovery. I knew Loving Energy would help with the latter!

That evening after going to bed, I checked on her. She was sobbing. Her biggest concern was wanting the baby's father (whom I will call Kevin) to know what was transpiring. I remember saying to her, "I know you believe in the Lord. I promise you Anna, Kevin will find out." After leaving her room (actually my son had given her his bedroom) I look up at the ceiling and said, God, if You are for real, you better help me out!" (I feel certain that like St. Thomas, we all have experienced a little doubt. After all, "Where there is doubt, there is no faith!")

About two weeks later, the phone rang. A young man's voice asked if Anna was there. I told him that she was babysitting and asked if I could take a message. He hesitated, then said, "Just tell her that Jake called." I wanted to respond, "Sure Kevin, I will be glad to!" So, you see, he found out through some good detective work, with the guidance of the Holy Spirit. The actual details of his discovery are too long to list. We invited him to our home for a few days, so he and Anna could talk.

In the meantime, Anna's parents would come visit her every other Sunday. One visit involved the presence of the lawyer. Again, it was voiced that the father of the baby was not to be contacted. I could feel grace from my friend, Loving Energy, so I immediately spoke up. What if, down the road, he finds out that he fathered this child? Let's say, he could have a legal right to parenthood. What about the child, the adoptive parents, Anna? The lawyer responded that they refer to these cases, as "high risk adoptions." I countered by saying, "I call it unethical, and I will not let that happen." Anna's mother started yelling at me and even took a swing. She missed.

Despite a few setbacks, we made it through the four challenging months. We even had Anna's thirteen -year-old twin sister stayed with us for two weeks to help her emotional state.

When delivery time came, I was with her through labor and delivery. I prayed with her during this time. She asked for a washcloth to cover her eyes during birth, because it was so difficult to chance seeing the baby. As I heard the baby's first cries, I thought how hard that must be for Anna. The doctor was very compassionate, as she asked the attending doctor to take the baby to another room. I thought, how sad both mother and father were not present for the new life to begin.

Our state law said that the biological parents had five days following the birth, to sign final adoption papers. The unethical lawyer wanted Kevin to sign a paper saying that he was not the father, since that was the wish of Anna's mother. Her mother said that if he didn't and showed up in court that she would not pay the lawyer's fees for the adoption. Luckily, the baby was born a few days after he had left for boot camp. The law allowed him to sign the paper before leaving that he was the biological father and that he was agreeable to the adoption. Therefore, he was spared a court appearance. Thank you, Holy Spirit! Anna did go to court to sign the necessary papers. The female judge hugged her and said, "Young lady, this is the greatest unconditional act of love you will ever commit."

The Holy Spirit presented me with what seemed like an insurmountable situation as my family's lives were challenged. Her Loving Energy expedited a Joyous Faith experience!

Since 1987, I have retold this story in every one of my classes. To this day, I am still touched!

REFLECTIONS FOR HUMILITY

Humility is refusing to get all tangled up with yourself. It's about surrender, receptivity, awareness, simplicity. Breathing in. Breathing out.

Cheryl Strayed

1. How do you define humility? In what ways do you demonstrate it in your life?

2. Read Luke 9:46. What message does it have for you in the way you live?

3. In Luke 18: 9–14, the Pharisee compares himself to the tax collector. Whom do you compare yourself to and how pleasing is that to God?

4. Here are two positive examples of humility that are found in the scriptures. Read Luke 7:1–10, the "centurion" and Luke 15:17 the "prodigal son"; what did you discover?

FROM THE HEART

- Jesus encourages us to seek the behavior of a servant (Luke 22:26).
- Some people think Joy comes from accumulating things; but the greatest Joy comes from helping others.
- Self-praise has no value.
- Focus on honorable behavior.
- "Let this mind be in you, which was also in Christ Jesus: who, being in the form of God, thought it not robbery to be equal with God: but made himself of no reputation, and took upon him the form of a servant, and was made in the likeness of men: and being found in fashion as a man, he humbled himself, and became obedient until death, even the death of the cross. Wherefore God also hath highly exalted him, and given him a name which is above every name…" Philippians 2:5–9 (KJV)

The best example of giving is found in Jesus Christ. He came into the world to serve, not to be served. Jesus told the disciples "…whoever wants to become great among you must be your servant, and whoever wants to be first must be slave of all." Mark 10:43–45 (NIV) In order to be like Him, we must be willing to deny self. This world is not our final destination. We want life eternally with God. The more we deny self, the more Christ increases in our lives. People will be drawn to you because your light will shine before men and give glory to God.

PRAYER

Lord, forgive me, for I have sinned against you. I am not a god; only you are, Father. How foolish, self-centered, and vain I have been to follow worldly guidelines to exalt myself. Your ways are not like the world. You are a holy God, and I am thankful because you provide the guidelines for my life, not the world. In our world, pride comes before a fall (Proverbs 16:18). Your word is knowledge, and now that I know better, I must do better, because in and of myself I can do nothing without you. I give you all the praise and glory for the things you have done in my life. Thank you for being the author and finisher of our faith and for blessing us every day. For all eternity, Amen!

"Which One Would You Choose?"

Joy	Happiness
Internal emotion	External emotion
Spiritual experience	Worldly experience
Lasting timeframe	Temporary timeframe
Rooted in Jesus Christ	Lacks depth
A gift from God	Dependent on gratification
Gratifying	Self-centered
Meaningful	Feels good
A meaningful choice	Chase after it
Connects people	Momentary connection
Exist in the good times and bad times	Fleeing and superficial

Inspired by: www.pediaa.com, Joy vs Happiness, August 2, 2018

In the introduction, I pointed out some differences between Joy and Happiness. In the testimonials, you see examples of why choosing Joy is so important. As you examine the lists above, keep in mind that Joy comes from knowing, trusting, and believing in Jesus Christ. The more we mature in our walk with Christ, the stronger we become in our faith. Continuously hearing the Word of God convinces us of the Sovereignty of God. With confidence in Him, we begin to walk boldly, believing and trusting in His Holy Word.

Happiness come from the world and is fleeting, temporary, and dependent on external circumstances. The world offers no guarantees, but Christ offers Joy and everlasting life. The Joy He provides the world, no one can take away John 16:22 (KJV). The world can't save us, but Christ can. Christ offers us over 8,000 assurances, while the world offers happenstances. The world can't give us Joy, but Christ can. The final decision belongs to you. Which one do you choose?

Chapter 5:

STEPS TO A JOYFUL LIFE

It's not too late. Time is not running out. Your life is here and now. And the moment has arrived at which you're finally ready to change.

Cheryl Strayed

The Mayo Clinic reports that the brain controls thought, emotions, behavior, movement, and sensation. Since the brain contains billions of nerve cells, communication may occur in a split second. Have you noticed, when in the midst of impeding danger, your body reacts quickly?

I like to walk. Sometimes cars or a dog will come to close to me. In a second, I automatically react to remain safe. When I am cooking sometimes, I accidently reach for a hot pan. Immediately, my brain cells let me know that I am in danger, and I release it. God created these bodies, and He considered everything we needed to live in this world. He is constantly guarding and protecting us. I am humbled by God's power and might.

In the article, Mind-Body Relationship In Psychology: Dualism vs Monism (June 16, 2023), some psychologists believe that it is naïve to think that the brain influences the body. As separate entities, the mind and body work together. They say one entity can influence the other.

Some psychologists also suggest what goes into our bodies impacts our minds and mental health. What we eat has the power to prevent or help reverse mental health challenges. People who eat healthy are less likely to suffer from anxiety and depression (*Psychology Today*, Aug 31, 2022).

When we accept Jesus Christ, His Holy Spirit lives in us. The Holy Spirit leads, guides, instructs, intercedes, and convicts us of our sins. Our bodies become the temple of God 1 Corinthians 6:19–20 (KJV). The first time I heard this scripture explained, the preacher did not dress the message up. He talked about sexual immorality, drugs and alcohol, smoking, adultery, pornography, and foul language. The church was so quiet you could hear pins fall. He emphasized each time we engage in these acts, the Holy Spirit knows. He's in you! You are not hiding or doing these sinful acts in secret. God sees (omnipresent) and knows (omniscient) everything. With the Holy Spirit, the things you used to do, you no longer desire to do. Old things become new 2 Corinthians 5:13 (KJV). Our old life is transformed into a new life with Christ. Our thoughts become His thoughts.

As God's children, the Holy Spirit reveals God's thoughts and plans. God wants us to experience His Joy and has laid out a plan for us in His Word. As you read and meditate on the steps to a Joyful Life, embrace each concept with prayer and know that the journey is a process. Believers are available to help you along the way. Go forth in faith knowing God is with you.

Renew The Mind

Now that you have accepted Jesus Christ, connect with a church ministry where you may grow in the Word of the Lord Jesus Christ and worship Him in spirit and truth. God wants to reveal himself to you. Walking in the fullness of the Lord will bless you, and your Joy will overflow.

> Whatever controls your mind controls your actions.
>
> Tony Evans

Renewing the mind allows you to align your words and thoughts with the Lord. Untruths are replaced with truths. It's a process, so don't become discouraged and decide to give up!

For example, a person may say, "I feel all alone since I became a Christian. There are no fun things to do." With a renewed mind, the truth would be that you are never alone. God is ever present and there are many Christians who are active and have fun. Begin to socialize with your new friends in Christ and accept invitations to events. My calendar is always full.

Keep your eyes on Jesus, the author and perfector of our faith Hebrews 12:2 (KJV) as He reveals himself in your life. When you go through the storms of life, don't dwell on the negative, use God's truth to replace feelings of doubt. Keep your eyes focused on Him, because the Holy Spirit inside of you will guide you in all things.

Do not allow yourself to be tossed "to and fro" about your belief in the Lord, Jesus Christ. Remember, Satan comes to rob, steal, kill, and destroy. Just stand firm in your belief!

Here are a few affirmations you may proclaim with authority daily to provide inner strength and encouragement:

I am a child of the King. (John 1:12)

I am free from sin and bondage. (Romans 6:8)

I am more than a conqueror in Christ Jesus. (Romans 8:37)

I can do all things through Christ that strengthens me. (Philippians 4:13)

He made me in His image, and He loves me. (Genesis 1:27)

I have peace that surpasses all understanding. (Philippians 4:7)

No weapon formed against me shall prosper. (Isaiah 54:17)

He will never leave me nor forsake me. (Hebrews 13:5)

I have joy down in my heart. (Romans 12:12)

I am strong in the Lord and in His mighty power. (Ephesians 6:10)

God has plans for me to prosper and have hope for the future. (Jeremiah 29:11)

God is my safe place; I go to Him because I trust Him. (Psalms 91:2)

As I seek the Lord, He hears me and delivers me from all my fears. (Psalms 34:4)

My favorite affirmation is this: For the Spirit God gave us does not make us timid, but gives us power, love and self-discipline. 2 Timothy 1:7 (NIV)

In the midst of my trials, Satan tries to make me doubt who God is in my life. I have to stand boldly and proclaim that God is in control. He is refuge and strength in times of need. Therefore, I can approach any situation with a calm, sound mind. Get thee behind me, Satan! I serve a Sovereign God!

As a Christian, there are expectations/disciplines that will help your walk in the fullness of the Lord. They are identified as inward disciplines, outward discipline and corporate discipline (George, Timothy, and McGrath, Alister. *For All the Saints Evangelical Theology and Christian Spirituality*, p. 179). As these disciplines are introduced, notice how they unfolded in the testimonials you read. Remember the Christian life is a growing process. We start out as babes in Christ, then mature to adults in Him. The information provided serve as orientation information for babes in Christ and a reminder for the adults.

RENEWING THE BODY

Do you not know that your bodies are temples of the Holy Spirit, who is in you and whom you have received from God? You are not your own 1 Corinthians 6:19 (KJV). Therefore, glorify God with our bodies.

We struggle with these bodies. For me it is a daily opportunity to make the right choices. Living on vegetables and fruits works for a while, but then the desserts creep in, along with the pancakes and syrup. Not to mention how irresistible fried chicken, pork chops with gravy, and fish are.

> Do you not know that your bodies are temples of the Holy Spirit, who is in you, whom you have received from God? You are not your own.
> 1 Corinthians 6:19 (NIV)

Renewing our bodies requires accepting the truths about the choices we make. The solution is to replace bad food choices with good choices. Anything worth having is worth fighting for. So, let's work toward making these temples, our bodies, acceptable.

In *Dr. Deanna's Healing Handbook*, author Deanna Osburn points out that it is essential to rethink how we care for our bodies. Due to new research findings on food and body exercise, we must be willing to look again at what we do to our bodies (*Dr. Deanna's Healing Handbook*, p.27). Today, we have access to more information than our parents or grandparents had. Renewing the mind and the body is a process that does not happen overnight. The renewal will take practice and commitment.

According to Dr. Deanna, the daily guidelines below are not optional, but essential for good health. They are as follows (*Dr. Deanna's Healing Handbook*, p.210):

1. Warm-ups help to increase the body's blood flow. In order to prevent muscle strain/stress, warm-up exercises heat up the muscles and prepare them for exercise and movement.
2. For the heart, brain, and lungs, aerobics is important because it allows oxygen to circulate through the body to provide energy.

>   There are other exercises to consider like jogging, swimming, walking, biking, treadmills, as well as outdoor workouts.
> 3. Muscle building/resistance training is usually included in most exercise classes to keep you toned and increase strength.
> 4. Drink 8 to 10 glasses of water a day. A popular trend among my peers is to carry water bottles, so you can drink throughout the day. Companies have designed bottles that carry 64–72 ounces of water with the times of consumption written on the bottle in 2 hours intervals.
> 5. Most Americans are unable to sleep because of the pressures and anxieties of life. A good night's sleep slows the aging process, boosts the autoimmune system, improves brain function, and reduces cortisol levels to help reduce stress.

St. Thomas Aquinas, an Italian priest, quoted St. Ambrose as saying, "sleep restores the tired limbs to labor, refreshes the weary mind, and banishes sorrow" (*How to be Happy: Saint Thomas' Secret to a Good Life*, p.123). Author Matt Fradd, host of the "Points with Aquinas" podcast points out that the body isn't a costume that we wear on earth. Lack of sleep may be detrimental to our souls. He reiterates that with the inventions of various time saving devices, we still fill our days with stuff (*How to be Happy: Saint Thomas' Secret to a Good Life*, 2021, p.123). Decide to turn the electronics off, consume no more caffeine, give thanks to God for a wonderful day, and relax in the arms of the Lord. There is an old adage that "everyone is better after a good night's sleep."

What you consume shows inside and outside of the body. NBC news report (March 10, 2016) that Brazilian and American researchers found that 50 percent of Americans eat processed foods. Nearly 60 percent of what Americans eat is junk — ultra-processed foods loaded with sugar, salt, fat and all the other stuff we are not to snack on that cause heart disease and diabetes to soar.

In the book *The Living Clearly Method* (2016), Hilaria Baldwin points out to gradually introduce healthy foods into your diet. Converting your diet immediately causes people to change their minds about healthy eating. The basic idea is for you to consume more greens/vegetables than a diet of fast foods and/or processed foods. When you eat, the body tells you what foods are not good for your body. Slow down when you eat and reflect afterward on the impact certain foods have on your body. The mind lets you know when you have consumed more than enough. After eating, stop and reflect.

Remember Daniel, who challenged the king's officer to allow him and his companions to eat vegetable and drink water, and they looked better than the King's men at the end of a 10 days period. Consider what you consume and make healthy choices. A diet of fast foods or processed foods is not good for your temple (body); consider vegetables, nuts, seeds, and low-fat options. As a result, the temple of God will be healthier inside and outside.

Inward Disciplines

The inward discipline incorporates meditation, prayer, fasting, and study. Richard Foster wrote that Christian disciplines lead to a mature experience, and Joy is ultimately found when the inner and outer disciplines are connected (*For All the Saints Evangelical Theology and Christian Spirituality*, p.178).

Meditation

Meditation provides an opportunity to hear God's Words and to walk in obedience to His Word. In a 21st Century world where everything is quick or instant, Christians are challenged to meditate. The psalmist says in 46:10: "Be still, and know that I am God; I will be exalted among the nations, I will be exalted in the earth." (NIV) During this process, we repent, obey, and change our behavior to align with what God would have us to do. Our hearts are open and receptive to forgive others as God has forgiven us.

Let go of the negative thoughts/baggage of the past; you have chosen a new life with Jesus. You are not a victim; you are a victor (Osteen, *It's On Its Way: Don't Give Up on Your Dreams and Prayers*, p.179). Therefore, victors are overcomers made in the image of God who will turn negatives thoughts and actions to positives (e.g., fear to faith; hate to love; weakness to strength).

Meditation may involve sitting quietly with God, talking to Him, seeking wisdom in His word, reading scriptures, listening to music, recording scripture verses, and/or placing them around the house and praying to become more sensitive to the guidance of the Holy Spirit.

Joshua 1:8 states why meditation should be foremost in our minds and hearts. The verse reads as follows:

"Keep this Book of the Law always on your lips; meditate on it day and night, so that you may be careful to do everything written in it. Then you will be prosperous and successful." Joshua 1:8 (NIV)

Prayer

Richard Foster and C. S. Lewis, who are recognized as early, foundational writers in this area, agreed that prayer is central to the Christian walk, because it communicates with the Father (who created us with the ability to communicate with Him), Son (who taught us how to pray), and the Holy Spirit (who intercedes on our behalf), known as the Trinity. Jesus taught us how to pray in the Model prayer.

> Until now you have not asked for anything in my name. Ask and you will receive, and your joy will be complete.

More importantly, a prayer should be honest and real. The length of the prayer does not determine a hierarchy of ability. In Philippians 4:6, the scripture says, "Do not be anxious about anything, but in every situation, by prayer and petition, with thanksgiving, present your requests to God" (NIV). It is a privilege to carry everything to God in prayer. Keep in mind that prayer is between you and God. He already knows your heart; therefore, pray earnestly, truthfully. Don't see prayer as an obligation to impress others. A prayer may be as simple as, "Lord, I need your help." "Father, I don't know what to do next, but I trust you to guide me."

I attended a birthday party and the guest of honor prayed and there were murmurs about the way he prayed. The Holy Spirit gave me these exact words, "He is praying to the Father and not to you!" There was complete silence. When you pray earnestly and openly from the heart, simply talk to God and tell Him what your specific concerns and thoughts are. Prayer has no time limits, specific posture, or a special place required. Just talk to God anytime, anyplace, for as long as you like. Remember, it's between you and God, anyway!

In the book, *For All the Saints For All the Saints Evangelical Theology and Christian Spirituality* (2013), Jesus tells his disciples that God answers **prayer**. The book of Luke demonstrates how prayers were answered. Here are a few examples taken from scripture:

1. In Luke 3:22, the spirit was present in the form of a dove, during the baptism of Jesus Christ.
2. Spiritual strength comes for those who ask Luke 22:39–46 (KJV).
3. In the Garden of Gethsemane, Jesus' prayer brings an angel to help Luke 22:43 (KJV).

4. God has assigned an angel to guard over you and work on your behalf. Powerful things happen in the spiritual world. Your strength doesn't exist in the physical world with your muscles and might; but in the spiritual realm where heaven moves on your behalf (Osteen, *It's On Its Way: Don't Give Up on Your Dreams and Prayers.* p.7; Evans, *Winning Your Spiritual Battles,* p. 20).

Henri J.M. Nouwen stated, "Prayer is Grace, a free gift from God to which we can only respond with gratitude" (*You Are the Beloved*, p.122). This author recommends you consider a prayer journal. Write down your prayers and how God personally answered them. I call it "counting your blessings day by day." You may want to make a list of things God has done for you today or this week and thank Him. Be grateful for the small things as well. Those little things may have saved you from experiencing some big issues in life. Since God is with us always, He is interceding on our behalf for He never slumbers or sleeps Psalms 121:1 (KJV). Go boldly before the throne of Christ and make your needs known Hebrews 4:16 (KJV).

For example, here are a few prayers of biblical characters in their time of need:

David was second King of Israel and was known for his warrior skills (David's victory over Goliath), writing of the psalms, his illicit affair with Bathsheba, and his love of God. He made many mistakes and endured many consequences, but always loved the Lord.

A prayer of David from Psalms 86:1–7

> [1] Hear me, LORD, and answer me,
> for I am poor and needy.
> [2] Guard my life, for I am faithful to you;
> save your servant who trusts in you.
> You are my God; [3] have mercy on me, Lord,
> for I call to you all day long.
> [4] Bring joy to your servant, Lord,
> for I put my trust in you.
> [5] You, Lord, are forgiving and good,
> abounding in love to all who call to you.
> [6] Hear my prayer, LORD;
> listen to my cry for mercy.

> ⁷ When I am in distress, I call to you,
>   because you answer me.

Hannah was the mother of Samuel. She was barren for many years, but continued to pray for a son. It was not easy for her to accept the fact that her husband's wives had children. However, in His own time, the Lord answered her prayer at a very old age, and she dedicated Samuel to the Lord.

Then Hannah prayed and said:

> "My heart rejoices in the LORD;
>   in the LORD my horn is lifted high.
> My mouth boasts over my enemies,
>   for I delight in your deliverance.
>
> "There is no one holy like the LORD;
>   there is no one besides you;
>   there is no Rock like our God."

Hannah's Prayer (1 Samuel 2:1–2).

These are just a few examples, while the Bible is filled with other examples of how Christian came boldly before the Lord. James 5:13 (NIV) states it very simply, "Is anyone among you in trouble? Let them pray." Prayers are strictly from the heart. Just tell God what is on your mind. You can go to Him at any time or place. He is always available to listen to you. For God wants a relationship with you.

Fasting

Fasting is about self-denial. According to Dr. Udoh in his sermon the *Power of Prayer and Fasting* (January 25, 2016), he points out the following:

1. Fasting is a spiritual weapon that God expects us to use. We are in a real spiritual battle that requires spiritual weapons.

2. Fasting breaks down strongholds and barriers in the spirit realm. The author suggests you tell God about the things in your life that you want to change in order to be more like Jesus. You need God's help.

3. Prayer with fasting enables us to see the unseen, hear the unheard, know the unknown, and understand the mysteries of God. The Bible becomes a living book.

4. Fasting releases the anointing: Moses ascended Mount Sinai and his 40-day fast produced more than a holy glow on his face; it also resulted in the giving of the law.

In Daniel 1:8–21, Daniel refused to eat the king's food and drink the wine because he did not want to defile his body. He asked the king's officials to give him and his companions vegetables and water for 10 days to see what the results would be. The chief official feared what the king would do to him if Daniel and his companions were not healthy like the other men. However, the chief official conceded and allowed the 10-day fast. When Daniel and his companions were compared to the king's men, they looked healthier and more well-nourished than the king's men. So, the royal food was removed and replaced with vegetables and water for the king's men. The main idea of fasting is to focus on God. During this time, we are looking and listening for a revelation from God.

> The main idea of fasting is to focus on God and not what you are eating.

Study

The Christian discipline of **study** helps to renew the mind and transforms it, by making us free. When we know the truth, we are made free John 8:32 (KJV). He has a plan for you. Reading the scriptures allows God to get closer to you, so you may know what He is truly about (Nouwen, *You Are the Beloved,* p. 23). God wants an unceasing dialogue with you. He asks that you pray without ceasing because His relationship with you is unconditional. He wants to hear your thoughts, dreams, challenges, and wishes. No conversation is prohibited. This thought reminds me of the song: *Have a Little Talk with Jesus,* written by Cleavant Derricks and sung by Brenda Lee. When you talk with Jesus, He helps to lift those burdens and concerns that weigh heavily on your heart and soul. You may talk to Him at any time or any place. He is always available to you.

The scriptures say, *"Do your best to present yourself to God as one approved, a worker who does not need to be ashamed and who correctly handles the word of truth."* 2 Timothy 2:15 (NIV) The Bible is God's plan for our life. We need to know that plan, so we will not follow false doctrine or be deceived.

In your Bible study groups, daily readings are assigned so you may carry the Word in your heart. Most classes provide a guide to discovering the Bible in a year. You need the word to fight off the enemy, who comes to try to steal your Joy. Spend time with the Lord every day! Remember, no one can steal your Joy unless you allow them. Stay focus on the main thing and that is Jesus Christ.

Outward Disciplines

There are four outward disciplines: simplicity, solitude, submission, and service.

Simplicity

God made man simple, the complexities of life are our own creation. When our focus is on Christ, we are able to let go of unimportant things. A simple life does not mean a boring life. I recall the time my husband entered the ministry. It was not a boring life. We saw miracles, wonders, and signs of Christ and discussed them often with great excitement and expectations. With great anticipation we would say, "What will God do next?" We could not wait to tell people about how God is working in our lives. Our lives were centered around Bible studies in the home, homeless work, and giving. To us this was simple compared to participating in "power" clubs: attending endless gatherings and trying to please the Joneses. We decided to let the Joneses have it and focused on what really mattered, following God's plan. Keeping it simple (KIS) took away the "clutter of life."

Solitude

Solitude does not mean being lonely. Instead, it requires separating ourselves from the busyness of the world. "Be still and know that I am God." In the stillness we hear and see the awesomeness of His power. On a sunny day, I sat looking out the window. I noticed animals that I never knew before coming out of the woods, looking around and going back to their shelter. I was mesmerized so I took pictures and asked neighbors to help me identify the animals. I read about these animals, but didn't know how they looked in real life. I thought, "God created these animals. They serve a purpose, too. How awesome and unique they are."

According to the United Nations, 8 billion people live on earth. Each person is uniquely created by God. No one has the same fingerprint, and the hairs on their heads are numbered. God knows and loves us all. So, when I look at people, I say, "God loves them, too, and wants them to spend eternity with Him. So, why would I think that I am better than anyone God has created?"

Submission

Submission means we are free to serve others versus doing what we want to do, all the time. Jesus Christ submitted to the Father. Whatever the Father called Him to do, He did it. Christ submitted to the Father. God has called us to allow Him to be the head of your life. It is a call to submission.

Submitting requires placing others first and helping them. Scriptures teaches us to yield to those in authority Hebrews 13:17(KJV). When I am driving on the expressway and look down at the speedometer to find out that I am 20 miles per hour over the speed limit, I submit to the law.

At work, there were times you wonder why your idea/s is/are not acceptable, but they become acceptable because someone different said it. You are called to submit to the leadership's decisions regardless.

Many people are lonely and need someone to talk to, while other may need a smile, a hand to hold, someone to talk to or a drink or water. Working with hospice, humility is an asset. I found people who needed someone to just visit them, sing a song, read mail, or just hold their hand. I was honored to submit to their needs.

During my life experience, this area of submission has caused many marriages to suffer. The scripture asks wives to submit to their husbands and husbands to love their wives as Christ loves the church.

The scriptures read as follows from Ephesians 5: 21–24 (NLT), "And further, submit to one another out of reverence for Christ. For wives, this means submit to your husbands as to the Lord. For a husband is the head of his wife as Christ is the head of the church. He is the Savior of his body, the church. As the church submits to Christ, so you wives should submit to your husbands in everything."

God has made the man the head of the household, and we have to trust God for what He says in His Word. This statement does not mean to accept an abusive relationship. However, it does mean consulting with him as decisions are made, show respect, demonstrate love, communicate often, and to be there for each other. In a world where most women are self-sufficient, this idea is hard for them to accept because they do not see the benefits. At first, I couldn't either, but I began to see many benefits, such as: my opinion weighing heavy on the decision-making side, because he was in charge, and he loved how I treated him. Secondly, nothing happened without him knowing about it. Thirdly, the door to communication was always open. So, we had a date night and he loved doing things together (tennis, walking, Bible study in the home, visiting, and entertaining). What I loved most was he would cook and help clean up. In the Bible, you do not pick and choose what you believe. The Bible is a book of Truth, not half-truths. That is why you walk by faith.

Service

Servicing others involve daily courtesies, acts of kindness (*For All the Saints Evangelical Theology and Christian Spirituality*, p.187). In the Sermon on the Mount, Jesus said, "Let your light so shine before men that they may see your good works and glorify your Father which is in heaven." Matthew 5:16(KJV) Once we accept Jesus as our Savior, we want to serve Him and show the world we belong to Him. There are many opportunities to let your light shine. Ask God to guide you in the process. Jesus' life was all about serving others, and we desire to be more like him.

> Jesus' life was all about serving others, and we desire to be more like him.

We live in a world that requires us to help each other as a demonstration of God's love. Serving others will cause you to grow. There are a lot of people who are hurting, grieving, anxious, confused, and need someone to care for them, but they are afraid to be honest about needing help. Before deciding where or how to serve, I recommend praying for guidance first.

In Exodus 17, Moses was standing on a hill with the staff of the Lord in his hand during a battle between Amalekites and the Israelites. As long as Moses held the staff of the Lord up in his hands, his people were winning. When he grew tired, they put a stone under him to sit, and Hur and Aaron held his hands up. The Israelites overcame the Amalekites. What would happen if no one decided to serve? Your service is important. It could mean the difference between life and death.

I have a strong desire to serve or help, so the world sees who is in charge of my life, even when it is difficult for me to hear due to severe hearing loss. I serve anyway in faith. Whether I am providing grief counseling, donating to the homeless, or greeting on Sunday, I find great Joy in serving others. The first question I'm usually asked is, "What church do you go to?" I consider it an opening to testify about God in my life and/or an opportunity to invite someone to my church. Once Joy enters your life, you look for opportunities to share from whence your Joy comes. The door will open for you to serve, and your service will become a door to testify about who Jesus is in your life. Recalling the blessings from your journal will keep your witnessing new and forever on your mind. Your service to God is a chance for someone else to join us in Heaven. What a Joy! I always have a story to tell.

Corporate Discipline

Corporate discipline is the coming together of the body of Christ, the church for confession, worship, guidance, and celebration. Keep in mind the church is filled with people who have experienced or still experience, trials and tribulations and will witness about the Grace and Mercy of God.

Confession

The discipline of confession is rooted in the scripture of James 5:16 (NIV), "Therefore confess your sins to each other and pray for each other so that you may be healed." In various churches this practice occurs differently, for example: some confess to a priest, others may confess to the church or confess only to God.

Worship

"God is spirit, and those who worship Him must worship in spirit and truth." John 4:24 (ESV) During worship, we demonstrate love, adoration, and praise to the Father. Chuck Swindoll (March 6, 2015. *The Discipline of Humility*. Dallas Theological Seminary) states the church is:

"Not a selfish group of people who come together to be entertained, but a body of selfless believers who are learning how to worship God as a lifestyle."

Man was made to worship, so he will worship something (e.g., money, sex, alcohol, drugs, house, car or education). During worship, we must give unto the Lord the glory due unto His name. The scriptures states, "Worship the Lord in the beauty of holiness." Psalms 29:2 (KJV) God is set apart from any evil and can cleanse us from any unrighteousness. All the earth is designed to praise the Lord. It is natural to worship God. If we don't worship Him, the stones will cry out. Luke 19:40 (paraphrase) How can we possibly fail in this important matter?

Webster defines worship as paying divine honor to the one who made us and has decreed how we shall worship Him. He wants us to worship Him in spirit and truth using your total being (body, mind, and soul). To worship

> Webster defines worship as paying divine honor.

requires a plan of action. The plan is to honestly seek him by opening our minds, hearts, and spirit. Think about the songs you sing. What do the words mean? Am I willing to commit to doing what the song says? Listen to the prayers you say, do you commit to those prayers? The Holy Spirit must have his way in your life for this to happen. There is power in worship. We do it to glorify, honor, praise, exalt, and please God. Therefore, we humble ourselves before the throne of Grace.

Isaiah 58:13-14 says, "…if you call the Sabbath a delight and the Lord's holy day honorable, and if you honor it by not going your own way and not doing as you please or speaking idle words, then you will find your joy in the Lord…."

He made you in love, to love, and there is no way you can love Him and not feel something. Tell God how much you love Him, and praise his holy name.

Guidance

This discipline involves another person mentoring someone else as they work to discern how God wants them to walk this life. The mentor or friend shares their life's experiences in an effort to enlighten others. All experiences are done in prayer bathed in humility and holiness.

Celebration

C.S. Lewis describes celebration as "inner health made audible." (*For All Saints*; p.192) Therefore, we rejoice in the Lord always. Rejoicing comes because we value the relationship with the Lord. The more we value him, the more intense the celebration of who He is occurs. 1 Corinthians 10:31 (KJV) states, *"Whether therefore ye eat, or drink, or whatsoever ye do, do all to the glory of God."*

In Conclusion

James 1:2–4 states, "Consider it pure joy, my brothers and sisters, whenever you face trials of many kinds, because you know that the testing of your faith produces perseverance. Let perseverance finish its work so that you may be mature and complete, not lacking anything." (NIV) In other words, testing is a blessing, because when the testing is over, we have "stood the test of time." As a result, we will "receive the crown of life, which God has promised to those who love him." James 1:12 (ESV)

Life on earth is certainly a test. God continually tests people's character, faith, obedience, love, integrity, and loyalty. The Bible uses words like "trials," "temptations," "refining," and "testing" over 200 times.

When you understand that life is a test, you realize that nothing is insignificant. Each day, hour, and second, equals a growth opportunity for you, as well. Every time you pass a test, God notices, and the results will affect your rewards in heaven for all eternity. Testing increases your faith to a higher level.

You have witnessed real-life examples of Joy in the lives of Christians. I know that you were blessed during the readings. In many instances, you saw yourself or loved ones in the writings. From this experience, you know that God is in control of every phase of your life and that He works things out in all situations. There are many reasons to praise and rejoice in who He is.

Approach trials and tribulations with confidence that God will never leave you nor forsake you. God does so much, for example: He saves, supports, strengthens, provides, encourages, guides, protects, intercedes, restores, comforts, cares, and loves you and the list goes on and on. So, you will experience combat between the spirit and the flesh. If you want the spirit to win, you must assist it by prayer (*Saint Thomas Aquinas' Secret of a Good Life, p 40*). According to Tony Evans, spiritual combat requires spiritual solutions, not physical. You may be very strong or physically fit, but that will not resolve your problems. You need power from the spiritual realm to battle for you. A lot of things happen that are Unseen; therefore, we need a God, who is sovereign and intercedes on our behalf.

This book was written to draw people to the Jesus Christ. In a world that confuses Joy with Happiness, we wanted you to know the truth. Joy is a gift of God, and you are invited to enjoy this gift. Once you receive the gift, your outlook on life will never

> "Just so, I tell you, there is joy before the angels of God over one sinner who repents."
> Luke 15:10 (ESV)

be the same. You will become a testimony of what Joy is. Share your story to help someone else. When God gives you a gift, He wants you to share it and not hide it under a bushel where it will grow dim and eventually fade away. Since you are connected to the vine (God), He wants you to bear fruit. Tell others about this Joy that is within you. God's desire is that all be saved! There are friends, family members, and neighbors who need a savior in their lives. Let's take someone with us to Heaven.

My prayer is that you chose Joy versus Happiness. Begin to follow the disciplines outlined in the last section. Pray that God will lead you to a place of Corporate Worship so that you will continue to grow and learn His will and plan for you. Let your light shine so the world may see the salvation of the Lord.

The past years of COVID have opened eyes as to how fragile life is. God has blessed you through the COVID-19 season. We prayed, cried out to Him, humbled ourselves, and he heard his people and began to heal the land. Since He has revealed himself in a special way in the last two years, let's take advantage of this opportunity to choose Him as Lord and Savior. God wants you to share His Joy with others. Let the world see that the Joy of the Lord is your strength. Spread His Word.

This journey with Christ is everlasting. There are no shortcuts. Keep your eyes focused on the right things and the right way! Remember who Jesus Christ is. If we hold on and don't give up, we will reap the harvest (Galatians 6:9). Don't be afraid; don't grow weary; don't give up. Seek the Lord with all your heart, mind, strength, and soul. He is always there for you. God says, "I have told you this so that my joy may be in you and that your joy may be complete." John 15:11 (NIV) The Joy of the Lord is your strength.

I HAVE A CHOICE TO MAKE

Therefore, my brothers and sisters, you have heard testimonials of what Joy looks like in the lives of Christians. This world is filled with challenges, hardships, violence, corruption, trials, and tribulations; however, we have a choice as to how we go through these times of uncertainty. Will we stand firm in the Lord or allow circumstances of life to "toss us to and fro," not knowing what to do next.

Some people would choose things in life that are temporary that make them happy like clothes, silver, cars, gold, houses, and land. What happens when those things are gone? Will you give up? Find more jobs to support your lifestyle? Will you lose hope when another trial or tribulation occurs?

If you decide to make Jesus your choice, you receive the gift of Joy that is eternal and nonconditional. Don't think that God does not bless his people with houses and land. The difference is that if they no longer have these things, God will continue to bless them. The Bible teaches us a lot about how God blesses his people. A popular story is the book of Job, which is about an upright man who had everything and loved the Lord. Satan asked God to remove these things to see if Job would continue to praise him. Job remains faithful although he lost home, family, health, riches, and respect of the community. Job's responses to these trials and tribulations were:

"Naked I came from my mother's womb, and naked I shall return there." Job 1:21 (NASB)

"The Lord gave, and the Lord has taken away; Blessed be the name of the Lord." Job 1:21 (NKJV)

The rest of the story reveals that Satan is a liar and God restores Job twofold.

The testimonials revealed that in our trials and tribulations, we find Joy in suffering, believing, giving and humility because of the gift given to us by Jesus Christ. We also found that you are never alone because God never leaves or forsakes you and there are others in the faith that will support, help and encourage you on your walk with Christ.

There is a need to renew your mind by not thinking as the world but to think as Christ. So, you will think on things that are true, noble, right, pure, lovely, admirable, excellent and praiseworthy (Philippians 4:8). In doing so you will find peace that only comes from God, the Father.

So, I rejoice in the Lord for this opportunity for you to make a choice this day as to **whom will you serve?** Most of us have encountered many of the situations in this book: sickness, loss of jobs and loved ones, loneliness, cancer, abuse, humbleness, care of loved ones, giving of self and resources, and serving others. The only way to go through these challenges is with Christ who gives us strength (Philippians 4:13). Decide today to make Jesus your choice. God says to you: "Here I am! I stand at the door and knock. If anyone hears my voice and opens the door, I will come in and eat with that person, and they with me."
Revelations 3:20 (NIV)

> **Joy is a gift from God, who assures us that He has total control of our lives. We are confident that all things will work for the good and make the decision to praise and worship Him at all times.**

INVITATION: A NEW LIFE IN CHRIST

Rev. Robert L. Byrd, Sr. (Notes)

God's Salvation is for His glory and the everlasting joy of His people.

What must I do now, since I have read the book? My response is to choose to receive the Lord Jesus Christ into your life. "Verily, Verily, I say unto thee, except a man be born again, he cannot see the kingdom of God." is Jesus' response John 3:3 (KJV)

> The Holy Spirit (God) bears witness to your Spirit that you are saved. He will allow you to take on the character of Jesus Christ and put you in the right place to represent Him.
>
> Dr. Walter Malone
>
> (Sermon: The Spirit of the Lord) 1-2-23

Why would a man/person desire to be born again? One reason is when we look at our current life, we see all the mistakes we've made. In most cases, our lives have been one failure after another one. Many of us are lost and without hope. We are truly in need of a new life, a new start, a new Hope.

Jesus offers the opportunity for you to be born again. You don't have to be stuck with a life of failure. Man is body, mind, and spirit. Jesus declares you must be born again. You must have a new spirit — why? The old one is dead, and a new one must be born.

Jesus says, "take my yoke upon you…my burden is light." Matthew 11 (KJV). The only requirement is to believe in the name of Jesus Christ. You become a new person. The "old you" will fade away and all things will become new. In others word, we have a new beginning and a fresh start. God will forgive you unconditionally for things that happened in the past. In fact, He forgives you and casts your sins into the sea of forgetfulness. He casts them as far as the east is from the west. Psalm 103:12 (KJV)

Ask Him to enter your life. He is waiting to receive you. God does not make it hard for you to become a Christian. Just confess with your mouth that you have sinned, believe in your heart that Jesus died for your sins, receive the holy spirit, and a new birth occurs. Things will never be the same, as you walk in the newness of Christ. There is nothing that God cannot help you through. What God is getting ready to do through you is miraculous because He will use you to help someone else to know who He is. What God is about to do with you is not based on your past, but your future.

Let's pray:

> *Dear God, I know that I am a sinner and I ask you to please forgive me for I have sinned against you. I believe in my heart that Jesus is your Son; He died for me on a cross, and you raised Him back to life. Jesus, I declare that you are my Lord, and I open my heart to you.*

Inspiration for Book

God's wonders, miracles, and signs never cease to amaze me, especially when they occur in my life. Walking in faith with God is an awesome journey. You think you have planned your day or your year, but God has something different and better for you.

Since retiring, I have my daily/weekly activities outlined, and fun is at the center of it all. Last spring (2022), I received a call that challenged me to do something for the world. The call, in my opinion, was so anointed and God centered that I was immediately convicted and said "yes" to the request with great humility.

Immediately, I knew that I was to write this book containing examples of Joy. Previously, I read a book by Kay Warren entitled *Choose Joy: Because Happiness Isn't Enough*. From my reading, I thought, "Wouldn't it be great for the world to see what Joy looked like in the lives of believers?" Therefore, the Lord used Dr. Rita Greer to light the fire of inspiration and make this thought a reality.

Dr. Greer's words convinced me so much that tears flowed, and I knew that there was no way I could delay or run from this obligation to influence and support mankind in a special way. I now understand how Jonah felt when God told him to go to Ninevah and tell the people about the things they were doing that were not pleasing in His sight; but he took detours in his life that caused a lot of suffering and tribulation. Well, God has a way of getting your attention. His plan for you will be completed regardless of the detours or stalls you create in life.

The scripture says: "To whom much shall be given, much is required." Luke 12:48 (KJV) This statement does not give you an option, but an obligation to those God has given gifts for his Glory. God gives us gifts to use, not to hide them under a bushel. Therefore, use what God has given you to make a difference. People need us (the light) to show that God is alive in this world (darkness). For some time, I knew that I needed to do something to draw people to God. The call from Dr. Greer lit the fire that got me out of my seat to begin making a difference. Even though it took one call from Dr. Greer, her commitment to help with meaningful and insightful advice continues

Dr. Rita Greer came into my life when I first sought employment in Louisville's Jefferson County Public Schools in the 1980s, and I have always admired her. She is now a retired educator who formally served in JCPS as a teacher and central office administrator, holding the positions of Human Resources Specialist, Data Management Coordinator, and Director of Human Resources as well as Special Projects Consultant upon her initial retirement. She is credited with the development of the Minority Teacher Recruitment Project, ACES—Alternative Certification in Elementary and Secondary—the only school-based certification program in Kentucky at that time; and numerous other recruitment and certification initiatives.

In 2010, she served as director of the Leadership Education doctoral degree (EDD) Program and Advanced Graduate Education Programs at Spalding University. She co-chaired the 15,000 Degrees Initiative, a project designed to encourage and support Metro Louisville's African Americans obtain degrees. During retirement, Dr. Greer continues to work as a consultant, an adjunct professor and on several boards. In 2020, Dr. Rita Greer published her first book entitled *Teacher Journeys: Memories, Reflections, and Lessons from 20th Century African-American Educators*. I was one of the educators who shared their stories.

God has a plan for each of our lives and that is **to live for Him and experience His Joy every day** (Jeremiah 29:11). When you are obedient to Him, God will use you for His Glory. Thank you, Dr. Greer for your obedience. It motivated, supported, encouraged, and showed me how God continues to use others to do great and wonderful things. From your call, we now have a body of work that shows what Joy is like in the lives of persons living in 2022 who have counted it all bliss when they encountered challenges and hardships. I know hearts will be touched, lives saved, and God glorified through the messages found in All Joy.

In your life, be receptive to the Dr. Greers of the world who challenge you for the good of others. Know that God is in the plan. God uses ordinary people to do extraordinary things. Be willing to say, "Yes! And thanks be to God! Amen."

About the Visionary Author

DR. LOUISE BYRD

Dr. Louise Byrd from Winston-Salem, North Carolina, where she graduated from Paisley Jr.-Sr. High School and North Carolina Central University, is now a retired educator from the Kentucky Department of Education (Highly Skilled Educator and District Achievement Gap Coordinator) and Jefferson County Public Schools, later obtained a Doctorate of Education from Spalding University and an adjunct professor at University of Louisville.

Her work has been with helping low-performing schools reach proficiency under No Child Left Behind. As a Highly Skilled Educator and District Achievement Gap Coordinator for the Kentucky Department of Education, her primary message was that all children want to be proficient learners and can accomplish this task with a caring, loving teacher with high expectations. She has spoken extensively on leadership in Kentucky, Alabama, Tennessee, New Jersey, and Florida.

She has conducted numerous workshops for local PTA and NAACP groups entitled," It takes a Village" and "Keepin' It Real." Dr. Byrd's message of leadership is published in an article, "Ten Things Great

Leaders Do?" (Kentucky Association of School Administrators, 2001). In her manual, *I Believe I Can Fly* (1999) she offers helpful lessons for the classroom generalists to bring the multiple intelligence of music into the curriculum that enhance learning. Her research, *Arts-Integrated Schools: Case Studies* (2000), show that schools can meet the needs of all children through an integrated method of instruction. In her children's book, *I Can Hear You Now* (2013), offers an opportunity for children and adults to partner in making guidelines that can have an impact in school, home and ultimately in their daily life. Her educational experience span four states and over 45 years.

Upon retiring, Dr. Byrd became director of the Champion Scholars Investigators Reading Program, an after-school program that assists children at the elementary grade levels (K–5) move to reading grade level. This program served five Jefferson County Public Schools and assisted approximately 120 students. Additionally, she works as a grief counselor, serves as a church greeter and spiritual partner, is a member of a diverse book club, enjoys line dancing and exercise classes, delights in Bible study classes, and formally volunteered with Hospice.

Being active in church started at an early age for Dr. Byrd. Going to Sunday School, church, and Bible study was a family expectation. Her 38 years marriage to Rev. Robert L. Byrd, Sr., enhanced the importance of studying the Word for he led studies daily and invited family, friends, and relatives to join. Their work together involved the homeless community, couple workshops, and devotions. Showing God's love, patience, forgiveness, understanding, kindness, peace, and self-control was their focus.

God has shown how His grace and mercy continue to sustain her in all situations. During her trials and tribulations, she has learned what people meant for evil; God turned it around for good. Counting it all Joy has been a wonderful learning experience in her life and wants the reader to learn more about God's Joy. Just as you hunger for physical nourishment, she wants you to seek spiritual nourishment that comes from spending time in the Word of God. The Christian walk is a journey that takes time. You must persevere. God does things on His time, not yours. During your journey, you will find God's **Wisdom** guiding you through the challenges of the world if you are obedient and remain close to Him.

BIBLIOGRAPHY

Achtemeier, Paul J. *Bible Dictionary*. Revised Edition Harper Collins, San Francisco, 1996, P.549

Baldwin, Hilaria. *The Living Clearly Method*. New York, NY: Rodale Inc., 2016.

Bible Study Fellowship. *Kingdom Divided*. Global Headquarters: 19001 Huebner Road San Antonio, TX USA 78258, 2021.

Elisabeth Elliot Foundation. Elisabeth Elliot. December 8, 2020. *Suffering Is Never for Nothing*. Vision Video. https://bit.ly/3LrbGIN

Evans, Tony. *Winning Your Spiritual Battles*. Eugene, Oregon, Harvest House Publishers, 2011.

Fradd, Matt. *How to be Happy: Saint Thomas' Secret to a Good Life*. Steubenville, Ohio: Emmaus Road, 2021.

Fritz Chery. Chuck Swindoll. Difference between Joy and Happiness. Nov 12, 2022. https://biblereasons.com/happiness-vs-joy

George, Timothy, and McGrath, Alister. *For All the Saints Evangelical Theology and Christian Spirituality*. Westminster: John Knox Press, 2013

Graham, Billy. May 29, 2021. What is the Difference Between Happiness and Joy? https://billygraham.org/answer/

Grief Share. *Your Journey from Mourning to Joy*. Church Initiative P. O. Box 1739 Wake Forest NC 27588-1739, 2007.

Harper Collins Bible Dictionary, Revised Edition. San Francisco Paul J. Achtemeir, p.549, 1996.

Holdren, Dr. Deanna & Dr. Linda Jeffrey. *Dr. Deanna's Healing Handbook*. WWW.DeannaHoldren.com, 2021.

Idleman, Kyle. *Don't Give Up*. Baker Books Grand Rapid MI, 2019.

Jesus Center. Francis Chan, Guest Speaker. Humility. 4-23-2023 https://www.jesuscenter.com/.

Joyce Meyers Ministries. Joyce Meyers. August 18, 2021. *Thoughts of Joy Part I. Enjoying Everyday Life*. JoyceMeyers.org

Joyce Meyers Ministries. Joyce Meyers. May 15, 2023. *Finding Joy in the Midst of Despair*. Podcast. JoyceMeyers.org

Jones, Nona. *Killing Comparison*. Zondervan, Grand Rapids, MI, 2022.

Kristenson, Sarah. April 26, 2022. Joy VS Happiness: 11 Important Differences Between Each-Happier Human. https://happierhuman.com/joy-vs-happiness/

Lama, Dalai; Desmond Tutu; & Douglas Abrams. *The Book of Joy*. New York: Penguin, Randon House, 2016.

Ligonier Ministries. R. C. Sproul. Sermon from Luke 14: 1-4. June 25, 2021. (1) The Gospel of Luke (Luke 1:1–4) — A Sermon by R.C. Sproul — YouTube.

Dr. Walter Malone. *The Spirit of the Lord*. Sunday Service Sermon. Canaan Christian Church. January 2, 2023.

Meyers, Joyce. *James*. New York, NY: Hachett Book Group, Inc., 2019.

Meyers, Joyce. *Be Joyful*. New York, NY: Hachett Book Group, Inc., 2022.

Morgan, Nick. How the Mind-Body Connection Works, *Psychology Today*, August 31, 2022. https://www.psychologytoday.com/us/blog/communications-matter/202208/how-the-mind-body-connection-works. Retrieved December, 2023

Murray, David. *The Happy Christian: Ten Ways to Be A Joyful Believer in a Gloomy World*. Nashville, Tennessee: Nelson Books, 2015.

Murray, Andrew. *Humility*. Nashville Tennessee: B and H Publishing Group, 2017.

New International Version. Gateway, https://www.biblegateway.com/versions/new-international-version-niv-bible. Retrieved June 2022–July 2023.

Nouwen, Henri J. M. *You Are the Beloved.* New York: Convergent Books, 2017.

Osteen, Lisa. *It's On Its Way: Don't Give Up on Your Dreams and Prayers.* New York, NY: Hatchett Book Group, Inc, 2021.

Simple Psychology. June 16, 2023. Mind Body Relationship in Psychology: Dualism vs Monism. https://www.simplepsychology.org/mindbodydebate.html. Retrieved December, 2023.

Strayed, Cheryl. *Brave Enough.* New York: Alfred Knopf, 2015.

Swindoll, Chuck. March 6, 2015. The Discipline of Humility. Dallas Theological Seminary. https://www.youtube.com/watch?v+EGOs7vH8RGQ

Swindoll, Charles R. *Why, God?* (Nashville, Tn: W. Publishing Group, 2011

The Father's House Ministry. Dr. Richard Udoh. Sermon *The Power of Prayer and Fasting* January 25, 2016. tfhconlinesermon.org

TD Jakes. Steps to Happiness and a Changed Mind. Podcast. April 15, 2017. https://www.youtube.com/watch?v=DTIdJ7-rhbs

TBN. Harper, Lisa. Sermon Are you strong enough to be Humble. July 3. 2022 www.lisaharper.net

TBN.T. D. Jakes. You Have to Keep Going. Full Sermon. January 28, 2023. http://www.tdjakes.org/

TBN. Jakes, T.D. April 12, 2019. Joy Co-Exist with Suffering. TBN.org/crushing

Tyler Wright, Lauren. Giving—The Sacred Art: Creating a Lifestyle of Generosity (The Art of Spiritual Living). Woodstock V: Skylight Paths Publishing, 2008.

Vaughn, Ellen. *Becoming Elisabeth Warren*. Nashville, Tn: B and H Publishing Group, 2020.

Warren, Kay. *Choose Joy.* Grand Rapids, MI: Revell Publishing, 2012.

Wilhite, Jud *Torn.* West Brook Multnomah Colorado Springs, Co, 2011.

William, Mark & Danny Penman. *Mindfulness.* New York, NY: Rodale Inc., 2011.

www.ingramcontent.com/pod-product-compliance
Lightning Source LLC
Chambersburg PA
CBHW081126170426
43197CB00017B/2765